PIES AND TARTS

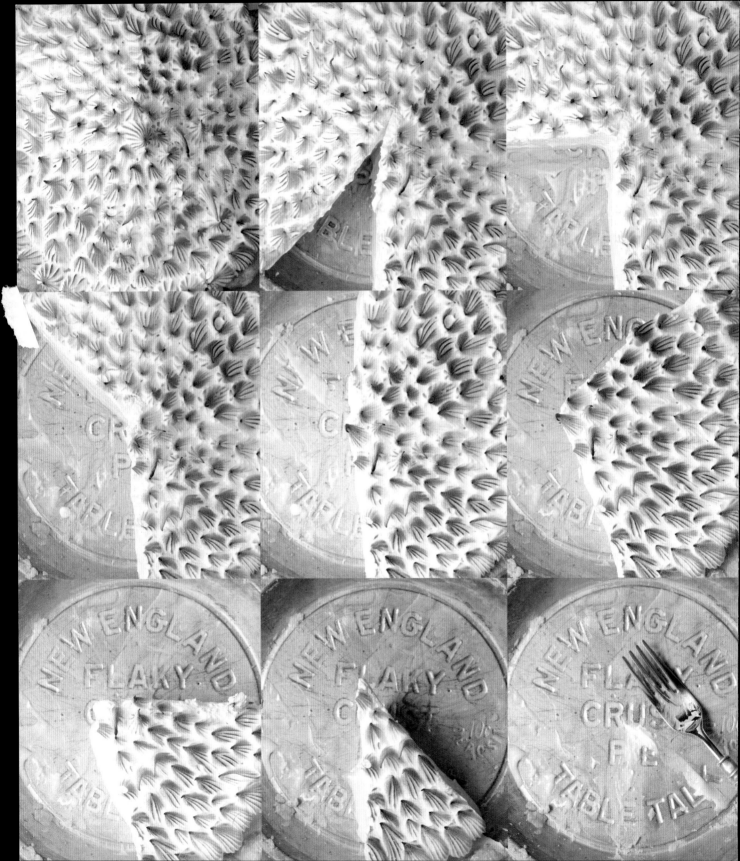

PIES AND TARTS

The Definitive Guide to Classic and Contemporary
Favorites from the World's Premier Culinary College

KRISTINA PETERSEN MIGOYA

PHOTOGRAPHY BY BEN FINK

THE CULINARY INSTITUTE OF AMERICA

BOSTON • NEW YORK • 2014

The Culinary Institute of America

President	Dr. Tim Ryan '77 CMC
Provost	Mark Erickson '77 CMC
Director of Publishing	Nathalie Fischer
Editorial Project Manager	Lisa Lahey '00
Editorial Assistant	Laura Monroe, '12

For information about permission to reproduce selections from this book, write to Permissions, Houghton Mifflin Harcourt Publishing Company, 215 Park Avenue South, New York, New York 10003.

www.hmhco.com

Library of Congress Cataloging-in-Publication Data
Migoya, Kristina Petersen.
  Pies and tarts : the definitive guide to classic and contemporary favorites from America's top cooking school / Kristina Petersen Migoya ; photography by Ben Fink.
    pages cm
  "The Culinary Institute of America"
  ISBN 978-0-470-87359-5 (cloth)
1. Pies. I. Title.
  TX773.M5327 2014
  641.86'52—dc23
                                    2013031653

Printed in China

TOP 10 9 8 7 6 5 4 3 2 1

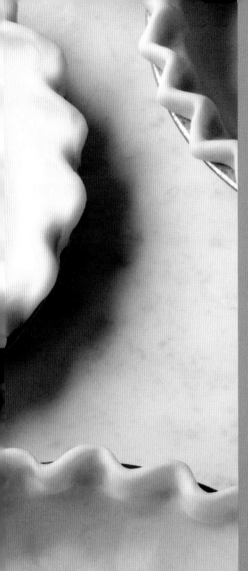

CONTENTS

ACKNOWLEDGMENTS

This book required many talented individuals to make it a reality and I am incredibly grateful to all of them.

First and foremost, I want to thank my husband, Francisco, for his unwavering support, patience, and encouragement throughout this project and in all of my life pursuits. Without him, this book would have been "just pie in the sky." You are amazing, chef. Special thanks to my daughter, Isabel, who happily tasted every test pie or tart and provided the inspiration for the Candy Bar Pie on page 223.

Tom Vaccaro, senior director for baking and pastry education, for his unflagging support and consistently positive attitude.

Dr. Tim Ryan, president of The Culinary Institute of America, and Mark Erickson, provost, for providing the opportunity and resources required for this book.

Nathalie Fischer, who was indispensable in making it all work together effortlessly.

Lisa Lahey, for the valuable advice and insights that enriched this book.

Erin McDowell, for her assistance and coordination of the photography, which helped make this book look beautiful.

Ben Fink, who understood my vision and helped me execute it through his visually stunning photos, and with a lot of laughs along the way.

Mark Furstenberg, owner of Bread Furst, for believing in me early in my career and putting up with my endless questions about the chemistry of bread.

And finally, thank you to my students at the CIA, who daily serve as inspiration to become a better educator.

INTRODUCTION

Long before I ever dreamed of writing a book about pies and tarts, I would stand in my grandmother's kitchen on a stool and "help" her make pies for family gatherings or celebrations. She was an expert baker and home cook, often not working from written recipes but rather from the look or feel of the ingredients as she was combining them. It is from these early childhood experiences that my love for and connection to these homespun, timeless treats was born.

Pie and tart making is quickly becoming a lost art. Most home bakers have difficulty producing consistent crusts and fillings, and it is my hope that this book will help not only explain but also demystify the fundamental techniques of making pies and tarts. There are many books that offer definitive advice regarding the "dos and don'ts" of the techniques of making pies and tarts, but ultimately, it is from the repetition of working with the ingredients, and to some degree "feeling" how they combine and work together, that your skills and understanding of pies and tarts will develop and evolve.

Traditionally, pies and tarts were made with ingredients readily available in most home pantries and without complex tools or unnecessary gadgets. That said, in order to create an exceptional pie or tart, I believe it is important to bake with high-quality ingredients and utilize seasonally available produce. Generally, fruits and vegetables are more abundant, less expensive, and better tasting if they are grown in your local area. Sourcing premium ingredients for your pies and tarts will certainly make a difference in flavor, texture, and quality.

All of the recipes included in this book give weight measures as well as volume. I have chosen to include weights because they are inherently more accurate than volume measurements and will produce a more consistent product. I encourage you to purchase a high-quality electronic scale, as they are inexpensive and readily available online or at kitchenware stores. This simple step of utilizing a scale for baking will help you produce better results faster.

Rustic to elegant, the recipes are designed to run the gamut of skills—from beginner to expert. I trust there is a pie or tart in this book that every reader will be able to make. On the pages that follow, you will find recipes that will allow you to create delicious and beautiful pies and tarts—easily and without fear.

Tools, Equipment, and Ingredients

The first step in crafting a superior pie, both in flavor and form, is to have a good understanding of your tools and equipment. Although our grandmothers and our great-grandmothers made delicious pies at home with little or no specialty equipment—other than years of accumulated experience—today we have a dizzying array of choices available to us. In my opinion, little, if any, specialty equipment is needed, but a few tools make the process of creating a pie simpler and easier for the home baker. So why not try them?

MEASURING TOOLS

In the United States, many home bakers rely on volumetric measures—measuring containers and measuring spoons—for portioning out ingredients for recipes. While using volumetric measures is what we have been taught to do, this method is inaccurate and inconsistent. Using a scale to measure ingredients by weight is the recommended and preferred method, and it is a method that you will find in this book. Understanding that you may not have access to a digital scale, however, the recipe ingredients in this book are provided in volume as well as weight.

Digital scale

A digital scale is indispensable in a professional bake shop and should be used in home kitchens as well. It is necessary to accurately and consistently weigh ingredients. Your digital scale should have a large, flat platform in order to easily accommodate a bowl; a legible readout displaying weight in pounds/ounces as well as grams; controls that are easy to use, including a tare/zero feature that allows you to "zero" the scale before adding additional ingredients; and a maximum capacity of 11 pounds.

Dry measuring cups

These typically come in sets of graduated volume amounts (⅛, ¼, ⅓, ½, ⅔, and 1 cup) and can be made from stainless steel or heavy-duty plastic. For accuracy, it is essential to have the ability to easily level the dry ingredients flush at the top edge; cups with spouts are not recommended. To measure dry ingredients such as flour or granulated sugar, dip the cup into the canister to fill, and then level the top with an offset spatula to remove the excess.

LIQUID MEASURING CUPS

A clear pitcher-style measuring cup with graduated fluid ounces and cups, made from heatproof glass, is the most versatile kind to use when working with liquids. To ensure an accurate reading of the measured ingredient, place the cup on a flat surface and view the liquid at eye level to compare it to the measurement markings.

MEASURING SPOONS

The same set of measuring spoons is used both for liquid and dry ingredients. It is essential to have a set that includes ⅛ teaspoon, ¼ teaspoon, ½ teaspoon, 1 teaspoon, 1½ teaspoons, and 1 tablespoon measures with a level, straight edge.

MIXING AND ROLLING EQUIPMENT AND TOOLS

PASTRY BLENDER

This inexpensive U-shaped tool is useful for combining chilled butter and flour in a mixing bowl to create a flaky pastry by hand. Select a cutter with steel blades or wires, and make sure that the handle is comfortable.

FOOD PROCESSOR

While not a mandatory piece of equipment for pie making, food processors certainly make the process easier. The blades of the processor efficiently cut butter into flour for pie and tart crusts. One downside to using a food processor to create a crust is that its motor generates friction and heat, which can soften or even melt the butter and can result in a dough that is overprocessed.

STAND MIXER

A stand mixer equipped with paddle and wire whip attachments is helpful for creating pie dough and finishing items for pies, such as meringues and whipped cream. The added benefit of a stand mixer when making dough is that there is little residual heat created during mixing, resulting in larger pieces of butter, which in turn create flakier crusts.

ROLLING PINS

Available in many shapes and materials, rolling pins are essential to pie making and are necessary for rolling dough evenly. The most common rolling pin material is hardwood, but for pie dough you might select marble or stainless steel, as these materials will remain cool and not transfer heat to the dough.

PIE-MAKING EQUIPMENT, CLOCKWISE FROM TOP LEFT: food processor, pastry bag and piping tips, traditional rolling pin, fine-mesh strainer, liquid measuring cup, silicone baking mat, bench scraper, bowl scraper, apple corer, apple peeler, rasp grater, kitchen torch, stand mixer, pie pan, pie birds, hand pie mold, pastry cutter, ceramic pie weights, metal pie weights, pie edge shield, dough docker, handheld lattice cutter, digital scale, dry measuring cups, pastry wheel, flan ring, pie crust pastry cutters, rubber spatula, offset spatula, rolling pin rings, straight rolling pin, tapered rolling pin, cherry pitter, cooling rack, instant-read thermometer, tart and tartlet pans, pastry brush, digital probe thermometer, oven thermometer

Straight pin

Typically made from hardwood, straight pins are also available in synthetic materials such as nylon or silicone. These French-style pins are approximately 20 inches in length and have no handles. Many professional bakers prefer using straight-cylinder pins because they make it easy to feel the thickness and evenness of the dough when rolling.

Tapered pin

This hardwood pin is a 19- to 21-inch cylinder with tapered ends and without handles. This style is most often used to roll out single rounds of dough as the tapered ends allow the pin to pivot with ease.

Traditional baker's rolling pin

Readily available, this pin is sturdy, typically made out of hardwood, and features offset handles with ball bearings. Additionally, these pins are available in marble and stainless steel; both can be refrigerated in order to maintain a cool temperature.

ROLLING PIN RINGS

These rubber rings are designed to slide onto both ends of a rolling pin so that dough can be rolled to a preselected and uniform thickness. (These rings cannot be used with a tapered rolling pin.)

BAKEWARE

Selecting bakeware for your pies and tarts is an essential step in creating a superior product. A pie or tart dough will bake differently depending on the kind of pan in which it is baked, and an inferior pan can adversely affect the crust of your pies and tarts. It is also important to use the correct size pan. There are a wide variety of materials being used today for bakeware. Each type has advantages and disadvantages.

Aluminum and *aluminum-coated steel* are the most common metals used for bakeware. They conduct heat efficiently and bake items evenly and quickly. *Shiny metal pans* reflect the oven heat away from the pan and slow down bake time, which can result in a soggy, underbaked crust. *Black* or *dark-colored metal pans* absorb heat and transfer it to the crust, typically browning crusts faster. The majority of pans have a *nonstick coating* that prevents the crust from sticking, but this coating can be scratched when cutting or serving the pie. The coating can also act as an insulator between the crust and the pan, making it more difficult to brown the crust.

Porcelain, ceramic, and *stoneware* are slow to absorb heat and bake a crust, resulting in longer bake times. Once hot, these materials readily retain their heat and transfer it evenly to the crust. An advantage of these vessels is that they can go from freezer to oven to table seamlessly. *Tempered glass pie pans* heat up very quickly and transfer the heat to the crust, baking it faster than metal pans. Glass pie plates are readily available and a popular choice. They have the added benefit of allowing the baker to see the browning of the bottom crust.

Silicone, recently introduced to the market, is being used for pie pans and a variety of other bakeware, such as cupcake pans. However, silicone is a poor conductor of heat and crusts will be slow to bake, although they will brown more evenly. Silicone pans need to be placed on a baking sheet for support, which can make transferring them to a cooling rack difficult; without the support of the baking sheet, the bottom of the flexible pan is more likely to buckle.

Pie pans

With sloped sides, this standard-size pie tin is available in several materials. Glass and aluminum pie pans are the most popular and readily available. They generally measure 9 to 10 inches, 1 to 1¼ inches deep, with a capacity of about 4½ cups.

Deep pie dishes

Typically made of ceramic or stoneware, these pie dishes are deeper and wider than a traditional pie pan, often 9½ inches, 2 to 3 inches deep, and with a capacity of 7 cups.

Flan rings

These are bottomless stainless-steel rings, available in several sizes and with straight sides or rolled edges. The standard depth is ¾ inch and diameters range from 2½ inches to 11 inches. Used with a baking sheet and parchment, these rings can be lined with tart dough and baked.

Tart and tartlet pans

These shallow tinned steel pans are available in a variety of shapes and sizes. The surfaces can be regular or nonstick, sides can be fluted or straight, and bottoms can be stationary or removable. The most versatile large tart pan is a 9-inch pan with a removable bottom that is easy to unmold.

Quiche dishes

These baking dishes are shallow, usually made of porcelain, and have decorative fluted edges. They are attractive for serving savory quiches. Typical quiche dishes measure 10 to 11 inches, 1 inch deep, with a capacity of 6½ cups.

Springform pans

These are round metal pans composed of two parts: a flat bottom and a deep, straight-sided outer ring with a metal clamp. When closed, the clamp tightens the outer ring and holds the bottom in place. Typically used for cakes, springform pans also are selected to bake deep quiches. Diameters range from 6 to 12 inches, with depths of 2½ to 3 inches.

BAKING AND SPECIALTY TOOLS

Apple corer

A hand tool used to remove the core of apples and pears. The stainless-steel tube is ½ to ¾ inch wide and 6 to 7 inches long with a serrated end for cutting.

Apple peeler

A hand-crank tool with a three-pronged arm that is inserted into the base of an apple or pear. When cranked, a small sharp blade efficiently peels the fruit while also coring and cutting the fruit into a spiral slice, which can then be cut into halves or quarters.

Cherry pitter

A specialty tool used to remove the pit from fresh cherries. The hollowed-out sphere holds a single piece of fruit. When squeezed, a plunger is forced through the fruit, ejecting the pit from the other side and leaving the fruit whole. Olives can be pitted in the same manner.

Citrus zester

A short, handheld stainless-steel tool with four to five sharpened holes at one end. When scraped over the rind of citrus fruits, thin strips of peel (zest) are removed and the bitter, white pith is left behind.

Cooling racks

Wire racks made from heavy-duty metal that allow air to circulate around and under baked goods. They are typically footed, can be rectangular or circular, and are available in a range of sizes.

Culinary torch

This handheld unit, fueled by a canister of butane, produces a small flame similar to a blowtorch. It is used to caramelize sugar topping and to quickly brown meringues.

Dough docker

A 3- to 5-inch-wide cylinder roller studded with metal or plastic spikes. This tool quickly pierces holes into dough, which reduces the chance of air pockets forming during the blind baking of pie and tart crusts. A tined fork will serve the same purpose.

Food mill

A food mill looks similar to a stainless-steel saucepan with a perforated bottom. It has a crank handle attached to an interior paddle blade. As the handle is turned, the paddle blade forces the food through a perforated disc and into a bowl below, while blocking any seeds or peels from going into the purée.

Handheld lattice cutter

A plastic or stainless-steel straight-edge rolling cylinder, 4 to 5 inches wide, with alternating blades attached to a handle. When rolled over dough, it creates a uniform crisscross, netlike pattern.

Hand pie molds

To form a shaped handheld pie, these plastic molds are lined with dough, filled with fruits or other filling, and pressed together. Available in various shapes.

Marble work surface

Marble is a preferred surface for rolling out pastry dough because it remains cool, thus preventing the fat from melting. Marble slabs can be purchased at kitchen-supply stores.

Offset spatula

An angled, round-tip metal blade with an offset handle. Because the handle is higher than the blade, the spatula can be used to smooth out fillings or toppings that are lower than the height of the pan. Offset spatulas are available in lengths ranging from 4 to 14 inches.

Parchment paper

A nonstick, grease- and heatproof baking paper used for lining baking pans and rolling out dough. The paper can be reused, will not burn in a conventional home oven, and is available in rolls or sheets.

Pastry brushes

These brushes are used to apply water, milk, or egg wash to crusts and to glaze finished pies. The bristles, made from materials ranging from silicone to nylon to natural boar bristles, are blunt and flat-edged and should be hand-washed with a detergent and allowed to air-dry after each use. Pastry brushes are available in several widths.

Pastry cloth and rolling pin cover

A large rectangular piece of canvas and stretchable rolling-pin cover, both made of cotton, prevent dough from sticking to the pin and the rolling surface. The cotton also absorbs some of the extra flour, which helps prevent the dough from becoming too tough.

Pastry cutters

Pastry crimper
A slotted rolling blade attached to a handle. When rolled along the edge of a double-crust pie or turnover, it seals or crimps together the crust.

Pie crust pastry cutters
Designed to cut out small decorative shapes of pie dough, these cutters are the size of small cookie cutters (1½ to 2 inches in length). The shapes can be layered on the edge of a crust or used to create decorative cutouts in a top crust.

Pastry wheel
A round stainless-steel rolling blade, straight or fluted, attached to a handle. When rolled through dough, it makes a continuous cut.

Pie top lattice cutter
A plastic cutter, 9 to 10 inches in diameter, with a decorative cutout design. Used on rolled pastry dough in a similar manner as a large cookie cutter to make the top crust of a double-crust pie.

Pie edge shield

Round metal or silicone shields, ranging from 9 to 10 inches in diameter, protect the decorative edge of a pie from overbrowning before the center is baked. These lightweight rings are available in adjustable or fixed sizes.

Pie vents

The traditional pie vent is a hollow porcelain or ceramic bird with an open mouth. A small arch on the bottom of the bird offsets it from the bottom crust of a fruit or meat pie. The function of a pie bird is twofold: venting steam from juices inside the crust and supporting the weight of the top crust.

Pie weights

These weigh down a bottom pie crust during blind baking to prevent it from buckling. Pie weights can be made of ceramic or aluminum, and also are available as a stainless-steel chain. Dried beans are an inexpensive alternative to store-bought weights and can be reused.

Piping bags and pastry tips

A pastry bag and basic set of tips are needed to create decorative garnishes on top of pies or tarts with whipped cream and meringues. Decorating bags are funnel-shaped, available in lengths of 7 to 24 inches, and are made of reusable plastic-coated fabric or nylon. Disposable plastic pastry bags also are available. Pastry tips are usually made of nickel-plated metal or chromed steel. They are tapered to fit tightly into the narrow end of the piping bag. A basic set of decorating tips should include an open star tip for making borders, stars, and rosettes; basket-weave flat tips for lattices and ribbons; and a plain round tip for borders and ropes.

Pizza stone

A pizza stone placed on the oven rack and thoroughly preheated will provide gentle radiant heat to a pie that is baked directly on top of it, helping to prevent a soggy bottom crust.

Rasp grater

Also known by the brand name Microplane, these handheld stainless-steel graters have sharp scalloped teeth that finely grate ingredients such as citrus zest, nutmeg, chocolate, or hard cheeses. They are available flat or curved.

Scrapers

Bench scraper
Also called a bench knife, this tool has a stainless-steel, rectangular straight-edge blade approximately 6 inches wide with an attached handle. It is used to remove sticky dough from work surfaces, to cut dough into portions, and to move ingredients into piles on the "bench" or work surface.

Bowl scraper
Similar in size and function to a bench scraper, but made of flexible plastic. The rectangular blade has a rounded edge that conforms to the shape of a mixing bowl and is used to scrape out dough, batter, and filling.

Sifter or strainer

Professional bakers use handheld, fine-mesh, heat-resistant strainers for many uses, including combining and aerating dry ingredients in place of a hand-operated canister-style sifter, draining and removing seeds or pulp from fruit juices, or removing inconsistencies from cooked fillings.

Silicone baking mats

Also known by the brand name Silpat, these flexible, nonstick, heat-resistant silicone mats are designed to withstand temperatures up to 500°F and are used to line baking sheets.

Silicone spatula

Flexible silicone spatulas are excellent for folding, stirring, blending, and scraping ingredients. These heat-resistant spatulas will not absorb flavors or odors.

Thermometers

Candy/Deep-frying thermometer
A thermometer that registers from 100° to 400°F with markings indicating important stages of sugar cooking that can also be used to monitor the temperature of cooking fats used for deep-frying.

Digital probe and instant-read thermometers
A digital probe thermometer has a metal probe attached to a handle. The probe is inserted into the center of the baked item and a digital readout on the handle provides a temperature reading. An instant-read thermometer is similar; it is a handheld thermometer that can have a dial or a digital face.

Oven thermometer
Temperatures in ovens can vary widely due to improper calibration or to oven thermostats that do not maintain a steady temperature. A metal mechanical standing or hanging thermometer is helpful, as it can be easily moved around the inside of the oven to check for temperature accuracy or hot spots.

Whisk

Also called whips, these handled, looped metal wires are available in several sizes and shapes. A balloon whisk has a spherical shape and is designed to incorporate air into egg whites or cream.

INGREDIENTS

Understanding how your ingredient selection affects your end product is essential for achieving consistent results in baking. The importance of selecting the highest-quality flour, fats, sweeteners, chocolate, nuts, and fruits cannot be ignored.

FLOUR

Flour is a key baking ingredient, especially for pie and tart crusts. The right flour yields a light, flaky, and flavorful vessel. *Wheat flour* is primarily protein and starch and is classified by its protein percentage. When wheat flour is combined with moisture, two of its proteins—glutenin and gliadin—combine to form a new protein called *gluten*. Gluten is responsible for creating an elastic, stretchable web in dough. Although this matrix is essential for baking bread, too much of it is less than desirable in pie and pastry dough. Low-protein flour creates delicate, tender crusts, and high-protein flour creates stronger, more elastic dough. Pie crusts require both of these qualities. As most national brands of all-purpose flour are a blend of low-protein flour and high-protein flour, they produce soft yet stretchable dough.

All-purpose flour

All-purpose flour is a blend of flours. Its protein content ranges from 10 to 12 percent. Select unbleached flour, as the process of bleaching whitens the flour, weakens the gluten proteins, and typically results in a heavy, off-tasting metallic crust. A word of caution: Not all regional brands of all-purpose flour perform the same way due to variations in the protein content in the wheat blends.

PROTEIN PERCENTAGES OF COMMON SUPERMARKET FLOURS

King Arthur, Unbleached	11.7%
Pillsbury, Unbleached, Enriched	10–11.5%
Gold Medal, Unbleached	10.5%
White Lily, Enriched, Bleached	8–9%

Whole-wheat flour

This flour is milled from the entire wheat kernel and includes both the germ and outer coating of bran (as opposed to all-purpose and other refined flours, which are milled only from the endosperm, or starchy center, of the kernel). Whole-grain flour adds a nutty flavor to crusts, and by volume or weight, one-quarter of the flour in most crust recipes can be replaced with whole-wheat flour without any adverse effect to the texture.

Meals and starches

Meals and starches are used like flour in many instances. Often the only difference between a flour and a meal is particle size. Meals, being of a larger particle size than flours, will lend a more granular texture to a dough or batter and to the resulting baked product. Processed and refined starches can also be used in place of flour, but are chiefly used in pies and tarts for their thickening abilities. In this book, they are used to set or give more substance or body to fillings, such as fruit fillings and custards. They result in a range of textures and consistencies once set.

Cornmeal

Ground from corn, this flour is manufactured in two main forms: stone ground and steel roller ground. Cornmeal made by millstones (stone ground) is usually coarser in texture and retains the germ and the hull of the seed, lending more flavor and texture to baked goods. Steel roller–processed cornmeal is more finely ground and uniform in texture, and the germ has been removed.

Oatmeal

Oat seeds are processed in several methods to produce a variety of products. The oat is rolled and steamed to make old-fashioned oats. Quick-cooking oats are produced in the same method as old-fashioned oats but are rolled thinner. Generally, quick-cooking oats and old-fashioned oats are interchangeable in recipes and will yield a similar flavor, although the finished texture will be slightly different due to the size of the flakes. Instant oats are made by precooking and drying the oats, and if used in baking will lose their texture and become mushy. If the oat is not steamed or rolled and instead cut into pieces, it yields steel-cut or Irish oats, which are not appropriate for baking.

Cornstarch

A popular and readily available starch taken from the center of a corn kernel, cornstarch is used as a thickener for fruit fillings and custards. When combined with fruit, it creates a semitranslucent, glossy, and smooth pie filling.

Tapioca

Three common forms of the starch-thickener tapioca are available: pearl, granular instant tapioca (sold under the brand name Minute and also called quick-cooking), and tapioca starch or flour. This starch is derived from the roots of the cassava plant, also called manioc or yucca, and is prized for its translucent, glossy appearance and neutral flavor in fruit pie fillings.

Granular quick-cooking tapioca is best used as a thickener in pies if it is finely ground into a powder in a clean coffee grinder or in a small food processor fitted with a blade. This additional step will ensure that the tapioca dissolves properly; otherwise it may create a gelatinous, lumpy texture when baked in the fruit filling. If it is quick-cooking but not granular, it must be combined with the fruit in layers and allowed to stand for a minimum of 30 minutes in order to fully dissolve.

Tapioca flour is processed into a fine, powdery flour, and this granulation allows it to easily be combined into fruit fillings without the additional step of grinding. If tapioca flour is being substituted for quick-cooking tapioca in a filling, increase the amount of flour by half, either by volume or by weight. For instance, if a recipe calls for 1 teaspoon of quick-cooking tapioca, use 1½ teaspoons of tapioca flour.

Fats

Fats are an essential ingredient in baking, directly imparting flavor and influencing tenderness and flakiness in pie and tart crusts. Most pie and tart crusts need to be made with a solid fat in order to create their characteristic tender and flaky texture. The role of fats in creating crusts is twofold: They coat the proteins in flour, preventing gluten development, which yields tenderness, and they produce flakiness by creating steam during baking, forcing apart the layers of pastry. A wide variety of fats are available for use in pastry making, each with its own advantages and shortcomings, but butter is used primarily for the pies and tarts in this book.

Butter
Butter is prized for its sweet, rich flavor and is the preferred fat for the crust recipes in this book, but its low melting point and overall makeup can make it difficult to work with. Unlike shortening or lard, butter is not 100 percent fat. It contains on average 80 percent butterfat, 10 to 16 percent water, and a small percentage of milk solids. The additional moisture in butter contributes to tough pastry dough if overworked during mixing, and the low melting point of 94°F allows the fat to melt into the flour as it is worked, changing the texture of the finished crust. Butter is produced as salted and unsalted, or "sweet." For baking, it is best to purchase unsalted butter, as manufacturers add varying amounts of salt, making it difficult to control the total amount.

Vegetable shortening
Shortening is made from hydrogenated vegetable oil and is 100 percent fat, white in color, and flavorless. The process of hydrogenation saturates fats in the oil and changes them from liquid to solid fat at room temperature, also raising the fat's melting point. As shortening is able to withstand higher temperatures and does not melt easily, it creates flaky and crisp yet tender pie crusts when used alone or in combination with butter.

Eggs

An essential ingredient in baking, eggs contribute flavor, richness, texture, and structure to baked goods. Eggs have a wide variety of uses in baking: acting as a binder and a thickener in cream pies and custard pie fillings, as a flavoring and binding agent in pie and tart doughs, and trapping air in egg whites for meringues.

STANDARD EGG SIZES AND WEIGHTS

SIZE	WEIGHT (UNSHELLED)	YOLK	WHITE
Medium	1.55 oz	0.52 oz	1.03 oz
Large	1.77 oz	0.59 oz	1.18 oz
Extra-large	2.05 oz	0.68 oz	1.37 oz
Jumbo	2.3 oz	0.77 oz	1.53 oz

Eggs are sold whole in a range of sizes, from jumbo to peewee. The most commonly available sizes are jumbo, extra-large, large, and medium. Most recipes call for large eggs. Eggs are also graded based on the interior and exterior quality of the egg when packed. The grades range from AA, which is the best, to grade B, which is the poorest quality. Most eggs sold in supermarkets are grade A, the middle grade.

When selecting eggs for purchase, check the sale date stamped on the package in order to select the freshest eggs possible. As an egg ages, both the white and yolk become looser and do not readily retain air and foam. Generally, eggs are packed and on the shelf within a week of being laid, and must be sold within thirty days from the date on the carton.

Dairy products

Milk

In the United States, milk and milk products are classified and standardized by the federal government. The milk fat content for fluid milk starts at a minimum of 3.25 percent for whole milk and ranges to less than ½ percent for skim milk.

If a recipe calls for milk, use whole milk unless otherwise specified. Milk with a lower fat percentage will negatively affect the texture, mouthfeel, and flavor of that product.

Evaporated milk A specialty canned unsweetened milk product produced by heating and removing water from whole milk until it contains twice the milk fat of whole milk. The resulting liquid is thick, with a slightly cooked milk flavor.

Sweetened condensed milk Condensed milk is produced in the same manner as evaporated milk, with the addition of approximately 45 percent sugar, creating a thick, sweet milk product.

Cream

Cream has multiple uses in baking: acting as the liquid base for cream and custard fillings, in whipped form to lighten the texture of cream pie fillings, and whipped and sweetened as a garnish for pies and tarts. In the

United States, there are three classifications of cream based upon the minimum milk fat content. Light cream has the lowest fat content, 18 to 20 percent, and is not suitable for whipping. Whipping cream must consist of a minimum of 30 percent but no more than 36 percent fat. Heavy cream contains the highest percentage, at 36 to 40 percent. When whipping cream, keep the bowl cool to help keep the fat from melting, as the friction from incorporating air can produce heat and melt the foam. Heavy cream is preferred for most of the recipes in this book; substituting another cream may affect the texture and balance of the end product due to the variances in fat content. Mascarpone, sour cream, and crème fraîche (described in the following entries) are all produced from cream.

Cultured dairy products

Buttermilk, yogurt, sour cream, and crème fraîche are all dairy products that have a characteristic sour and tangy flavor due to the addition of a bacterial culture or lactic acid. After the addition of the culture, these products are heated, allowing the bacteria to convert the sugars to lactic acid, resulting in a pleasant tart flavor and prolonged shelf life.

Buttermilk In times past, buttermilk was the by-product of making butter; however, modern buttermilk is produced through the addition of a bacterial culture to whole, low-fat, or nonfat milk, giving it a thickened, tangy flavor.

Yogurt A cultured dairy product made from whole, low-fat, or nonfat milk to which a bacterial culture is added

Mascarpone This Italian cheese has a high butterfat content ranging from 70 to 75 percent. It is an ivory-colored, firm-bodied, mildly sweet cheese. However, mascarpone is not technically a cheese, as it is produced by the addition of an acid to cream, which is heated, causing it to thicken.

Crème fraîche A cultured dairy product widely used in France and traditionally produced by allowing the natural bacteria present in unpasteurized cream to thicken and sour it at room temperature. In the United States, crème fraîche is made from cream containing 30 to 40 percent butterfat, and is produced with the addition of a bacterial culture. Crème fraîche has a mildly tangy, nutty flavor with a smoother, richer texture than sour cream.

Sour cream The characteristic tangy flavor is created by adding lactic acid to cream containing 18 to 20 percent fat to thicken it. Often gums, gelatin, or starches are added to create a gelled consistency. Low-fat or light sour cream has a fat content of approximately 10 to 11 percent, and often can be used as a substitute for full-fat sour cream in fillings and garnishes without compromising flavor or texture.

Fresh cheeses

These cheeses are moist and very soft. They have a flavor that is generally termed mild, but fresh cheese made from goat's milk may be slightly tangy and strong. Fresh cheeses are unripened, high in moisture, and generally have a fresh flavor and creamy texture.

Cream cheese With a mild, slightly tangy flavor and smooth, creamy texture, cream cheese is produced from cream that must contain a minimum of 33 percent milk fat. A lower-fat version of cream cheese is available and is labeled Neufchâtel or low-fat cream cheese; it contains a minimum 20 percent milk fat. Both types of cream cheese often have stabilizer and gums added to increase firmness and creaminess.

Ricotta An Italian soft cheese with a slightly creamy, grainy texture and a mildly sweet flavor that is produced from adding bacteria or enzymes to whole or part-skim milk.

Fruits and vegetables

In pies and tarts, fruits and sometimes vegetables are often the focal point and contribute flavor, texture, and color. Generally speaking, purchasing produce when it is at its best in your locality, from local growers, will result in a superior pie or tart. However, while seasonality and locality are important considerations when selecting fruits and vegetables for pie and tart making, they are no guarantee of quality. Fresh produce is extremely perishable, and improper selection or storage can negatively affect your finished pie or tart.

When selecting fresh produce for purchase, look for mature fruits or vegetables at the height of their season. Always use your senses, as the aroma of the fruit is generally a good indicator of ripeness. When possible, taste the product to evaluate its sweetness or tartness. Produce charts are often helpful in determining what is in season in a particular month, but climatic conditions can affect the start or end of a growing season, which in turn affects the harvest timeline and availability. Fruits are the ovaries that surround or contain the seeds of plants. Dried fruits have more intense flavor than their fresh counterparts and may be used in savory or sweet cooking or baking.

The process of ripening generally softens the texture of fresh fruit, and the fruit becomes juicier and sweeter. However, not all fruits ripen after harvest and some fruits must be purchased fully ripe. Fruits that ripen after harvest include apples, pears, bananas, kiwis, apricots, peaches, nectarines, and plums. Fruits that do not ripen after harvest include berries, citrus fruits, cherries, figs, grapes, and pineapples. Before use, always wash all fruits or vegetables to remove dirt and microorganisms, especially if the produce will be consumed uncooked.

Almost any selection of vegetables can be used in making savory pies and tarts, but there are a few that are commonly used in making pies and tarts as dessert too; the few that are discussed on the pages that follow fall into this category.

SEASONAL AVAILABILITY OF FRUITS AND VEGETABLES

FRUIT/VEGETABLE	JAN	FEB	MAR	APR	MAY	JUNE	JULY	AUG	SEP	OCT	NOV	DEC
Apples	○	○	○	○	○	○	○	●	●	●	●	●
Apricots					○	●	●	●				
Blackberries					○	●	●					
Blueberries						●	●	●				
Citrus (oranges, lemons, and limes)	●	●	○	○	○	○	○	○	○	●	●	●
Cherries						●	●	●				
Cranberries										●	●	●
Figs, Mission					○	○	●	●	○	○	○	
Grapes, Concord									●	●		
Peaches				○	○	●	●	●	○	○		
Pears	●							●	●	●	●	●
Plums					○	●	●	●	○			
Pumpkins							○	●	●	●		
Raspberries						●	●	●	●			
Rhubarb				○	●	●	○	○	○			
Strawberries				●	●	●						
Sweet Potatoes	○	○	○	○	○	○	●	●	●	●	○	○

○ Available but not in season   ● In season, best quality

Dried fruits

Dried fruits are often used to add texture and concentrated flavor to pies and tarts. The most common dried fruits are raisins, cherries, figs, and cranberries. With the exception of raisins, these fruits often have sugar added to them before drying in order to keep them soft and moist. When purchasing dried fruits, select moist fruits and keep them in sealed packages or containers. If buying fruits in bulk, be sure to taste them for freshness. Often, dried fruits are plumped with a liquid before they are added to a filling; see note on page 157 for a description of that process.

Apples

Over 2,500 varieties of apples are grown in the United States, but only one hundred varieties are grown commercially, and those are only available in specific regions. Each variety has its own characteristic flavor, aroma, color, and texture. Not all apple types are good for baking, as some varieties lose their texture and fall apart, or the flavor of the apple is overly sweet or excessively sour, or the aroma of the apple is not prominent. Try combining different varieties of apples grown in your region to create a unique and distinctive apple pie.

BEST APPLES FOR BAKING PIES AND TARTS

VARIETY	EAST	MIDWEST	WEST	AVAILABILITY	FLAVOR/AROMA	BAKING CHARACTERISTICS
Cortland	●	●		September–April	Sweet, hint of tart	Retains shape, ¾-inch slices, resists browning, good for open tarts
Golden Delicious	●	●	●	Year-round	Sweet, gingery, strong pearlike aroma	Retains shape, resists browning, good for open tarts, use less sugar
Granny Smith	●		●	Year-round	Tart, sour, little aroma	Retains firm shape, ¼-inch slices, tends to brown excessively
Ida Red	●	●	●	October–April	Tangy, sweet	Retains shape, increase thickener
Jonagold	●	●	●	October–June	Tart but sweet, strong pearlike aroma	Retains shape, ½-inch slices
Northern Spy	●		●	October–June	Tart, acidic, sweet	Retains shape
Rome Beauty	●	●	●	September–April	Mild, sweet yet tart, little aroma	Combine with tart apples, retains shape

When selecting apples for purchase, choose those varieties appropriate for baking, and make sure they have smooth, bruise-free skin and have an appropriate skin color.

The chart opposite lists commonly available apple types that are highly recommended for use in baking pies and tarts.

Bananas

One of the world's largest fruit crops, bananas are available year-round. Bananas are a difficult fruit to work with in pies and tarts because their flesh discolors, turning brown soon after peeling. Bananas are perfectly ripe when their skin becomes freckled with light brown spots. Once ripened, they can easily be stored whole in their skin in the refrigerator. The skin turns black, but the fruit remains perfectly ripe.

Berries

When fresh berries begin to appear in the markets, they are a harbinger of spring and of the bounty of the fruits yet to come. The first berries of the season are typically strawberries in late spring; the season closes with the arrival of cranberries in early fall.

Most berries can be purchased year-round, but berries purchased outside of locally grown seasons do not match the bright color, sweet flavor, or tender texture of those in season. As an alternative to bland, flavorless, out-of-season berries, purchase and freeze field-ripened berries while they are at the height of their season. To freeze berries, rinse them and allow to air-dry on clean towels, then freeze them in a single layer on a baking sheet. After 2 to 3 hours, remove the berries from the tray and store them in sealed containers or freezer bags.

When selecting berries for purchase, choose berries with color appropriate to their variety, without mold or signs of shriveling. As berries do not ripen after harvest, the flavor should be sweet, not tart, and they should have a fragrant aroma. If storing berries in the refrigerator, store them in a single layer. Do not rinse them until you are ready to use them; the moisture will hasten their decay.

Blackberries When fully ripe, blackberries have a glossy blue, almost black hue, without any signs of red or green color, and should be firm and plump. If baked in a pie, these berries tend to become "jammy" and sweet, and each berry contains many seeds, which can affect the texture of the filling. Blackberries sold in pints are equal to approximately 1½ cups.

Blueberries This deep, dark purple to blue-black berry is pea-size, with a frosty bloom. This dusty color is a good sign of freshness, as is a firm, smooth, and plump skin without any red or green tint. Blueberries have an excellent balance of sweetness and tartness. Blueberries sold in pints are equal to approximately 3 cups; and 1 pound of fresh blueberries is about 2¾ cups of berries.

Cranberries Smooth, glossy red, firm cranberries are extremely bitter and best combined with other sweeter fruits to balance their tartness. Cranberries are also available in dried form, both sweetened and unsweetened. Fresh cranberries are generally sold in 12-ounce packages; each package is equal to 2½ to 3 cups.

Raspberries These berries are the cousin of blackberries and are similar in construction, but with a hollow core. Raspberries are usually red in color, but a golden variety is also available. They should be plump and without an attached stem or hull, which usually indicates an unripe fruit lacking sweetness or flavor. Raspberries are sold in pints that are equal to 1½ cups.

Strawberries Choose fully ripened, red berries with stem and hull still attached and without yellow shoulders. They should have a sweet aroma and a firm but yielding texture. Strawberries that are available year-round are cultivated to withstand travel and tend to be mealy and tasteless. They do not compare to the sweet flavor and juicy texture of local berries in season. Rinse strawberries with their stems and hulls attached; without them, the berries can quickly become waterlogged. Strawberries are typically sold in pint baskets equal to 2 cups, or quart baskets equal to 4 cups.

Citrus

Citrus fruits are prized for their acidity, distinctive aroma, and fresh, bright flavor—either as an accent or as the centerpiece in pie and tart fillings. The zest is the thin outer layer of the rind, which contains the natural oils and the bright color of the fruit. Between the rind and fruit lies the white pith, which is bitter and unpleasant.

Purchase citrus fruits that feel firm and heavy for their size, indicating freshness due to high moisture content. The fruit's exterior should have a shiny, almost oily, bright rind color with no signs of mold. Seasonal availability varies according to the type of citrus, but generally, the quality of these fruits improves significantly in the winter months.

Lemons Thick-skinned varieties of lemons yield less juice than the thinner-skinned fruits. Lemons are widely available year-round.

Limes Limes are a brightly colored, deep green fruit widely available year-round, and are considered the most acidic of all citrus fruits. The most common lime is the Persian. Another widely recognized variety is the Key lime, which is smaller and rounder than a Persian lime and yellow-green with brown splotches on the leathery rind. The Key lime is tarter and has a more complex acidic flavor.

Oranges Smooth, thin-skinned, small- and medium-size juicing varieties, such as Valencia, are best for obtaining a balanced acidic yet sweet juice. Blood oranges are another variety, with a unique maroon to deep purple flesh and a distinctive raspberry aroma.

Coconuts

Botanically speaking, the coconut is not classified as a nut but rather as a fruit. Common coconut products include: dried sweetened or unsweetened flakes, coconut milk, and coconut cream. Desiccated coconut is a flaked and unsweetened product with a concentrated coconut flavor. Sweetened coconut is produced by cooking it with sugar and drying the grated flakes. It can be produced untoasted or toasted, and is often used as a garnish.

Two liquid coconut products are available for use in pies and tarts: coconut milk and coconut cream. Coconut milk is an unsweetened product made by heating grated coconut, which extracts the flavor and oil, and infusing it into water. The resulting liquid is then filtered. It can be purchased canned or frozen. Coconut cream is the unsweetened fat from the coconut milk.

Figs

Black Mission figs are the most popular variety available and have dark purple to light red flesh with a delicate, sweet flavor. As figs will not ripen after harvest, select soft fruit with the stem still attached and no signs of bruising. The fruit should have a sweet aroma and a small amount of syrup at the opening on the base. Figs have a very high sugar content, which, combined with a thin, delicate skin, make these fruits extremely perishable. Three to 4 medium figs equal approximately 1 cup.

Grapes

Grapes are an often overlooked fruit in baking, as they tend to be used only as a garnish to top fresh fruit tarts. Yet grapes can be used alone or in combination with another fruit to make delicious and distinctive pie fillings. When selecting grapes, choose those that are plump and firmly attached to a green, pliable stem. Concord grapes are a seeded variety ranging from dark blue to purple, with sweet fruit and thin, tart, frosty skin. They make excellent pie fillings but have a short season and are available only in August, September, and October. One pound of grapes is 3 to 3½ cups.

Kiwis

A small, oblong, fuzzy, brown fruit with a brilliant green (or sometimes gold) interior, kiwis are used most often as a garnish for fruit tarts. Kiwis will ripen at room temperature, and when ripe will give slightly to pressure. Once ripe, the fruit can be stored in the refrigerator for up to 4 weeks.

CITRUS YIELDS FOR ZEST AND JUICE

- *Lemon: 2 teaspoons of juice and 1 to 2 teaspoons of zest*

- *Lime: 2 teaspoons of juice and approximately 1 teaspoon of zest*

- *Orange: ¼ cup juice and 4 to 5 teaspoons of zest*

Pears

Pears lend a sweet flavor and creamy texture to pies and tarts, and can easily be combined with more assertive fruit and nut flavors without "disappearing." Select fruit that is firm, underripe, and hard, with smooth skin. Pears are harvested before they ripen, and not all pear varieties change color or aroma when ripe. To check ripeness, press the flesh near the stem; if it yields to gentle pressure, the fruit is ripe.

Pale green or red Anjou pears have a sweet, mellow flavor with a hint of citrus, and their firm flesh retains its shape when baked. Bosc pears have a long, tapered neck, long stems, and skin that is russet yellow–cinnamon brown. When ripe, the flesh is crisp yet creamy and honey sweet, but the peel should be removed as it can be bitter and tough. The Bartlett pear is unique in that its color turns from bright green to golden yellow as it ripens. Its creamy, sweet, and aromatic flesh retains its shape when baked.

Three medium pears will equal approximately 1 pound.

Pumpkins

Sugar pumpkins (also termed pie or cheese pumpkins) are smaller, sweeter, and more tender and flavorful than pumpkins used for carving Jack-o'-lanterns. The flesh of this variety of pumpkin has a creamier, less stringy flesh. Choose smooth, deep orange pumpkins that are heavy for their size and without cracks or soft spots. While using in-season fresh pumpkins is a pleasure, excellent pies can be made from canned pumpkin purée, as it is difficult to obtain consistent flavor and texture in your pies with fresh pumpkin purée. The approximate yield of a sugar pumpkin 6 to 8 inches in diameter is 15 ounces or 1¾ cups of pumpkin purée.

Rhubarb

An extremely tart, astringent, long-stalked vegetable, rhubarb ranges in color from pale speckled pink to bright red. Long considered a spring vegetable, it is now grown in hot-houses and is widely available year-round, but is best from April to September. Select crisp, thick stalks free of mold or dark spots. Rhubarb can be easily combined with fruits, or used alone as the centerpiece of a pie or tart, but either way requires a substantial amount of sweetener to make it palatable. To freeze rhubarb, rinse the stalks and air-dry them on clean towels, then chop them into 1- to 2-inch segments and freeze them in a single layer on a baking sheet. After 2 to 3 hours, remove the rhubarb from the tray and store in sealed containers or freezer bags. One pound of rhubarb will yield 2½ to 3 cups chopped rhubarb.

Stone fruits

Stone fruits are aptly named after the large, hard pit, or stone, common to these varieties. A stone fruit will be classified as either *freestone* or *clingstone* depending on how easily the pit separates from the fruit. These fruits are generally only available in the summer months, and will soften once picked but not increase in sweetness. They should be firm and vibrantly colored, with no hint of green, and the aroma should be sweet and full. To properly ripen stone fruits, spread them out in a single layer to prevent bruising, and avoid refrigeration, which can accelerate spoiling.

Apricots Apricots are the first stone fruit of the season and they are fully ripe when the fruit yields to gentle pressure. The fruit should have a sweet aroma and gold to deep orange skin without traces of green. Once apricots are ripe, their shelf life is very short, but they can be refrigerated to halt ripening for up to 2 days. The weight of 6 to 7 medium apricots is approximately 1 pound.

Cherries There are two basic types of cherries, sweet and sour (sometimes called tart). Sweet cherries are primarily eaten fresh, while tart cherries are used for pies. Tart cherries are darker in color and firmer in texture than sweet cherries, and have higher acidity. Cherries will not ripen once picked, so select cherries that are ripe and sweet, plump, and glossy with green stems attached. Do not wash cherries until just before use. It is most efficient to pit cherries with a hand-operated pitter. To freeze cherries, rinse them and remove the stems, air-dry the fruit on clean towels, pit the stones, and freeze the cherries in a single layer on a baking sheet. After 2 to 3 hours, remove them from the tray and store them in sealed containers or freezer bags.

The yield of a 1-quart basket of cherries is approximately 3 to 4 cups.

Peaches and nectarines Peaches are the fuzzy cousin of the nectarine, with many similarities in skin color, flavor, as well as flesh color. Peaches and nectarines can be either yellow or white and categorized as either freestone or clingstone. For baking, freestone are best as they are easily removed from their stone and are generally sweeter and juicier than clingstones.

Peaches and nectarines are picked when ripe, and green peaches and nectarines are definitely unripe; however, color is not a good indicator of how ripe the fruit is. Different varieties have varying amounts of red blush in their coloring. The sweet, ripe aroma of a peach or nectarine should be distinct and apparent and the fruit should be plump and firm, but not hard, and free of bruises. Be sure your peaches and nectarines are ripe before you refrigerate them as the cool temperatures can cause the fruit to become mealy.

Two medium peaches or nectarines will yield approximately 1 cup of sliced peaches or nectarines.

Plums In the United States, over 150 plum varieties are cultivated, but only about twenty varieties are grown commercially. Generally, oval or egg-shaped plums with dark blue, black, or purple skins are best for baking. The firm texture and low moisture of the fruit allows it to retain its shape and texture when baked, and the sweet but tart flavor combines well with other fruits. Choose plums that are firm and plump, as the fruit ripens at room temperature and the flesh will become slightly soft, especially at the tip end.

Sweet potatoes

Much confusion exists when sweet potatoes are referred to as yams and vice versa. A true yam is darker, less sweet, and drier than a sweet potato—and not widely available in this country. For baking, the thinner skin Jewel and Beauregard sweet potatoes are the best due to their moist texture and deep orange color. When selecting sweet potatoes for pie filling, purchase firm, heavy potatoes without soft spots or mold. The equivalent of 1½ pounds of sweet potatoes will yield approximately 2 cups of cooked and mashed sweet potatoes.

CHOCOLATE

Bewildering arrays of cocoa and chocolate products exist and vary widely in quality and availability. The first step in properly selecting these products is to understand the makeup of each and their uses.

Bittersweet/semisweet chocolate

Often simply called dark chocolate, the FDA regulates that this type of chocolate must contain at least 35 percent of cocoa solids from the bean. On average, most brands contain about 50 percent added sugar, with the remaining balance containing both cocoa solids and cocoa butter (the fat from the cacao bean). Although brands vary, bittersweet chocolate contains an average of 46 percent sugar by weight, and semisweet contains an approximate average of 57 percent sugar.

Cocoa powder

Cocoa powder is produced by removing the cocoa butter from unsweetened chocolate and grinding the resulting dry cake into powder. Two types of cocoa powder are available: natural cocoa powder and Dutch-processed cocoa powder (sometimes termed alkalized). Each has a distinct color and flavor. Natural cocoa powder is untreated and very acidic, resulting in a redder, lighter, and less chocolate-flavored product. Dutch-processed cocoa powder is less acidic (or more alkaline), which can result in a smoother and darker product and less bitter chocolate flavor.

Chocolate baking chips

Molded, flat-bottomed, teardrop-shaped bits can be made from a variety of chocolates and some nonchocolate substances, such as peanut butter. As they do not contain a significant amount of cocoa butter, these chips do not readily melt when exposed to heat; therefore, they do not lose their shape. They are not recommended for melting, or when chocolate is the primary ingredient in a pie or tart, as when making chocolate custards and other fillings.

Milk chocolate

Milk chocolate is a light-colored, sweet chocolate, often with sugar as its main ingredient. On average, milk chocolate in the United States contains only 10 percent cocoa solids, with the remaining 90 percent made up of sugar, milk solids, and often vanilla.

White chocolate

Containing only cocoa butter, sugar, milk solids, and often vanilla, white chocolate is not considered a "real" chocolate as it does not contain cocoa solids. Essentially, white chocolate is milk chocolate without the cocoa solids, and it is often paired with more assertive flavors, as its predominate flavor is vanilla.

Unsweetened chocolate

Unsweetened chocolate is often referred to as baking chocolate. It is made from roasted cocoa beans and contains approximately 50 percent cocoa solids from the bean, and 50 percent cocoa butter, with no added sugar.

Nuts and specialty nut products

A wide variety of nuts are available for use in pies and tarts, and each type lends its flavor and crunchy texture to fillings and crusts, or as a garnish or a decorative element. Frequently used nuts are almonds, hazelnuts (filberts), walnuts, pecans, peanuts (not botanically classified as a nut but as a legume), macadamias, pistachios, and pine nuts. Many forms of nuts are available, including whole, chopped, sliced, slivered, and blanched; they can also be ground into flours, butters, or pastes.

When purchasing nuts, select the freshest nuts possible, sealed in vacuum packages or cans, as unshelled nuts are high in fats and oils and exposure to light or heat causes them to turn rancid quickly. If buying nuts in bulk, be sure to taste them for off flavors due to poor turnover or storage. Generally, if stored in sealed, airtight containers, unshelled nuts can be refrigerated for up to four months or frozen up to one year without affecting their flavor or quality. Specialty nut products include nut meals or flours, butters, and pastes. For nut meals or flours, the skin is usually removed from the raw nut, and the nut is blanched and then ground coarsely into meal or finely into flour. The most common nut flours and meals are almond and hazelnut, although others are available. Nut butters and pastes are made by crushing or finely grinding nuts until the natural oils are released, creating

REMOVING THE SKINS OF NUTS

The thin outer skin of some nuts can add an astringency to a crust or filling and discolor it. The thin skins of peanuts and hazelnuts can easily be removed by briefly heating them, then placing them in a mesh strainer and rubbing them against the sides of the strainer. An alternative is to place the nuts in between two clean kitchen towels and rub them together, separating the skins from the nuts. Heavier nut skins, such as almond or pistachio skins, can be removed by blanching the nuts in hot water until the skins loosen, then immediately rinsing them in cold water and draining them.

TOASTING NUTS

Toasting nuts greatly enhances their flavor and texture. To brown less than 1 cup of nuts on the stovetop, heat an ungreased heavy-bottomed skillet over medium heat, add the nuts, and toast, stirring frequently, for 4 to 8 minutes. Watch carefully and do not allow the nuts to burn. For larger quantities, preheat the oven to 350°F, and spread the nuts in a single layer on a shallow heavy-gauge baking pan. Toast the nuts in the oven for 5 to 10 minutes, stirring often.

When toasting nuts, their doneness should be judged by their color and aroma rather than by texture, as nuts are less brittle when warm and will become crisp as they cool. Remove the nuts from the pan or the oven when a toasted aroma is present and the nuts are one shade lighter than desired, as the nuts will continue to brown as they cool. Chopping nuts when warm will produce a cleaner cut, and will produce fewer flakes and crumbs.

a creamy, butterlike paste, sometimes with sugar added. Peanut butter by far is the most familiar nut butter, but many others are becoming readily available, such as cashew, hazelnut, and almond. Marzipan is made with almond paste, to which sugar is added until it becomes a malleable dough.

SALT

An often overlooked ingredient, salt acts as a flavor enhancer when properly paired with sweet flavors; more important, it suppresses bitterness, allowing more desirable flavors to become more pronounced.

Table salt
While fine-grained, these uniform, cube-shaped crystals are the densest of all the salts and are the slowest to dissolve. Select a table salt without added iodine for baking; the iodine yields a mineral aftertaste, and many manufacturers add sugar to mask this undesirable flavor.

Kosher salt and other coarse salts
A coarse-grained salt, the particles are produced in large flakes. Choose a coarse granular or flaked salt for garnishing as it will not readily dissolve on the surface. Kosher salt and table salt cannot be substituted for each other in equal amounts; the particle size of each salt varies by manufacturer. The recipes in this book have been developed and tested using kosher salt.

SWEETENERS

Sweeteners are divided into two main categories: crystalline sugar and sugar syrups. Most crystalline sugar is refined from either sugar beets or sugarcane, and several different varieties and types are available for use. Sugar must be stored in an airtight container as it tends to absorb moisture and clump.

Sugar and sugar syrups are key ingredients in baking, serving numerous functions, but are best known for lending sweetness and flavor to fillings as well as contributing to tenderness in pie and tart crusts.

Crystalline sugars

Granulated sugar The most commonly used sugar, regular white granulated sugar is also the least expensive sugar and imparts the least amount of flavor. As granulated sugar is the most neutral of the crystalline sugars, it allows the flavors of other ingredients to dominate.

Brown sugar Brown sugar is regular granulated sugar with less than 10 percent of molasses added to darken and deepen the flavor. Two types of brown sugar are available, light and dark, and they can be used interchangeably with the only consequence being a color change in your finished product. There is little if any difference in the amount of molasses added to light brown sugar and dark brown sugar; the only difference is that dark brown sugar has added caramel coloring to darken the sugar.

If your brown sugar has dried out, microwave it on low for 2 to 3 minutes before using, and store it with a slightly damp paper towel in a sealed container.

Confectioners' sugar The finest ground, powdered white sugar is combined with cornstarch to prevent clumping

Decorative sugars These sugars are larger and coarser in particle size than granulated sugar. Three main varieties can be used: sanding sugar, which has glistening, clear particles; pearl sugar, which is white and opaque; and turbinado sugar, which is partially refined and tan-brown in color, often sold under the brand name Sugar in the Raw. As these sugars are larger, they tend not to melt as easily in the heat of the oven, and thus are used to add a decorative element, texture, and sweetness to the top of pies.

Maple sugar A granular sugar made from maple syrup that has been reduced until all the water has evaporated and the sugar has crystallized. Maple sugar cannot be substituted for other sugars as it is extremely sweet, containing almost twice the sweetness of white granulated sugar.

Sugar syrups

Corn syrup Two forms of corn syrup are available, both processed from cornstarch. Light corn syrup is a clear, light-colored, mild sweetener with vanilla added. Dark corn syrup has a deep brown color and a stronger, more assertive flavor as it is a mixture of corn syrup and refiners' syrup (a form of molasses), with added caramel coloring.

Honey A liquid sweetener produced by bees, each honey has a unique flavor, primarily due to the flower source. It is available from specific flower nectars, such as orange blossom, or sold as a blend.

If your honey has crystallized, place the jar (with the lid off) in a saucepan filled with an inch of water and set it over low heat, stirring the honey often. Or heat the jar in the microwave in 10-second intervals, stirring after each interval, until liquid.

Maple syrup A liquid syrup produced from the heating and evaporation of water contained in maple sap. Maple syrup is available in several grades: Grade A (light, medium, and dark amber—each with an increasingly more assertive maple flavor and amber color) and Grade B (very dark, with an intense maple flavor that is best for baking).

Molasses A by-product of the sugar-refining process, molasses is a thick, dark brown syrup. Three types of molasses are available: Light or mild molasses is from the first boiling of the sugarcane juice, dark molasses is from the second, and blackstrap molasses is from the third. As more sugar is extracted from the sugarcane juice, each resulting molasses becomes less sweet, stronger, more bitter, and darker in color.

SPECIALTY ITEMS

Coffee or espresso powder

A jarred instant or freeze-dried powdered coffee or espresso product can be added to lend coffee flavor to fillings. Best used when combined with a hot liquid in concentrated form (at a 3 to 1 ratio) and then added to a recipe as an extract.

Cream of tartar

A powdered by-product of the wine-making process, cream of tartar is a concentrated acidic ingredient. When whipping egg whites, cream of tartar helps to stabilize the egg proteins, creating a glossier, higher-volume meringue, and prevents weeping after baking.

Gelatin

An odorless, flavorless product derived from animal bones and skins, gelatin helps to stabilize and thicken no-bake fillings made with whipping cream or puddings. Two forms of gelatin are available: powdered and leaf (sometimes called sheet) gelatin.

Spices and extracts

Spices and extracts are meant to complement or add an element of flavor to a baked good, without overwhelming or overpowering other ingredients.

The most common spices in baking are cinnamon, nutmeg, allspice, cloves, and ginger. Nutmeg is best grated whole as the fresh flavor is essential. When selecting and using spices, always check for their distinct aroma when opening a container.

Extracts are available in two forms—pure and imitation. Pure extracts are essential oils extracted from fruit rinds, nuts, and herbs, and dissolved in alcohol. Imitation extracts are synthetic compounds made from chemicals in combinations that imitate natural flavors. Like pure extracts, they are also dissolved in alcohol. Always use pure, never imitation, extracts for the best flavor.

Vanilla beans

The vanilla bean originates from the vanilla flower, which is a member of the orchid family. The beans are picked green and cured to create a dark chocolate–colored brown pod with floral and honey flavors. When purchasing vanilla beans, select beans that are fresh, plump, and moist, with a sheen on the pod.

TECHNIQUES

Making pies and tarts is a timeless art, and until recent times was a craft handed down from one generation to another. Today, we turn to books and other sources to help educate ourselves about the ingredients, techniques, and methods used to make these pastries.

By all accounts, the word *pie* is derived from "magpie," a diminutive bird that gathers a wide variety of items to line its nest, just as a pie crust is lined with all manner of fillings. In their earliest form, pies contained a variety of savory ingredients, such as meats, cheeses, and sauces, enclosed in a pastelike crust that was rendered hard and inedible when baked. This early form of the pie was termed a *coffin* as the "pastry" that encased the ingredients acted as a baking pan, similar to our modern-day casseroles.

Today's pie crusts are an edible container baked in a pan, filled with either savory or sweet fillings, and often covered with an additional pastry crust or other topping. Pies are served from the pan in which they were baked and are considered somewhat informal and rustic. Simply defined, tarts have an open-faced, shallow-bottomed crust, typically sweeter than pie pastry, filled with either a sweet or savory filling. Tarts are unmolded from their pans before serving as the sturdier crust allows for easy removal, and are generally more formal in presentation than pies.

The process of baking pies and tarts at home is part alchemy and part science. But it is also important to remember that making pies and tarts at home should be a pleasurable and enjoyable process. Even if the final outcome is less than perfect, it will most likely still taste delicious.

The various techniques in this book can be used to create nearly endless varieties of pies and tarts: crusts that are flaky or mealy, tender and sweet, prebaked or unbaked—filled with fruit, pudding, nuts, chocolate, or baked custard and topped with a double crust, whipped cream, streusel, latticework, meringue, or simply presented with no topping at all. The chapters in this book are organized based on the ingredients used and the method by which they are prepared: fruit, cream, custard, chocolate and nut, and savory.

THE DOUGH AND CRUST:
THE BASE OF ALL PIES AND TARTS

For many home bakers, creating a flavorful, tender pie or tart crust is a fearful and challenging process filled with questions. How is it that some home bakers consistently produce flaky, crispy, and tender crusts or shells while others consistently find this task so daunting? As pie and tart dough is produced from a few relatively simple ingredients—flour, fat, water, and salt—what are the secrets to creating great crusts?

Pastry doughs are commonly referred to as rubbed doughs. The texture of these doughs is developed by rubbing a solid fat and flour together, leaving pieces of the fat visible. The size of the fat pieces in the rubbed dough in part determines the final texture of the baked pastry. The fat coats and separates the protein links in the flour. Thus, when an ice-cold liquid is added, long protein chains called *gluten* are prevented from forming and the fat pieces remain solid. When pastry dough is baked, the fat melts and creates open pockets, and the liquid contained in the dough turns into steam, forcing apart the layers of dough and creating a flaky crust.

Within the pastry dough category, there are two types of rubbed doughs: mealy and flaky.

MEALY DOUGHS

Mealy dough, which is sometimes referred to as "short" dough, bakes into a crust with a crumbly yet melt-in-your-mouth tenderness that is achieved by rubbing the fat into the flour, leaving some pieces smaller than peas. When a liquid is added to mealy dough pieces, the flour is almost fully coated by the small pieces of fat and not able to fully absorb the liquid into the dough, which creates a crumbly yet tender texture. Mealy dough is appropriate for all types of pies and tarts, especially those requiring a blind-baked crust (see page 54), as its finer and tender texture is fairly durable.

FLAKY DOUGHS

Flaky dough is created by leaving larger pieces of fat, about the size of a pea, hazelnut, or small walnut, in the flour mixture. Flaky dough will bake into a crust that flakes apart into thin, delicate sheets. These types of crusts are best suited for pies and tarts in which the filling is baked in the crust. Flaky doughs are not suitable for blind-baked crust recipes because the flaky texture tends to leak fillings and juices.

To create an exceptionally flaky and tender crust, it is necessary to create distinct pockets of fat in the dough, so that as the fat melts, the steam forces apart the layers of dough as described on the previous page. The temperature of the ingredients and the manner in which the ingredients are incorporated are the keys to producing a flaky crust.

Temperature

If a flaky crust is desired, the fat should remain cold and solid. If the weather is warm, it can also be helpful to chill your bowl and your flour. The temperature of the added liquid—water, cream, milk—must be ice cold to prevent the fat from melting. If the fat chunks melt before the dough is baked, the flour will absorb the fat and the result will be a mealy crust rather than the desired flaky crust.

Mixing the Dough

The manner in which the dough is mixed is essential, whether it is by hand or in a food processor or stand mixer. The first step is to cut the solid pieces of fat quickly into the flour and salt mixture. The flour should coat the pieces of fat but not become thoroughly combined with them; the mixture should not be smooth and homogeneous. Next, the smallest amount liquid possible should be added, just enough to bring the flour-fat mixture together into a dough but still keep the fat solid. Gently incorporate the liquid without overworking the mixture, or the fat could melt. Refer to page 40 for detailed step-by-step instructions and photos for mixing pastry dough.

SELECTING INGREDIENTS

Flour, fat, and liquid are the building blocks of pie and tart doughs. The ways in which they interact with each other, as described above, create the structure, texture, and flavor of the finished crust.

Flour

When choosing flour for pie and pastry doughs, unbleached all-purpose flour is best, as it has the ideal balance of protein and starch needed to create a dough that holds together without becoming tough, yet remains tender without falling apart. Unbleached flour has a natural off-white hue. Since chemically bleaching flour not only affects the color but the flavor as well, bleached all-purpose flour is not recommended.

Fat

Baking fats, such as butter, vegetable shortening, lard, margarine, and other fats, can all be used in rubbed doughs (see page 17). While butter is preferred for flavor, it has a lower melting point than shortening, making it imperative that the butter be kept very cold before it is added to the dough and while it is being cut into the flour.

Many bakers prefer using a combination of half shortening and half butter to create pastry dough that is sturdier, holds its shape better, and is easier to work with, yet retains the characteristic flavor of an all-butter crust. Cream cheese and mascarpone can also be used in addition to butter; besides adding their own distinct flavors, the higher percentage of fat in these cheeses contributes to an extremely tender crust.

Liquid

The most common liquid used in pastry dough is water, but other liquids can be used. Water creates crispiness in dough, and needs to be added with care. If there is too little liquid in the pie dough, it will not easily combine or will fall apart. Too much liquid will cause the dough to become tough. The dough should be just moist enough to hold together when pinched. When buttermilk, vinegar, and lemon juice are used in a crust, they impart tangy flavor and provide acidity that weakens the gluten (protein) structure in the flour slightly, making the dough less elastic and easier to roll out. Cream can also be used, providing additional fat and resulting in softer, richer dough. Liquor such as vodka can be used to replace a portion of the water in pie dough. As vodka consists of approximately 60 percent water, it provides proportionally less water to the dough, thus preventing the formation of gluten and creating a tender, flaky structure.

MIXING

Pie and tart doughs can be made by three different methods: by hand, in a food processor, or in a stand mixer with a paddle attachment.

Although making pastry dough by hand is time-consuming, when you are learning how to make dough it is helpful to make it by hand in order to develop a feel for the various stages of development.

Making pastry dough in a food processor is the easiest method. However, there are two disadvantages to this method: The fat can accidentally be too thoroughly blended, resulting in a less flaky crust. Additionally, the ingredients can heat up very quickly in a food processor, which can result in the fat melting. It is a good idea to chill the bowl, blade, and dry ingredients before making dough in a food processor.

Finally, a stand mixer outfitted with a paddle is an easy way to make dough and does not readily heat up the ingredients. The bowl, paddle, and ingredients should be thoroughly chilled, and you must be careful not to overmix. If properly used, the stand mixer breaks the fat into irregular pieces without melting, which results in a flaky pastry.

TIPS FOR SUCCESS

- *If not weighing dry ingredients, use the "dip, sweep, and level" measuring-cup method described on page 4.*

- *Keep your equipment, ingredients, and dough cold.*

- *Dough should look a bit ragged, with irregular pieces of butter scattered throughout.*

- *Always allow the dough to rest in the refrigerator (see page 43).*

MIXING DOUGH

1 For flaky dough, cut the butter into the flour by hand, or blend it using a food processor or stand mixer, until the butter forms irregular chunks about the size of peas or small walnuts.

2 For mealy dough, mix the butter into the flour until the dough resembles sand.

3 Gradually add ice-cold water or other liquid to the flour-butter mixture.

4 As you mix the dough, it will begin to form into a shaggy mass.

5 The dough has reached the right consistency when it can be easily pressed together into a dough mass.

6 Press the finished dough into a round disc and wrap in plastic wrap. Refrigerate at least 45 minutes to let the dough rest.

Mixing by Hand in a Bowl

Combine flour, salt, and sugar (if using) in a bowl and stir to combine. Cut the cold butter into ¾-inch pieces and use a pastry blender or your fingers to incorporate the butter into the flour until the butter is no larger than small walnuts but no smaller than peas. Work quickly, as the butter may soften as you work to blend it. The butter will be irregular in size and the mixture slightly ragged, but as you become more experienced working with pastry dough you will instinctively know the proper size of the butter pieces. Sprinkle a small amount of ice-cold liquid over the mixture and blend to combine. Continue to add the liquid in small amounts, until the mixture transitions from a slightly powdery appearance with butter chunks to a gravelly, rough dough. *At this stage, do not add too much liquid or overwork the dough, as it will cause your crust to become tough.* The dough is finished when it just holds together when pressed to the side of the bowl. Shape and press it into a ragged ball (or two, if making a double crust). Turn out the dough onto a work surface, and press and flatten it into a 5- to 6-inch-diameter disc. (For a double crust or lattice, divide the dough into two discs—a little less than half for the top crust or lattice and a little more than half for the bottom crust.) Wrap the dough in plastic wrap and chill for at least 1 hour, or preferably overnight (see page 43 for the role of resting and chilling).

Mixing in a Food Processor

In the bowl of a food processor fitted with the steel cutting blade, combine the flour, salt, and sugar (if using). Place the work bowl in the freezer for 30 minutes, chilling the ingredients and bowl. Return the bowl to the food processor and pulse for 15 to 20 seconds to combine the dry ingredients. Cut the cold butter into ¾-inch pieces. With the food processor off, add half of the cold butter and pulse for 3 to 5 seconds. Add the remaining cold butter and pulse for 4 to 5 seconds. The mixture should appear rough, with irregular pieces of butter approximately the size of small walnuts. With the food processor off, add 2 tablespoons of ice-cold liquid, then pulse for 3 to 5 seconds just to combine. The dough should appear slightly sandy, with the pieces of butter no larger than peas. Check the dough by pressing it to the side of the bowl. If it does not hold together, add 2 more tablespoons of liquid and check it again. *Do not add too much liquid or overwork the dough as it will cause your crust to become tough. Do not allow the mixture to form a ball or mass of dough in the bowl. If this occurs, you have overmixed the dough, and it will be tough.* If the dough stays together when pressed to the side of the bowl, remove it from the bowl and turn it out onto a work surface, then press and flatten it into a 5- to 6-inch disc. (For a double crust or lattice, divide the dough into two discs—a little less than half for the top crust or lattice and a little more than half for the bottom crust.) Wrap the dough in plastic wrap and chill for at least 1 hour, or preferably overnight (see opposite for the role of resting and chilling).

Mixing in a Stand Mixer

In the bowl of a stand mixer, combine the flour, salt, and sugar (if using) and place the bowl in the freezer for 30 minutes. Fit the mixer with the paddle attachment and place the bowl on the mixer stand. Mix on low speed for 15 seconds just to combine the dry ingredients. Cut the cold butter into ¾-inch pieces. With the mixer off, add the butter to the mixing bowl, then turn the mixer to medium speed and mix for 1 to 2 minutes, just until the butter is broken up into pieces no larger than small walnuts but no smaller than peas. Sprinkle approximately 1 tablespoon of ice-cold liquid over the mixture and mix on low speed for 30 to 60 seconds to combine. Continue to add the liquid 1 tablespoon at a time until the mixture transitions from a slightly powdery appearance with butter chunks to gravelly, rough dough. *At this stage, do not add too much liquid or overwork the dough as it will cause your crust to become tough.* If the dough just holds together when pressed to the side of the bowl, shape and press it into a ragged ball (or two for a double crust). Turn out the dough onto a work surface, then press and flatten it into a 5- to 6-inch disc. (For a double crust or lattice, divide the dough into two discs—a little less than half for the top crust or lattice and a little more than half for the bottom crust.) Wrap the dough in plastic wrap and chill for at least 1 hour or preferably overnight (see opposite for the role of resting and chilling).

The Role of Resting and Chilling Dough

Chilling pie dough is very important. It allows the dough to relax, making it less elastic and easier to roll out; prevents shrinkage and slumping of the dough during baking; holds shaped decorative edges better; and helps develop flavor in the dough. Chilling also resolidifies the fat in the dough to ensure a flakier crust. Rolling out well-chilled dough is easier, too, as the cold dough requires less dusting flour and is less likely to stick to the rolling surface.

You should chill a pie or tart dough for a minimum of 1 hour, but pastry dough can be refrigerated for up to 3 days or frozen for up to 4 months. After removing chilled pastry dough from the refrigerator, allow it to sit at room temperature for 10 to 15 minutes before rolling. Allow frozen dough to defrost for several hours or overnight in the refrigerator. If it is still too cold and hard to roll, set it out at room temperature until it becomes pliable and workable.

Preparing to Roll Dough

Rolling doughs can be a frustrating and exasperating process. With their high fat content and delicate structure, they are susceptible to tearing or ripping, especially if they are too warm and the fat has begun to melt. Alternatively, if they are too cold, these doughs can crack during rolling.

The first step of successfully rolling out pastry dough is to ensure that the dough has been properly shaped into a 5- to 6-inch disc, rested, and chilled. If your dough has been in the refrigerator for more than an hour, give it 10 or 15 minutes at room temperature to soften. The dough is ready to be rolled out if an indentation appears when pressed with your finger. If you prefer not to wait, you can use the rolling pin to work and soften the dough until it is ready for rolling.

The dough must be kept cool to the touch. Work quickly to prevent the dough from softening. If the dough is becoming too warm, refrigerate it to cool it down. Use flour with restraint, using just enough to lightly dust the rolling surface and the dough. When too much dusting flour is used, it can make the dough dry and tough.

Choosing a Rolling Surface

Any flat, hard level surface will work and there are many different materials to choose from: a marble countertop or pastry board; a canvas pastry cloth on a countertop; or a piece of hardwood, lightly dusted with flour and anchored to the countertop with a piece of rubber-mesh nonslip shelf liner. Some home bakers prefer to roll out the dough between two sheets of floured parchment or waxed paper. This allows for easy transfer of the dough from the work surface to the pie or tart pan.

Size and Thickness of the Rolled Dough

Before rolling, it is important to determine the necessary final rolled dough size, depending on the type of pie and tart you are making and the shape and size of your pan. The crust should be rolled to ⅛ inch thick. Rubber rolling pin rings (see page 8) are useful and clever items that help you gauge the thickness of your dough. Below is a chart to assist you in determining the necessary diameter of the rolled dough. However, if the dough has not been chilled in the refrigerator for an hour or more, add 1 inch to the listed measurements to accommodate any shrinkage during baking.

SIZE OF ROLLED-OUT DOUGH

TYPE OF PAN	SIZE AND DEPTH	SINGLE	DOUBLE (BOTTOM)	DOUBLE (TOP)	LATTICE
Pie pan	9–10 inches wide, 1–1¼ inches deep	14 inches	13 inches	13 inches	13 inches
Deep pie dish	9½ inches wide, 2–3 inches deep	15–16 inches	15-16 inches	15 inches	13 inches
Quiche dish	10–11 inches wide, 1–1½ inches deep	15 inches	-	-	-
Springform pan	9 inches wide, 2½ inches deep	16 inches	-	-	-
Fluted tart pan (with or without removable bottom)	9½ inches wide, 1 inch deep	13 inches	-	-	13 inches
Tart/Flan ring (9½-inch)	9½ inches wide, 1 inch deep	13 inches	-	-	13 inches
Tart/Flan ring (11-inch)	11 inches wide, 1 inch deep	15 inches	-	-	13 inches

ROLLING OUT DOUGH

PATCHING AND SAVING SCRAPS

Tears or splits that occur during rolling can be repaired easily by gently pressing the dough back together. If irregular cracks form, press the dough together to patch, angle your rolling pin to the area that needs to be repaired, and gently roll over the surface. If larger gaps form, they can be patched with trimmings cut from the overhanging dough.

If using scraps to make decorative cutouts for the edges of a pie (see page 52), pile the scraps together, wrap them in plastic wrap, gently press them together into a disc, and refrigerate for 20 to 30 minutes before rolling out the dough and cutting out shapes.

1 Place the rolling pin in the center of the dough, with one end of the pin at 9 o'clock and the other at 3 o'clock. Applying firm, even pressure with the rolling pin, roll outward from the center. Never roll over one section in the same direction repeatedly, as this can toughen the dough.

2 Rotate the dough 90 degrees to the right when rolling. This allows you to evenly roll the dough in all directions, creating a consistent thickness and preventing the dough from sticking.

3 As you rotate the dough, frequently check the uniformity of the thickness by running your forefinger and thumb together with the dough in between. Adjust the rolling pin pressure as needed. If the dough is rolled too thick, it may not bake properly. If rolled too thin, it may rip or tear. In order to avoid an irregular shape, press the dough inward and together to maintain a circular shape while rolling.

RIGHT: Fold the dough into quarters from the center of the dough, forming a wedge shape. Gently transfer the dough to the pan, placing the pointed tip at the center of the pan, and unfold the dough to cover the pan.

FAR RIGHT: Position the rolling pin 2 inches from the edge of the dough, fold the edge over the pin, and roll it up. Move the rolling pin over the pan, align the edge of the dough on the pin with the edge of the pan, and unroll the dough over the pan.

BOTTOM RIGHT: Place the pan near the rolled dough round and gently put your hands under the dough. Use the backs of your hands to slide and move the dough to the pan.

Transferring Dough to the Pan

Transferring rolled dough from your work surface to the pie or tart pan can be daunting, but can be simply done by using one of the three methods shown on this page.

FITTING THE DOUGH

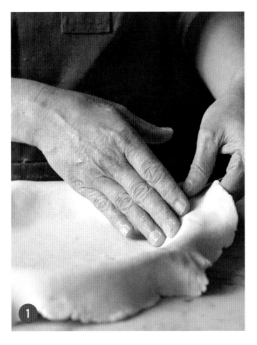

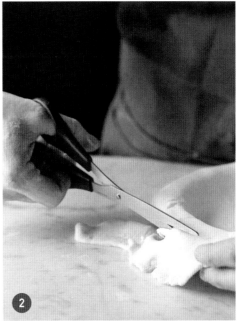

1 Gently lift the dough and set it into the pan, pressing it into the edges of the pan. Do not force or stretch the dough or it may shrink during baking.

2 Trim the dough using a pair of scissors, leaving 1 to 2 inches overhanging, depending on the type of decorative border around the edge of the pan.

3 Gently fold and press the extra dough under the inside of the pan edge to form a thick border. (If using a top crust, leave the edge unfolded.) Refrigerate the formed shell for 1 hour and then place it in the freezer 30 minutes before blind baking (see page 54), or before filling and baking.

Fitting the Dough to the Pan

Once you have transferred the dough to the pan, properly fitting the dough before blind baking or filling the crust helps to ensure the beauty of the finished pie. It is important not to stretch the dough, or it may shrink during baking.

LINING A TART PAN

1 Gently lift the dough and press it into the creases of a lightly buttered or greased tart pan. Take care not to force or stretch the dough, or it may shrink during baking.

2 For a flush edge, roll a rolling pin over the tart pan to cut the dough against the edge of the pan, or trim the edge with a paring knife, as shown.

LINING A TART PAN

Tart dough tends to rip and tear more easily than pie dough, so it is important to fully support it while transferring it to the pan. Once you have transferred the dough to the pan, press it gently into place: Starting in the middle of the pan, press out any visible air bubbles, gently lifting and supporting the dough as you smooth it into place. When you reach the edges, press your finger gently into the fluting in a rocking motion from the bottom to the top to press out any air bubbles. Take care not to force or stretch the dough or it may shrink during baking. If the dough gets too warm, return it to the refrigerator for a few minutes to chill. For a

flush edge, trim the edges as shown above. If you are using a bottomless tart ring, set it on a baking sheet before lining it with dough. Before partially or fully blind baking or filling and baking, it is important to chill the formed shell for a minimum of 30 minutes (see page 43 for more on the role of relaxing and chilling the dough).

MAKING DOUBLE-CRUST PIES

Double-crust pies start in the same manner as single-crust pies: First, follow the methods described on pages 45 to 47 to roll out the bottom crust and fit it into the pan. Next, roll out a top crust to the desired

MAKING DOUBLE-CRUST PIE

diameter (see the chart on page 44) to make either a top crust or a lattice. Once assembled, double-crust pies must have vents cut into the top crust to create a pathway for the steam and moisture to escape from the filling. You can do this with a knife or using small decorative cutters or a handy specialty tool called a pie-top lattice cutter (see page 12; cut shapes before transferring the top crust to the pie). Pie birds (see page 12) are another method of allowing steam and moisture to exit a pie, but can be difficult to use with juicy fillings. Practically speaking, simply cutting vents into the top crust serves the same purpose.

1 Transfer the top crust to the filled pie, carefully settling the crust over the filling and being careful not to stretch or thin the crust. Trim both edges to approximately ½ inch and press the edges of both the top and bottom crusts together to seal them. Fold the dough under to make it flush with the edge of the pan, press the edge flat, and form a decorative edge as desired (see page 52).

2 Using a sharp knife, cut four to eight slashes running from the center to the edge, into the top crust.

3 For an appealing finish, use a pastry brush to apply an egg wash (see page 295) to the top crust, then sprinkle with decorative sugar, such as sanding sugar, pearl sugar, or turbinado sugar.

1 Using a sharp knife or a straight-edge or fluted pastry cutter and a ruler, cut 10 or more ¾-inch strips of dough (for a tightly woven lattice top, cut twenty-four ½-inch strips). Gently arrange half of the strips over the top of the pan, spacing them evenly.

2 Turn the pan 90 degrees and fold back alternating strips to a little more than halfway. Place the first perpendicular strip onto the pie, slightly off center, and then carefully fold each strip back to the edge of the pan. Repeat, folding back the alternating strips and adding the next strip.

FORMING A LATTICE CRUST

Lattice top crusts are most often associated with pies that contain a very juicy fruit filling, such as berries, cherries, or peaches, as the open design readily allows steam to evaporate during baking. Lattice work can also be used to lend a decorative element to top other types of pies or tarts—as in the classic jam-filled tart Linzer Torte (page 127). Lattice tops should not be used for raw, uncooked fruit fillings that are piled above the rim of the pie pan because, when baked, the fruit will shrink and the lattice will collapse. To begin, roll out a single crust to a circle approximately 11 inches in diameter (see page 45).

3 Working back and forth, continue to weave the strips through each other by folding alternating strips back and then unfolding them over each added strip.

4 Trim off the excess at the ends of the strips, leaving a 1-inch overhang of dough, and fold the dough to seal. Flute or crimp the edges as desired (see page 52).

DECORATIVE LATTICES

Lattices can be arranged directly on top of a pie or tart filling, or first on a piece of parchment paper or waxed paper and then transferred to the pan over the filling. To add a special touch to a pie or tart, you can adapt and vary the classic lattice into any of the following formations:

Tightly woven lattice: Strips are woven more tightly together, covering the filling completely.

Extra-wide woven lattice: The strips are cut twice as wide (around 2 inches) and then woven together.

Unwoven overlaid lattice: Strips are first laid in one direction and then a second layer is positioned on top to form a diamond pattern. They are not woven together.

Twisted lattice: Strips are twisted into spirals and then laid perpendicular to each other to resemble a lattice.

Shingled cutouts: Decorative cutouts such as stars, scalloped rounds, or leaves are arranged in an overlapping pattern on top of the filling.

Pie-top lattice cutter: A large round cutter (see page 12) is used to cut a pattern into the top crust.

Cutout pattern: Small decorative cutters, such as rounds, diamonds, squares, or other shapes, are used to cut a pattern into the top crust.

These toppers are best used on flat-rimmed ceramic pie plates and should always be frozen prior to placing it on the filling. On a lightly floured piece of parchment paper, roll out the dough as described on page 45 and cut a circle of dough 1 inch larger on all sides than the pie plate. Using a pastry brush, lightly brush the outer edge of the dough circle with water. Fold back the outer 1 inch of the dough. Flute the edge of the dough as desired. Use a paring knife to cut decorative vents into the top, pressing the vents open if needed. Transfer to a flat baking sheet, brush with egg wash, and freeze for a minimum of 30 minutes, or until firm, before using.

FORMING DECORATIVE EDGES

The finished edges of double- or single-crust pies can be decoratively shaped to add a signature or artful flair. These not only serve to please the eye, but they also act as a barrier, preventing the filling from spilling or leaking during baking.

Although some people use the terms interchangeably, crimping and fluting are different methods for decoratively sealing the edges of a pie. Crimping means to seal a pie with the tines of a fork or a special pastry crimping tool (see page 12); a uniform texture is pressed into the edge. Fluting means to form regular patterns in the dough edge by pressing the dough between your fingertips.

When a pie dough has a high fat content, it is helpful to use well-floured fingers to shape decorative edges. The additional flour can help to retain the shape of the decorative edge during baking. After forming edges, always refrigerate the pie or tart for a minimum of 1 hour or place the unfilled shell in the freezer for 30 minutes to help keep the shell from slumping or losing its shape when exposed to the heat of the oven.

Fork Crimping

Dip the tines of a fork in flour. Press the tines into the edge of the dough at regular intervals to form a straight crimp pattern. For a crisscross pattern, press the tines into the edge at a 45-degree angle in one direction at regular intervals, then repeat in the opposite direction.

Fluted Edges

Lightly flour your hands. Working quickly to prevent the dough edge from becoming too soft, gently press the inside dough edge with the index finger of one hand while simultaneously holding the outside of the dough rim between the index finger and thumb of your other hand, pressing to form a pointed, rippled V pattern around the edge. To form an angled edge, gently pinch the dough edge between the knuckle of your index finger and thumb at a 45-degree angle while simultaneously slanting the dough to form an angled pattern around the edge. For a scalloped edge, gently press the inside dough edge with the index finger of one hand while simultaneously holding the outside of the dough rim between the index finger and thumb of your other hand, forming a wavy scalloped pattern around the edge. To add a four-prong pattern, make a scalloped edge as described above. Using the tines of a fork dipped in flour, press a four-pronged pattern onto the inside curve of each of the scallops at regular intervals.

Cutout Edges

To make a checkerboard edge, working quickly to prevent the dough edge from becoming too soft, use a sharp knife to cut the edge of the dough at 1-inch intervals. Fold every other cut flap of dough on the edge of the pie pan toward the inside to create a checkerboard pattern. To make a decorative edge with cutout shapes, roll chilled dough scraps to ⅛ inch thick. Use a

FAR LEFT:
FORK CRIMPING
crisscross crimping
(top), basic crimping
(bottom)

LEFT:
FLUTED EDGES
(clockwise from
top): fluted V-edge,
fluted edge with four-
pronged pattern, fluted
scalloped edge, fluted
angle edge

BOTTOM LEFT:
CUTOUT EDGES
cutout shape edge
(top), folded edge or
checkerboard (bottom)

lightly floured cutter to cut out the desired shapes and attach them to the dough edge using cold water or egg wash, pressing lightly to adhere. For a braided edge, roll out chilled dough scraps in the same manner and then, using a sharp knife, cut out ¼-inch strips of dough and gently braid three pieces together to form a braid. Add more pieces as needed to make the braid long enough to completely encircle the edge of the dough. Attach the braid to the dough edge using cold water or egg wash, pressing lightly to adhere.

Forming Crumb Crusts

Many pies feature crusts made from a mixture of ground cookies, nuts, or crackers combined with a fat, usually melted butter. Sometimes egg whites are added to help the crust hold together, and sugar and spices can be added for sweetness and flavor. These crusts can be either unbaked or baked, but baking lends flavor, holds the crust together, and creates a crunchy, crispy texture.

These crusts are often used in combination with moist and creamy fillings as they do not readily absorb liquid and remain crisp and crunchy during refrigeration. To make a crumb crust, pulse the nuts, cookies, or crackers (with sugar or spices, if desired) in a food processor until finely ground. Alternatively, the ingredients can be placed in a resealable plastic bag and gently crushed with a rolling pin. Transfer the crumb mixture to a bowl and work in the melted fat, stirring to combine and coat the crumbs. Press the crumb mixture evenly over the bottom and up the sides of a lightly buttered (or sprayed) baking pan. If baking the crumb crust, first refrigerate it for 10 to 15 minutes. This will help the butter resolidify and prevent the crust from shifting during baking.

Blind Baking

Many pie and tart shells require partial baking (par baking) or fully prebaking the empty crust prior to filling. This method is termed *blind baking*. A pie or tart shell can benefit from partially baking before filling if it will be filled with a fruit that produces a significant amount of moisture during baking, or a liquid filling such as custard. Otherwise the liquid will prevent the crust from fully baking and create a dense and gummy bottom crust. Additionally, a shell may be fully baked if it contains a filling that does not require further cooking.

When blind baking a crust, it is essential to fully chill the formed shell in the refrigerator for at least 1 hour, or in the freezer for 30 minutes, prior to baking to ensure that the shell will retain its shape. To prevent the sides from collapsing and the bottom crust from rising and creating irregular bubbles in the shell, it must first be pricked at regular 1-inch intervals with the tines of a fork; this is known as *docking* the dough. The pastry shell must be lined with parchment paper (you may also use foil or a round fluted-style coffee filter). It is helpful to spray the parchment with nonstick cooking spray to keep it from sticking to the dough. Fold and fit the paper to the slope of the pan and avoid using waxed paper as a liner; it is not designed to withstand the high temperature of the oven. Fill the pie shell with weights. Weights can range from inexpensive and reusable dried beans or rice to specialty ceramic or metal baking weights (see page 13). Cover the surface of the bottom crust with weights until they just come up the sides. Do not overfill or the weights will make indentations in the crust.

When blind baking a pie or tart shell, first line the shell with parchment that has been lightly oiled or sprayed and fill with pie weights. Remove the parchment and weights after the first 10 to 15 minutes of baking.

The oven should be preheated 15 to 20 minutes before baking and should initially be set at a higher temperature for the first 10 to 15 minutes of baking to create a crispy bottom crust. The weights are then gently removed and the oven temperature is reduced.

For a partially baked shell that will continue to bake after filling, bake only for 5 to 10 minutes after removing the weights, or until the bottom crust is a pale, golden brown. Then add the filling and bake according to the instructions. For a fully baked shell, bake approximately 10 to 15 minutes, or until the crust is a light golden brown. If the edges of a pie or tart shell are beginning to brown excessively, cover them with a foil ring or a pie edge shield (see page 12).

Sealing a Bottom Crust

When filling a prebaked or par baked pie or tart crust with a wet filling, it is helpful to create a barrier between the liquid filling and the crust to prevent the custard or the fruit juices from causing the crust to become soggy and dense. Sealers, such as egg wash, egg whites, or a flour-and-water paste, can be brushed onto the bottom crust after the weights are removed during blind baking. As the crust continues to bake, the sealers form a barrier. The flour-and-water paste is best utilized for sealing any cracks visible in a bottom crust. For more information on egg washes, see page 295.

Other sealers, such as chocolate or preserves, can be applied after the crust is fully baked. These preserve the crispness of the crust and create a flavorful barrier.

TECHNIQUES FOR FILLINGS

A wide variety of methods and techniques are utilized when making the fillings for pies and tarts, including fruit fillings, custards, and pastry creams and similar cooked fillings. Mastering these techniques will help you create consistently delicious and well-executed pies and tarts.

Fruit Fillings

The best fruit pies and tarts are made with fresh fruits at their peak of ripeness, and should be prepared—and of course consumed—on the same day as baking. Though delicious, they are not without their frustrations. Fruit pies require a starch to thicken the fruit filling, which can either be precooked on the stovetop prior to baking, or baked in the oven. Precooking the fruit softens it, releases juices, evaporates moisture, and allows the filling to thicken, all of which help prevent a soggy bottom crust and a filling that does not properly set. Berries and cherries benefit from precooking; apples, apricots, pears, and peaches do not require precooking, as their juices will readily evaporate. However, the moisture content in fresh produce can vary, making it sometimes difficult to get the balance of fruit and thickener just right. Remember that while achieving the perfect slice is desirable, the flavor—and the pleasure of a juicy, fruit-laden pie from your own kitchen—is more important.

Custards

Baked custards and boiled cream pie fillings are two types of custard fillings for pies and tarts. They are not complicated, generally consisting of pantry ingredients (eggs, milk or cream, sugar, and sometimes starch) that most home bakers have on hand, yet understanding the proper methods of incorporating these key ingredients is vital to producing a pie or tart with a crisp bottom and a smooth, creamy filling.

Baked custards, such as pumpkin pie, have no added starch and are instead thickened only with eggs—either whole eggs, or yolks for a richer filling. Baked custards can be prepared either cold or warm, as described below.

Cream pie and tart fillings differ from baked custard fillings in that they are thickened with a starch on the stovetop, and then poured into a prebaked crust or shell. Often cream pies are referred to as "icebox" or "refrigerator" pies, as they are chilled to help to set the filling. This results in neat, clean slices. These types of custards are referred to as *boiled* custards.

When making either type of custard pie, it is key to have all of your ingredients and equipment prepared and at hand, and to have a clear understanding of the step-by-step method. All of the steps in the procedure must be followed exactly or the custard may not set properly or may become curdled.

Two Methods of Preparing Baked Custards

There are two methods of preparing baked custards—cold and warm. To prepare a custard filling using the *cold method*, all of the ingredients are simply stirred together and then poured into the formed pastry shell and baked. While this method is simple and straightforward, custard pies and tarts made in this manner often have dense and gummy bottom crusts. The *warm method* requires the dairy—cream and/or milk—to be heated with half of the sugar in a heavy-bottomed pot until the sugar has dissolved. In a separate bowl, the eggs and the remaining sugar are combined. Stirring continuously, add one-third of the hot dairy mixture to the egg mixture to equalize the temperature of the eggs and thus prevent "scrambling" them. Pour the tempered eggs back into the pot with the hot dairy mixture and stir to combine. Immediately pour the mixture into a hot, partially baked crust and place it in the oven with the bottom rack set in the lowest position, or bake on a preheated pizza stone.

Baked Custards

Custard fillings must be baked very carefully at a low temperature to avoid overheating, which can curdle the custard and create a grainy and watery filling. Yet the shell requires high heat in order to create a crisp, not soggy, crust. Preventing a sodden, gummy crust is one of the most common challenges when making a baked custard pie, but following the tips given at right will help.

Boiled Custards

Boiled custards consist of milk and/or cream, eggs, and sugar, and are stabilized with a starch. Unlike custard fillings baked in the oven, boiled custards are prepared on the stovetop, and they must be stirred constantly

- *Fully blind bake the pie shell.*

- *After removing the pie weights, seal the bottom crust with egg white wash, or seal the cooled crust with white or dark chocolate, if compatible.*

- *Boil the custard rapidly for at least 1 minute to thicken the starch and remove the starchy flavor.*

- *To prevent a skin from forming on the custard, place plastic wrap directly on the surface.*

- *Refrigerate the assembled pie or tart for 4 hours to fully set before serving.*

while coming to a full boil in order to activate the starch and thicken the filling.

To prepare boiled custard filling, in a heavy-bottomed pot, bring 90 percent of the cream and/or milk and half of the sugar to a rolling boil, stirring to melt and dissolve the sugar. In a separate bowl, stir together the starch and the remaining cream and/or milk. Then add the eggs and sugar. Stirring continuously, add one-third of the hot milk mixture into the egg mixture to temper the eggs. Return the tempered egg mixture to the pan with the remaining hot milk mixture. Bring the mixture back to a boil for at least 1 minute, stirring continuously. Remove the pan from the heat and add extract or butter if directed in the recipe. Pour into the pie or tart shell and cover with plastic wrap to cool.

Chiffon Pies

Chiffon pies are an American invention that first appeared in the 1920s. A chiffon filling is a custard, typically thickened with a starch and lightened with whipped egg whites, whipped cream, or both, and often stabilized with gelatin. The chiffon filling is then poured into a prebaked crust. They are never baked; they are always refrigerated to achieve their firm, sliceable shape. Chiffon pies and their fillings are not difficult to prepare, but the ingredients are temperature sensitive and should be handled properly.

Gelatin If used in small amounts, gelatin lends body to fillings, and in greater amounts sets a filling until it is firm and sliceable. Gelatin is a flavorless and colorless ingredient that is derived from animal collagen and is available in two forms: powdered and sheet (also called leaf gelatin). When exposed to cooling temperatures, the protein works to create a tangled semisolid web of the liquids in a mixture.

To use powdered or sheet gelatin, it first must be rehydrated or soaked in cool water for approximately 10 to 15 minutes or it will cause clumping when added to other ingredients. This is referred to as *blooming* the gelatin. After the gelatin is soaked, it must be heated in order to melt it. The gelatin then can be incorporated into the chiffon filling base. Since gelatin begins to set when cooled, it is important that the gelatin is warmer than the base in order for it to be properly incorporated. Also, since gelatin begins to set almost immediately after incorporation, it is key to have all of your ingredients and equipment prepared and at hand, and to have a clear understanding of the step-by-step method in the recipe before you begin preparing the pie.

Meringues, from left to right: soft, medium, and stiff peaks

MERINGUE

Whipping egg whites with sugar creates a delicate yet stable structure called meringue. Egg whites are approximately 90 percent water and 10 percent protein. When the whites are beaten, the protein strands begin to bond with each other, creating a web holding the air bubbles and the liquid together. With continued beating, the proteins continue to link, forming a stable foam. Any added sugar also acts to stabilize egg whites, as it melts and surrounds the air bubbles, helping to hold the matrix in place.

To best create a stable meringue, there are several rules and precautions to follow. First, ensure that the egg whites do not come in contact with any fats, whether from the yolks or from your equipment, as fats coat the proteins and prevent them from readily forming a foam. Be sure the bowl and whisk are free of grease. When separating eggs, note that the yolks and whites separate cleanly when refrigerator-cold as the yolks are firmer and do not easily break. However, temperature can affect the ability of the egg whites to foam; the colder their temperature, the longer the foaming time. Bring the whites to room temperature (68°F) before whipping. Choose a stainless-steel or copper bowl, if available, and a balloon whisk, if whipping by hand, to achieve the best volume. Another technique for stabilizing egg whites is to add a small amount of an acid, such as cream of tartar, to the whites. This strengthens the protein links and creates a thicker, more stable foam. A good rule of thumb for adding cream of tartar as a stabilizer is to add ⅛ teaspoon for every two egg whites.

Stages of Whipping

When whipping egg whites, there are three stages of foam development: soft peak, medium peak, and stiff peak. Egg white foams will have a stronger structure and more volume if foamed slowly at the beginning until frothy, and then finished at higher speeds. To determine the stage of whipping, lift the whisk out of the bowl. A soft-peak meringue will not create a point at the end and will cling to the surface of the whisk or beater. A medium-peak meringue will form a peak but will droop slightly at the end. A stiff-peak meringue will form a sharp point at the end of the whisk or beater. If a meringue appears dull or lumpy, it has been overwhipped and may be saved by adding another egg white and whipping to the desired stage.

Types of Meringues

There are three types of meringues: common (or French), Swiss, and Italian. Swiss and Italian meringues are cooked meringues and are the most stable, making them the best suited for toppings. They are also used for lightening creams and fillings. Common meringues are used to aerate or lighten preparations that are to be further baked.

> **Common Meringue** A *common meringue,* also called *French meringue,* is made by simply whipping egg whites with sugar added until the desired volume is reached. This type of meringue is the easiest to form but the least stable.
>
> **Swiss Meringue** *Swiss meringue* is formed when the egg whites and sugar are heated together, while whisking, over a hot water bath to 140°F. The meringue is then whipped either by hand or with a mixer to the desired volume. The heating of the whites creates a cooked meringue that is safe to consume and that is more stable than the common meringue.

Italian Meringue An *Italian meringue* is made by beating the egg whites with a mixer and heating the sugar and water together to 240°F to create a sugar syrup that is poured into the whites while whipping. This meringue is the most stable of the three types of meringues; additionally, it is safe to eat because the hot sugar syrup has effectively cooked the egg whites.

Whipped Cream

Whipped cream is formed when air is incorporated into cream through whipping. The fat helps to stabilize the air bubbles as they form. A seemingly simple process, there are several considerations to keep in mind when whipping cream.

When choosing cream for whipping, it is ideal to choose a cream with a fat content of 30 percent or more (see page 18). Temperature is also important: As the fat begins to warm up, it melts, and then a structure is either unable to form or it collapses. Chilling your equipment, tools, and cream helps ensure that the cream will stay cold enough to remain solid.

It is essential to avoid overwhipping; if it is agitated for too long, the whipped cream may become granular and curdled and the end result is butter. A good strategy to avoid overwhipping is to use an electric mixer to foam the cream to soft peaks, and then finish whipping by hand.

Avoid using confectioners' sugar as you will need to use twice as much as the required amount of granulated sugar to achieve the same sweetness, and this affects the texture and flavor of the whipped cream. When adding granulated sugar to whipping cream, add it at the beginning of foaming to allow the particles sufficient time to dissolve, preventing a grainy texture.

Folding

The technique of folding is used when handling delicate foams such as whipped cream or egg foams, and when incorporating them into heavy ingredients such as custards, fruit purées, or chocolate. The goal of folding the airier ingredients into the heavier ingredients is to lighten and decrease the denseness of the mixture without deflating the lighter ingredient. To lighten a cooled base, use a balloon whisk and a large stainless-steel bowl to incorporate one-third of the whipped mixture (either cream or egg whites) into the base, and then switch to a broad rubber spatula to gently fold in the remaining aerated ingredients. Working quickly, rotate the bowl as you gently fold in the aerated mixture with a circular sweeping motion, ensuring an even consistency and color. When folding whipped mixtures into custards, it is important that they are slightly warm instead of cold; otherwise it will be difficult to incorporate the foam evenly and smoothly.

PIE AND TART CRUSTS

ALL-BUTTER PIE DOUGH

An all-purpose buttery and flaky pie pastry made with butter as the sole fat. The key to the flakiness is threefold: the size of the butter pieces; the proper mixing of the dough to prevent the butter from completely blending into the flour; and keeping the butter cold throughout mixing. For step-by-step photos, refer to pages 40 and 41.

YIELD/PAN SIZE	INGREDIENTS	VOLUME	OUNCES
One disc, enough for one single-crust pie or tart	All-purpose flour	1½ cups	7
	Kosher salt	½ tsp	-
	Sugar	½ tsp	-
	Unsalted butter, cold, cut into ¾-inch cubes	½ cup (1 stick)	4
	Water, ice cold, plus more as needed	1 to 2 tbsp	-

YIELD/PAN SIZE	INGREDIENTS	VOLUME	OUNCES
Two discs, enough for two single-crust pies or one double-crust pie	All-purpose flour	3 cups	14
	Kosher salt	1 tsp	-
	Sugar	1 tsp	-
	Unsalted butter, cold, cut into ¾-inch cubes	1 cup (2 sticks)	8
	Water, ice cold, plus more as needed	⅓ cup	3.5

To make by hand:

1 Combine the flour, salt, and sugar in a large bowl. Scatter the butter pieces over the dry ingredients.

2 Using a pastry blender or by rubbing the mixture between your fingers, quickly cut or rub the butter into the ingredients until it is in pieces no larger than small walnuts, but no smaller than peas.

3 Sprinkle half of the ice-cold water over the butter mixture. Using your hands or a rubber spatula, lightly toss the mixture to incorporate the water. Do not overwork the dough, or the butter may melt. Continue to add water in small amounts until the

*For single-crust pie
dough: Omit the
sugar in step 1, and
reduce the butter
to 6 tablespoons (3
ounces). Add 1 cup
(3 ounces) grated
cheddar after cutting
in the butter in step
2. Increase the water
to ¼ cup (2 ounces),
or more as needed.
For double-crust pie
dough, use ¾ cup
butter (1½ sticks/
6 ounces), 2 cups
(6 ounces) cheddar,
and ½ cup water.*

dough is rough but pliable and just holds together when pressed to the side of the bowl. The mixture should not form a ball or mass of dough in the bowl.

4 Turn the dough out onto a lightly floured work surface. Shape the dough into one or two 5- to 6-inch discs, depending on whether you are following the single- or double-crust recipe. Wrap disc(s) tightly in plastic wrap. Chill the dough in the refrigerator for at least 1 hour, or preferably overnight.

To make using a food processor:

1 In the bowl of a food processor fitted with the steel cutting blade, combine the flour, salt, and sugar. Process for a few seconds to combine the dry ingredients.

2 With the food processor off, add half of the butter. Pulse for 3 to 5 seconds, or until the dough is rough and pliable. With the food processor off, add the remaining butter and pulse for 4 to 5 seconds, or until the mixture appears rough, with irregular pieces of butter approximately the size of small walnuts.

3 With the food processor off, sprinkle approximately half of the ice-cold water over the mixture. Pulse for 3 to 5 seconds, or until just combined. Check the dough by pressing it to the side of the bowl. If it does not hold together, add a small amount of ice-cold water, pulse for 3 to 5 seconds, and check it again. The dough should just hold together when pressed to the side of the bowl. It should not form a ball or mass of dough in the bowl.

4 Turn the dough out onto a lightly floured work surface. Shape the dough into one or two 5- to 6-inch discs, depending on whether you are following the single- or double-crust recipe. Wrap disc(s) tightly in plastic wrap. Chill the dough in the refrigerator for at least 1 hour, or preferably overnight.

To make using a stand mixer:

1 In the bowl of a stand mixer, combine the flour, salt, and sugar.

2 Place the bowl in the freezer for 30 minutes, or until the bowl and ingredients are well chilled.

3 Remove the bowl from the freezer and place it on the mixer. Using the paddle attachment, blend the dry ingredients on low speed for 15 seconds, or until combined. With the mixer off, add the butter pieces to the mixing bowl. Mix on medium speed for 1 to 2 minutes, or until the butter is in pieces no larger than small walnuts, but no smaller than peas.

4　With the mixer off, sprinkle approximately half of the ice-cold water over the mixture. Mix on low speed for 30 to 60 seconds, or until just combined. Continue to add water in small amounts until the dough transitions from a slightly powdery appearance with chunks of butter to that of a rough and pliable dough. The dough should just hold together when pressed to the side of the bowl. It should not form a ball or mass of dough in the bowl.

5　Turn the dough out onto a lightly floured work surface. Shape the dough into one or two 5- to 6-inch discs, depending on whether you are following the single- or double-crust recipe. Wrap disc(s) tightly in plastic wrap. Chill the dough in the refrigerator for at least 1 hour, or preferably overnight.

UNBAKED SINGLE CRUST *On a lightly floured work surface, roll out the dough to a ⅛-inch thickness (see chart, page 44, for size guidelines for various pie and tart pans). Transfer the dough to the pan of your choice and fit it into the pan, crimping, fluting, or trimming the edges as desired. Chill the crust in the refrigerator for at least 1 hour and then transfer it to the freezer for at least 15 minutes before baking.*

UNBAKED DOUBLE CRUST *Follow the instructions above to form an unbaked bottom crust. Trim the edge to overhang the edge of the pan by about ½ inch. Chill the crust until ready to use. Leave the second disc wrapped and chilled until ready to use.*

BLIND-BAKED SINGLE CRUST *Preheat the oven to 400°F. Place the docked, chilled crust on a baking sheet, line the chilled crust with lightly oiled or sprayed parchment and fill with weights. Partially blind bake the crust until it is a matte, pale golden color, 15 to 20 minutes. Lower the oven temperature to 350°F. Remove the weights and parchment and bake until lightly browned, about 10 minutes more. Remove the crust from the oven and place it on a cooling rack.*

GRAHAM CRACKER–CRUMB CRUST

Graham crackers come in a variety of flavors, including honey graham, chocolate, and cinnamon. If you do not have a food processor to create crumbs, use a resealable bag and a rolling pin to finely crush the crackers.

YIELD/PAN SIZE

9-inch pie or tart pan

INGREDIENTS	VOLUME	OUNCES
Graham cracker crumbs (from 8 to 9 sheets)	1 cup	4
Light brown sugar, packed	2 tbsp	1
Unsalted butter, melted and cooled	4 tbsp (½ stick)	2

1 Preheat the oven to 350°F. Using a pastry brush, lightly coat a pie or tart pan with softened butter and dust it with flour.

2 Combine the crumbs with the sugar in a bowl and rub with your fingers to incorporate.

3 Add the melted butter to the mixture and mix thoroughly until all the crumbs are moistened. Squeeze the mixture together in your hand. If it holds together in a clump, it is thoroughly mixed.

4 Using your fingers, press the crumb mixture evenly over the bottom and up the sides of the prepared pan.

5 Refrigerate or freeze for at least 30 minutes, or until firm. Bake for 8 to 10 minutes, or until lightly browned, or fill the crust unbaked, as directed in the pie or tart recipe.

NO-BAKE CHOCOLATE COOKIE–CRUMB CRUST

This unbaked crumb crust has chocolate in the mix to boost the flavor. Use this recipe when making delicious and easy summertime no-bake icebox pies, such as Candy Bar Pie (page 223) or Chocolate Any (or No) Nut Pie (page 215). As when making the Cookie-Crumb Crust (opposite), it is essential to use crisp, not soft-baked, cookies.

YIELD/PAN SIZE	INGREDIENTS	VOLUME	OUNCES
9-inch pie pan	Unsalted butter	4 tbsp (½ stick)	2
	Roughly chopped bittersweet chocolate (not more than 65% cacao, if marked)	-	1
	Crisp chocolate wafer cookie crumbs, or chocolate graham cracker crumbs (from 8 to 10 graham-cracker sheets)	1¼ cups	7

1 In a medium saucepan, melt the butter over low to medium heat. Remove the pan from the heat and add the chocolate. Allow the mixture to stand for 5 minutes and then gently stir to incorporate until smooth and creamy.

2 Place the crumbs in a medium bowl and add the melted butter and chocolate mixture. Mix thoroughly until all the crumbs are moistened. Squeeze some of the mixture in your hand. If it holds together in a clump, it is thoroughly mixed.

3 Using your fingers, press the crumb mixture evenly over the bottom and up the sides of the pan.

4 Refrigerate or freeze for 30 minutes to 1 hour, or until firm.

COOKIE-CRUMB CRUST

This master crumb crust recipe can be made with a variety of cookies, including oatmeal, gingersnap, chocolate, and sugar cookies. Be sure to select crispy, dry cookies and avoid soft or filled ones. A crust prepared with them will not hold together and will remain soft, even when the formed crust is baked. If using the volume measurements for this recipe, make sure the cookies are finely ground, and do not shake or pack the crumbs when measuring them.

YIELD/PAN SIZE	INGREDIENTS	VOLUME	OUNCES
9-inch pie or tart pan	Finely ground cookie crumbs	1¼ cups	7
	Sugar	2 tbsp	-
	Unsalted butter, melted and cooled	6 tbsp (¾ stick)	3

1 Preheat the oven to 350°F. Using a pastry brush, lightly coat a pie or tart pan with softened butter and dust it with flour. Set aside.

2 Place the crumbs in a bowl and add the sugar and melted butter to the mixture. Mix thoroughly until all the crumbs are moistened. Squeeze some of the mixture in your hand. If it holds together in a clump, it is thoroughly mixed.

3 Using your fingers, press the crumb mixture evenly over the bottom and up the sides of the prepared pie or tart pan. This crumb crust will remain dry and sandy prior to baking.

4 Chill in the refrigerator or freezer for 30 minutes to 1 hour, or until firm. Bake for 8 to 10 minutes, or until lightly browned, or fill unbaked as directed in the pie or tart recipe.

VANILLA TART DOUGH

Rich and sweet, this vanilla dough has the consistency of a rolled cookie dough. It is delicate and may tear and crack during rolling; to repair it, simply press the edges of the torn dough together to reseal the gap. In order to prevent shrinkage of the crust during baking, this recipe uses confectioners' sugar and a small amount of cornstarch, but it is also important to freeze the preformed tart or tartlet shells prior to baking. For tips on lining tart pans, see page 48.

YIELD/PAN SIZE

One disc, enough for one 9- to 11-inch tart or twelve 3¼-inch tartlets

INGREDIENTS	VOLUME	OUNCES
Unsalted butter, softened	½ cup (1 stick)	4
Confectioners' sugar, sifted	½ cup	2.7
Large egg	1	-
Vanilla extract	1 tsp	-
All-purpose flour	1½ cups	7
Cornstarch	1 tbsp	-
Kosher salt	½ tsp	-

1 In the bowl of a stand mixer fitted with the paddle attachment, combine the butter and sugar. With the mixer on low speed, cream together the butter and sugar until well combined, 4 to 5 minutes. Raise the mixer speed to medium and mix, scraping down the sides of the bowl as necessary, until the mixture is well combined and light in color, about 5 minutes.

2 In a small bowl, whisk together the egg and vanilla. With the mixer on medium speed, gradually add the egg mixture to the butter mixture and mix, scraping down the sides of the bowl as necessary, until the mixture is smooth and well blended, 3 to 4 minutes.

3 Turn off the mixer and add the flour, cornstarch, and salt all at once. Pulse the mixer until the dry ingredients are moistened and then mix on low speed for 1 minute, or until just combined. Do not overmix.

4 Turn the dough out onto a lightly floured work surface. Shape the dough into a 5- to 6-inch disc and wrap it tightly in plastic wrap. Refrigerate for at least 1 hour, or preferably overnight, until firm.

SPICE TART DOUGH *Follow the recipe, adding ½ teaspoon ground cinnamon, ¼ teaspoon freshly grated nutmeg, and ¼ teaspoon ground cloves in step 3 along with the flour, cornstarch, and salt.*

CITRUS TART DOUGH *Follow the recipe, adding 1 teaspoon lemon zest or 1 teaspoon orange zest in step 2 along with the egg and vanilla.*

UNBAKED TART SHELL *On a lightly floured surface, roll out the dough to a ⅛-inch thickness (see chart, page 44, for size guidelines for various pie and tart pans). If making tartlets, it may be necessary to reroll the scraps: Stack the scraps, gently press them together, chill, if necessary, and roll out the re-formed dough. Transfer the dough to the pan of your choice, fit it into the pan, and trim the edges. Refrigerate the crust at least 1 hour or freeze at least 30 minutes or until ready to use.*

BLIND-BAKED TART SHELL *Preheat the oven to 400°F. Line the docked, chilled crust with lightly oiled or sprayed parchment and fill with weights. Partially blind bake the crust until it is a matte, pale golden color, 15 to 20 minutes. Lower the oven temperature to 350°F. Remove the weights and parchment and bake until lightly browned, about 10 minutes more. Remove the crust from the oven and place it on a cooling rack.*

CHOCOLATE TART DOUGH

Cocoa powder imparts a rich chocolate flavor to this cookie-style rolled dough. This dough is fragile, so be sure it is well chilled prior to rolling and handling.

YIELD/PAN SIZE

One disc, enough for one 9- or 11-inch tart

INGREDIENTS	VOLUME	OUNCES
Unsalted butter, softened	½ cup (1 stick)	4
Sugar	½ cup	3.5
Large egg	1	-
Milk	1 tbsp	-
All-purpose flour	1 cup	4.6
Dutch-process cocoa powder, sifted	¾ cup	2.5
Kosher salt	½ tsp	-

UNBAKED TART SHELL

On a lightly floured surface, roll out the dough to a ⅛-inch thickness (see chart, page 44, for size guidelines for various pie and tart pans). Transfer the dough to the pan of your choice, fit it into the pan, and trim the edges. Refrigerate the crust at least 1 hour or freeze at least 30 minutes or until ready to use.

1 In the bowl of a stand mixer fitted with the paddle attachment, combine the butter and sugar. With the mixer on low speed, cream together the butter and sugar until well combined, 4 to 5 minutes. Raise the mixer speed to medium and mix, scraping down the sides of the bowl as necessary, until the mixture is well combined and light in color, about 5 minutes.

2 In a small bowl, whisk together the egg and milk. With the mixer on medium speed, gradually add the egg mixture to the butter mixture and mix, scraping down the sides of the bowl as necessary, until smooth and well blended, 3 to 4 minutes.

3 Turn off the mixer and add the flour, cocoa powder, and salt all at once. Pulse the mixer until the dry ingredients are moistened and then mix on low speed for 1 minute, or until just combined. Do not overmix.

4 Turn the dough out onto a lightly floured work surface. Shape the dough into a 5- to 6-inch disc and wrap it tightly in plastic wrap. Refrigerate for at least 1 hour, or preferably overnight, until firm.

BLIND-BAKED TART SHELL *Preheat the oven to 400°F. Line the docked, chilled crust with lightly oiled or sprayed parchment and fill with weights. Partially blind bake the crust until it has a matte appearance and chocolate aroma, 15 to 20 minutes. Lower the oven temperature to 350°F. Remove the weights and parchment and bake for 10 minutes more. Transfer to a wire rack to cool.*

PRETZEL TART DOUGH

A simple press-into-the-pan dough. Both crunchy and salty, this dough is best combined with chocolate and/or peanut butter no-bake or refrigerator pies or tarts, such as Chocolate Any (or No) Nut Pie (page 215) or Chocolate Truffle Tart (page 242). Be sure the pretzels are broken or crushed into very small pieces, or the crust will not come together properly.

YIELD/PAN SIZE
One 9- or 11-inch tart shell

INGREDIENTS	VOLUME	OUNCES
Unsalted butter, softened	½ cup (1 stick)	4
Sugar	½ cup	3.5
Large egg, lightly beaten	1	-
All-purpose flour	1¼ cups	5.75
Finely crushed pretzels (⅛-inch pieces)	1 cup	3

1 Using a pastry brush, lightly coat a tart pan with softened butter and dust it with flour. Set aside.

2 In the bowl of a stand mixer fitted with the paddle attachment, combine the butter and sugar. With the mixer on low speed, cream together the butter and sugar until well combined, 4 to 5 minutes. Raise the mixer speed to medium and mix, scraping down the sides of the bowl as necessary, until the mixture is well combined and light in color, about 5 minutes.

3 With the mixer on medium speed, gradually add the egg to the butter mixture and mix, scraping down the sides of the bowl as necessary, until smooth and well blended, 3 to 4 minutes.

4 Turn off the mixer and add the flour all at once. Pulse the mixer until the flour is moistened. Add the crushed pretzels and mix on low speed for 1 minute, or until just combined.

5 Press the dough evenly over the bottom and up the sides of the prepared pie or tart pan and refrigerate or freeze for 1 hour, or until firm.

BLIND-BAKED TART SHELL *Preheat the oven to 400°F. Line the chilled tart shell with lightly oiled or sprayed parchment and fill with weights. Bake until golden brown, about 15 minutes. Lower the oven temperature to 350°F. Remove the weights and bake for 5 to 15 minutes more. Let cool completely before filling.*

NUT TART DOUGH

A simple and quick nut dough with no rolling necessary: just mix, press into the tart pan, chill, and bake. This recipe can easily accommodate the nut of your choice—almonds, hazelnuts, macadamias, pecans, walnuts—just be sure to lightly toast the nuts before grinding them for the fullest flavor (see page 30 for instruction on toasting nuts).

YIELD/PAN SIZE
One 9- or 11-inch
tart shell

**SALTY PEANUT
TART DOUGH**

*Follow the recipe for
Nut Tart Dough,
using finely ground
salted dry-roasted
peanuts.*

**BLIND-BAKED
TART SHELL**

*Preheat the oven
to 400°F. Line the
chilled tart crust
with lightly oiled or
sprayed parchment
and fill with weights.
Bake until golden
brown, about
15 minutes. Lower
the oven temperature
to 350°F. Remove the
weights and bake for
5 to 10 minutes more.
Let cool completely
before filling.*

INGREDIENTS	VOLUME	OUNCES
Unsalted butter, softened	4 tbsp (½ stick)	2
Sugar	¼ cup	1.8
Large egg, lightly beaten	1	-
Vanilla extract	1 tsp	-
All-purpose flour	¾ cup	3.5
Kosher salt	¼ tsp	-
Finely ground toasted nuts	¾ cup	3.15

1 Using a pastry brush, lightly coat a tart pan with softened butter and dust it with flour.

2 In the bowl of a stand mixer fitted with the paddle attachment, combine the butter and sugar. With the mixer on low speed, cream together the butter and sugar until well combined, 4 to 5 minutes. Raise the mixer speed to medium and mix, scraping down the sides of the bowl as necessary, until the mixture is well combined and light in color, about 5 minutes.

3 In a small bowl, combine the egg and vanilla. With the mixer on low speed, gradually add the egg mixture to the butter mixture and mix, scraping down the sides of the bowl as necessary, until the mixture is smooth and well blended, 2 to 3 minutes.

4 Turn off the mixer and add the flour and salt all at once. Pulse the mixer until the flour is moistened. Add the ground nuts and mix on low speed for 1 minute, or until just combined.

5 Press the dough evenly over the bottom and up the sides of the prepared tart pan and refrigerate or freeze for at least 1 hour, or until firm.

LINZER TORTE DOUGH

Traditionally, this delicate, buttery, shortbread-type tart dough contains finely ground toasted almonds and is spiced with cinnamon and clove. Be sure the dough is as cold as possible when rolling it out, forming the lattice, and lining the pan, or it will fall apart and tear.

YIELD/PAN SIZE

Two discs, enough for one 9- or 11-inch double-crust tart

INGREDIENTS	VOLUME	OUNCES
Unsalted butter, softened	¾ cup (1½ sticks)	6
Sugar	½ cup	3.5
Egg yolks, lightly beaten	2	-
Water, plus more as needed	1 to 2 tbsp	-
All-purpose flour	1½ cups	7
Almonds, blanched, toasted, and finely ground	1½ cups	6
Ground cinnamon	1 tsp	-
Ground cloves	¼ tsp	-
Kosher salt	½ tsp	-

1 Preheat oven to 350°F. Using a pastry brush, lightly coat a tart pan with softened butter and dust it with flour. Set aside.

2 In the bowl of a stand mixer fitted with the paddle attachment, cream the butter and sugar on low speed until well combined, 4 to 5 minutes. Raise the speed to medium and mix, scraping down the bowl as necessary, until well combined and light in color, about 5 minutes.

3 In a small bowl, combine the egg yolks and water. With the mixer on low speed, gradually add the egg mixture to the butter mixture and mix, scraping down the sides of the bowl as necessary, until smooth and well blended, 3 to 5 minutes.

4 Turn the mixer off and add the flour, almonds, cinnamon, cloves, and salt. Pulse the mixer until the dry ingredients are moistened, then mix on low speed until just combined.

5 Turn the dough out onto a lightly floured work surface and shape it into two 5- to 6-inch discs. Wrap each disc tightly in plastic wrap and refrigerate for at least 1 hour, or preferably overnight, until firm.

CREAM CHEESE DOUGH

This dough is incredibly easy to make and to work with. If you have had trouble with pastry dough in the past, this recipe yields a no-fail flaky, tender crust. It browns easily in the oven and is perfect for hand pies or juicy fruit pies.

YIELD/PAN SIZE	INGREDIENTS	VOLUME	OUNCES
One disc, enough for one 9-inch single-crust pie	All-purpose flour	1½ cups	7
	Kosher salt	½ tsp	-
	Cream cheese, cold, cut into ¾-inch cubes	½ cup	4
	Unsalted butter, cold, cut into ¾-inch cubes	½ cup (1 stick)	4
	Water, ice cold	1 tbsp	-
	Fresh lemon juice	1 tsp	-

1 In the bowl of a stand mixer fitted with the paddle attachment, combine the flour and salt.

2 Blend the dry ingredients on low speed until combined, about 15 seconds. With the mixer off, add the cream cheese pieces to the mixing bowl and combine on medium speed until the mixture resembles cornmeal, 2 to 3 minutes. Add the butter pieces and combine on medium speed until the mixture appears rough, with irregular pieces of butter no larger than small walnuts and no smaller than peas, 2 to 3 minutes.

3 Sprinkle the ice-cold water and the lemon juice over the mixture and mix on low speed for 30 to 60 seconds, or until just combined. Continue to mix until the dough is rough but pliable. The dough should just hold together when pressed to the side of the bowl. It should not form a ball or mass of dough in the bowl.

4 Turn out the dough onto a lightly floured work surface. Shape the dough into a 5- to 6-inch disc and wrap it tightly in plastic wrap. Refrigerate for at least 1 hour, or preferably overnight, until firm.

PARMESAN PASTRY DOUGH

When baked, the browned bits of Parmesan scattered throughout this crust create pockets of rich, sharp flavor and aroma.

YIELD/PAN SIZE

One disc, enough for one 9-inch single-crust pie

INGREDIENTS	VOLUME	OUNCES
All-purpose flour	1 cup	5
Kosher salt	¼ tsp	-
Unsalted butter, cold, cut into ¾-inch cubes	6 tbsp (¾ stick)	3
Parmesan, finely grated	¼ cup	1.5
Water, ice cold, plus more as needed	1 to 2 tbsp	-

1 In a large bowl, combine the flour and salt. Scatter the butter pieces over the dry ingredients.

2 Using a pastry blender or by rubbing the mixture between your fingers, quickly cut or rub the butter into the dry ingredients until it is in pieces no bigger than small walnuts but no smaller than peas. Add the cheese and toss gently to combine.

3 Sprinkle half of the ice-cold water over the butter mixture. Using your hands or a rubber spatula, lightly toss the dry mixture to incorporate the water. Do not over-work the dough, or the butter may melt. Continue to add water in small amounts until the dough is rough but pliable and just holds together when pressed to the side of the bowl. The mixture should not form a ball or mass of dough in the bowl.

4 Turn out the dough onto a lightly floured work surface. Shape it into a 5- to 6-inch disc and wrap it tightly in plastic wrap. Refrigerate for at least 1 hour, or preferably overnight, until firm.

CORNMEAL PASTRY DOUGH

This crispy cornmeal crust was developed to be used for both savory and sweet pies. It is especially good paired with stone fruit pies and galettes—just be sure to purchase a high-quality, stone-ground fine cornmeal for the best flavor.

YIELD/PAN SIZE

One disc, enough for one 9-inch single-crust pie

INGREDIENTS	VOLUME	OUNCES
All-purpose flour	1¼ cups	5.75
Finely ground cornmeal	¼ cup	1.5
Kosher salt	½ tsp	-
Sugar	¼ tsp	-
Unsalted butter, cold, cut into ¾-inch cubes	½ cup (1 stick)	4
Water, ice cold, plus more as needed	3 to 4 tbsp	-

1 In a large bowl, combine the flour, cornmeal, salt, and sugar. Scatter the butter pieces over the dry ingredients.

2 Using a pastry blender or by rubbing the mixture between your fingers, quickly cut or rub the butter into the dry ingredients until it is in pieces no bigger than small walnuts but no smaller than peas.

3 Sprinkle half of the ice-cold water over the butter mixture. Using your hands or a rubber spatula, lightly toss the dry mixture to incorporate the water. Do not overwork the dough, or the butter may melt. Continue to add water in small amounts until the dough is rough but pliable and just holds together when pressed to the side of the bowl. The mixture should not form a ball or mass of dough in the bowl.

4 Turn the dough out onto a lightly floured work surface. Shape the dough into a 5- to 6-inch disc and wrap it tightly in plastic wrap. Refrigerate for at least 1 hour, or preferably overnight, until firm.

SWEET CORNMEAL CRUST *Follow the recipe for Cornmeal Pastry Dough, increasing the sugar in step 1 to 1 tablespoon.*

EMPANADA DOUGH

For the most authentic, best flavor, this dough should be made with masa harina, a flour made from corn that can be found in most supermarkets or Latin markets. If you cannot locate it, the masa harina can be replaced with flour.

YIELD

One disc, enough for about 2 dozen 4½-inch empanadas

INGREDIENTS	VOLUME	OUNCES
All-purpose flour	1½ cups	7
Masa harina	½ cup	2.5
Kosher salt	½ tsp	-
Unsalted butter, cold, cut into ¼-inch cubes	½ cup (1 stick)	4
Large egg	1	-
Water, ice cold, plus more as needed	½ cup	4

1 In the bowl of a food processor fitted with the steel cutting blade, combine the flour, masa harina, and salt. Pulse for 15 to 20 seconds.

2 With the food processor off, add 4 tablespoons of the butter. Pulse for 3 to 5 seconds, or until the mixture appears rough and pebbly. With the food processor off, add the remaining 4 tablespoons butter. Pulse for 4 to 5 seconds, or until the mixture appears rough, with irregular pieces of butter approximately the size of small walnuts.

3 With the food processor off, add the egg and 2 tablespoons of the ice-cold water. Pulse for 3 to 5 seconds, or until just combined. Check the dough by pressing it to the side of the bowl. If it does not hold together, add a small amount of water (about 2 tablespoons), pulse for 3 to 5 seconds, and check it again. The dough should just hold together when pressed to the side of the bowl. It should not form a ball or mass of dough in the bowl.

4 Turn out the dough onto a lightly floured work surface. Shape the dough into a 5- to 6-inch disc and wrap it tightly in plastic wrap. Refrigerate for at least 1 hour, or preferably overnight, until firm.

FRUIT

APPLE PIE

During the fall apple season, there are countless varieties of apples available in local markets, such as Cortland, Northern Spy, or Jonagold. These and many other regional varieties are all good choices for making pie. If none of these varieties is available, a good substitute is a combination of the widely available and flavorful McIntosh and the tart Granny Smith.

MAKES
One 9-inch pie

CRUST
All-Butter Pie
Dough, Unbaked
Double Crust
(page 64)

INGREDIENTS	VOLUME	OUNCES
Apples, peeled and cut into ¼-inch slices	4 to 5	3 lb
Fresh lemon juice	2 tsp	-
Granulated sugar	¾ cup	5.3
All-purpose flour	2 tbsp	-
Ground cinnamon	2 tsp	-
Freshly grated nutmeg	¼ tsp	-
Ground allspice	¼ tsp	-
Kosher salt	¼ tsp	-
Egg wash (page 308), as needed		
Sanding or granulated sugar, as needed		

1 Preheat the oven to 375°F and set the rack in the lowest position.

2 Roll out the dough for the top crust to ⅛ inch thick. Using a pastry wheel, cut twelve 1-inch-wide strips of dough. Set aside.

3 In a medium bowl, combine the apples, lemon juice, granulated sugar, flour, cinnamon, nutmeg, allspice, and salt. Toss to combine. Immediately transfer the apples into the prepared bottom crust, arranging and pressing them to eliminate gaps and air pockets.

4 Brush the edge of the bottom crust with water and gently weave and arrange the dough strips on top of the filling to create a lattice top (see page 50). Trim the edges flush with the edge of the bottom crust and press them to seal. Turn the edge under and decoratively crimp the edges as desired.

5 Place the pie on a rimmed baking sheet. Brush the lattice top with egg wash and sprinkle liberally with sanding or granulated sugar.

6 Bake for 30 minutes, then rotate the pie and reduce the oven temperature to 350°F. Continue baking until the filling is bubbly and thick, 60 to 70 minutes more. Remove the pie from the oven and place it on a cooling rack. Let cool for 2 to 3 hours. The filling will continue to thicken and set as the pie cools.

APPLE RAISIN PIE   *In a small saucepan, heat ½ cup apple juice over medium heat to just under a boil. Remove the pan from the heat and add ¾ cup raisins (or dried sweet cherries or cranberries) to the warm juice, cover the pan, and let sit for 10 to 15 minutes, or until the raisins are soft. Drain off the juice and cover the pan, allowing the raisins to rehydrate for 4 hours, or until plump. (This method prevents the dried fruit from losing their flavor in the juice or weeping into the filling.) Follow the recipe for Apple Pie, adding the raisins to the apple mixture in step 3.*

TIPS FOR SUCCESSFUL APPLE PIES

If you have access to a local orchard or a farmer's market, ask which regional varieties make the best pie.

Peeling, coring, and slicing apples can be a tiresome process. A hand-cranked apple peeler/corer/slicer (see page 10) is a helpful aid, especially when making multiple pies.

Always wait to toss the apples with the sugar until you are ready to assemble the pie; otherwise the sugar will draw out the moisture from the fruit and make it sloppy and difficult to handle.

To keep the top crust or the lattice from puffing above the fruit (known as "tenting") on double-crust apple pies, substitute 3 tablespoons all-purpose shortening for an equal amount of the butter in the crust. The addition of shortening makes the dough more flexible and less brittle. This will allow the top crust to settle with the apples while baking.

Cool the pie to room temperature before slicing. This allows the filling to properly set.

If you are serving leftovers the next day, refresh the pie by rewarming it in the oven (see page 301).

SALTY CARAMEL APPLE PIE

The flavor combination of caramel and apples is a natural pairing that has become a popular choice for pies—a trend that hopefully is here to stay. The salt in this recipe enhances the flavors. Use a high-quality flaked sea salt, such as Maldon.

MAKES
One 9-inch pie

CRUST
All-Butter Pie Dough, Unbaked Double Crust (page 64)

INGREDIENTS	VOLUME	OUNCES
Unsalted butter	4 tbsp (½ stick)	2
Heavy cream	½ cup	4.2
Light brown sugar, packed	1¼ cups	9.7
Water	¼ cup	2
Vanilla extract	1 tsp	-
Kosher salt	1 tsp	-
Apples, Golden Delicious, peeled and cut into ¼-inch slices	4 to 5	3 lb
Fresh lemon juice	2 tsp	-
Granulated sugar	¼ cup	1.8
Cornstarch	¼ cup	1
Ground cinnamon	2 tsp	-
Freshly grated nutmeg	⅛ tsp	-
Egg wash (page 308), as needed		
Sanding sugar, as needed		
Flaked salt, as needed		

1 Preheat the oven to 375°F and set the rack in the lowest position.

2 In a small, heavy-bottom saucepan, combine the butter and cream and bring to a simmer. Remove from the heat and set aside.

3 In a heavy-bottom medium saucepan, combine the brown sugar and water, stirring continuously over medium heat to dissolve the sugar. If the sugar is melting unevenly, gently tilt or swirl the pan to evenly distribute the sugar. Cook until the mixture registers 240°F on a candy thermometer.

4 Remove the pan from the heat and slowly stir the heavy cream and butter into the sugar until smooth. Be careful, as the hot mixture will bubble up. If the caramel mixture seizes (begins to recrystallize and harden), return it to the heat and continue to stir until smooth. Remove the pan from the heat and stir in the vanilla and salt. Reserve ½ cup of the caramel sauce for serving with the pie, and use the remaining for the assembly.

5 In a medium bowl, combine the apples, lemon juice, granulated sugar, cornstarch, cinnamon, and nutmeg. Toss to combine.

6 Layer half of the apples in the prepared bottom crust, arranging and pressing them to eliminate gaps and air pockets. Pour one-third of the remaining caramel sauce over the apples. Layer the remaining apples on top of the caramel sauce, again arranging and pressing them to reduce gaps and air pockets. Pour the remaining caramel over the top layer of apples.

7 Roll out the dough for the top crust to ⅛ inch thick. Using a pastry wheel, cut twelve 1-inch-wide strips of dough. Brush the edge of the bottom crust with water, and gently weave and arrange the dough strips on top of the filling to create a lattice top (see page 50). Trim the edges flush with the edge of the bottom crust and press them to seal. Turn and decoratively crimp the edges.

8 Place the pie on a rimmed baking sheet. Brush the lattice top of the crust with egg wash and sprinkle liberally with sanding sugar and flaked salt.

9 Bake until the filling is bubbly and thick, 50 to 60 minutes. Remove the pie from the oven and place it on a cooling rack. Let cool for 2 to 3 hours. The filling will continue to thicken and set as the pie cools.

10 Serve with the reserved caramel sauce on the side, or drizzle the sauce over each slice.

APPLE SLAB PIE

If you prefer a higher ratio of crust to filling, then slab pies are for you! The filling is thick enough to allow you to easily eat a slice "out of hand" without utensils. They are also convenient to serve as they can be sliced easily into narrow pieces or wedges to feed a crowd.

MAKES
One 5½ by 17-inch slab pie

CRUST
All-Butter Pie Dough, double crust (page 64; form the dough into one disc instead of two in Step 4)

TOPPING
Vanilla Icing Glaze (page 312; optional)

INGREDIENTS	VOLUME	OUNCES
Apples, Golden Delicious, peeled and cut into ¼-inch slices	4 to 5	2 lb
Fresh lemon juice	2 tsp	-
Granulated sugar	1 cup	7
All-purpose flour	3 tbsp	-
Vanilla extract	1 tsp	-
Ground cinnamon	1 tsp	-
Freshly grated nutmeg	⅛ tsp	-
Egg wash (page 308), as needed		
Sanding or granulated sugar, as needed		

1 Preheat the oven to 375°F and set the rack in the lowest position.

2 Dust a 13 by 18-inch sheet of parchment paper with flour. On the parchment paper, roll out the dough to ⅛ inch thick. Using a pastry wheel, trim the dough to 10 inches by 17 inches. Slide the parchment paper with the dough onto a rimmed baking sheet and refrigerate for 30 minutes, or until firm.

3 In a medium bowl, combine the apples, lemon juice, granulated sugar, flour, vanilla, cinnamon, and nutmeg. Toss to combine. Immediately layer the apples over half of the chilled pie dough lengthwise, leaving a ½-inch border on three sides. Arrange and press the apples gently to eliminate gaps and air pockets. Brush the ½-inch border lightly with water and fold the top half over the filling, pressing the edges to seal. Using the tines of a fork, gently press and crimp the edges.

4 Brush the top crust with egg wash. Using a paring knife, cut 6 or 7 vents in the top crust at 2- to 3-inch intervals. Sprinkle the top crust liberally with sanding or granulated sugar.

5 Bake until the filling is bubbly and thick, 45 to 50 minutes. Remove the pie from the oven and place it on a cooling rack. Let cool for 2 to 3 hours. The filling will continue to thicken and set as the pie cools.

6 If desired, glaze the pie with Vanilla Icing Glaze, using a fork to drizzle the icing over the top of the slab pie. Allow to set 1 to 2 hours before serving.

MANY BERRY PIE

At the height of the summer, many different types of berries are available. This pie allows you to pick and choose from the season's best offerings. Here we have chosen blueberries, raspberries, and blackberries, but strawberries or other local berries, such as boysenberries or marionberries, work just as well. If you prefer to use frozen berries, be sure to partially defrost and drain them before mixing the filling.

MAKES
One 9-inch pie

CRUST
All-Butter Pie Dough, Unbaked Single Crust (page 64)

TOPPING
Streusel (page 304)

INGREDIENTS	VOLUME	OUNCES
Blueberries, rinsed and picked over for stems	3 cups (1 pint)	16
Raspberries, rinsed	1½ cups (1 pint)	16
Blackberries, rinsed	1½ cups (1 pint)	16
Sugar	¾ cup	5.3
Cornstarch	3 tbsp	-
Fresh orange juice	1 tbsp	-
Orange zest	2 tsp	-
Kosher salt	¼ tsp	-

1 Preheat the oven to 375°F and set the rack in the lowest position.

2 In a medium bowl, combine the blueberries, raspberries, blackberries, sugar, cornstarch, orange juice, orange zest, and salt. Toss to combine. Transfer the filling to the prepared bottom crust. Top with the streusel.

3 Place the pie on a rimmed baking sheet. Bake until the filling is bubbly and thick, 60 to 70 minutes. Remove the pie from the oven and place it on a cooling rack. Let cool for 2 to 3 hours. The filling will to continue to thicken and set as the pie cools.

RHUBARB PIE

This recipe was handed down to me from my mother. Every spring we would make pies from the prolific plants given to us by her mother, always topped with Brown Sugar and Oat Streusel to offset the tartness.

MAKES
One 9-inch pie

CRUST
All-Butter Pie
Dough, Unbaked
Single Crust
(page 64)

TOPPING
Brown Sugar and
Oat Crumble
(page 307)

INGREDIENTS	VOLUME	OUNCES
Rhubarb, cut into ½-inch pieces	4 cups	18
Sugar	1¼ cups	8.75
All-purpose flour	½ cup	2.2
Kosher salt	¼ tsp	-

1 Preheat the oven to 375°F and set the rack in the lowest position.

2 In a medium bowl, combine the rhubarb, sugar, flour, and salt. Toss to combine.

3 Transfer the filling to the prepared bottom crust. Top with the crumble.

4 Place the pie on a rimmed baking sheet. Bake until the filling is bubbly and thick, 45 to 50 minutes. Remove the pie from the oven and place it on a cooling rack. Let cool for 2 to 3 hours. The filling will continue to thicken and set as the pie cools.

STRAWBERRY RHUBARB PIE *Prepare a double crust using All-Butter Pie Dough (page 64) and fit the bottom crust into a pie pan and chill. Follow the recipe for Rhubarb Pie, reducing the rhubarb to 2 cups and adding ¾ pint (about 2 cups) strawberries, hulled and halved, in step 2, and ½ teaspoon orange zest to the sugar. Pour the filling into the prepared bottom crust.*

Roll out the dough for the top crust to ⅛ inch thick. Using a fluted pastry wheel, cut ten 1-inch-wide strips of dough. Brush the edge of the bottom crust with water, and gently weave and arrange the dough strips on top of the filling to create a lattice top (see page 50). Trim the edges flush with the edge of the bottom crust and press to seal. Turn and decoratively crimp the edges. Brush with egg wash (page 308), and sprinkle liberally with sanding sugar or granulated sugar.

STRAWBERRY BALSAMIC PIE

The pairing of balsamic vinegar and strawberries under this pie's lattice top is a delightful and unusual combination. Modena vinegar, which is wood-aged, is best. The length of time for aging depends on the type you buy. It also has the darkest color and richest flavor.

MAKES
One 9-inch pie

CRUST
All-Butter Pie
Dough, Unbaked
Double Crust
(page 64)

INGREDIENTS	VOLUME	OUNCES
Strawberries, fresh, hulled and halved, or frozen, halved	4 cups (1 qt)	32
Cornstarch	⅓ cup	1.75
Granulated sugar	¾ cup	5.3
Balsamic vinegar	2 tbsp	-
Egg wash (page 308), as needed		
Sanding sugar or granulated sugar, as needed (optional)		

1 Preheat the oven to 375°F and set the rack in the lowest position.

2 Roll out the top crust to ⅛ inch thick. To make the crust pictured, use a pie-top lattice cutter (see page 12): Lightly coat the cutting edges of the pie-top cutter with flour. Place the cutter on your work surface, cutting edges facing up. Transfer the dough onto the cutter. Roll a rolling pin over the dough, applying enough pressure to cut out the lattice.

3 In a medium bowl, combine the strawberries, cornstarch, granulated sugar, and vinegar. Toss to combine. Immediately transfer the mixture to the prepared bottom crust.

4 Brush the edge of the bottom crust with water. Gently transfer the cutout top crust to the pie. Trim the edges flush with the edge of the bottom crust and press to seal. Turn and decoratively crimp the edges.

5 Brush the top crust with egg wash and, if desired, sprinkle with sanding sugar or granulated sugar.

6 Place the pie on a baking sheet. Bake until the filling is bubbly and thick, 45 to 50 minutes. Remove the pie from the oven and place it on a cooling rack. Let cool for 2 to 3 hours. The filling will continue to thicken and set as the pie cools.

SOUR CHERRY PIE

The fresh sour-cherry season is a short and fleeting one. Though they are often too fragile to ship very far, if you are lucky enough to find these tart deep red or dark purple–black pie cherries at a local farmer's market, purchase them! They can also be found canned or frozen. Two varieties are Montmorency and Morello.

MAKES

One 9-inch pie

CRUST

All-Butter Pie Dough, Unbaked Double Crust (page 64)

INGREDIENTS	VOLUME	OUNCES
Sour cherries, Morello or Montmorency; pitted if fresh; drained if canned or frozen, ¼ cup of juice reserved	5 cups	2 lb
Water, if using fresh cherries	2 tbsp	-
Cornstarch	⅓ cup	1.75
Granulated sugar	1¼ cups	8.8
Fresh lemon juice	2 tsp	-
Kosher salt	¼ tsp	-
Egg wash (page 308), as needed		
Sanding sugar or granulated sugar, as needed		

1 Preheat the oven to 375°F and set the rack in the lowest position.

2 Add the cornstarch to the reserved juice, if using frozen or canned cherries, or water if using fresh, and stir to combine. Set aside.

3 In a medium saucepan, combine the cherries, sugar, lemon juice, and salt, stirring to combine. Bring to a gentle simmer over medium heat, and simmer, stirring, for 15 to 20 minutes, until reduced and thickened. Remove the pan from the heat and stir in the cornstarch mixture. Return the pan to the stovetop and bring to a simmer over medium heat. Cook for 3 to 5 minutes, until clear and thick. Remove the pan from the heat and allow to cool for 30 to 45 minutes, or until cooled to room temperature. Transfer the cherry mixture to the prepared and chilled bottom crust.

4 Roll out the top crust to ⅛ inch thick. Using a pastry wheel, cut fourteen 1-inch-wide strips of dough. Brush the edge of the bottom crust with water and gently weave and arrange the dough strips on top of the filling to create a lattice top (see

page 50). Trim the edges flush with the edge of the bottom crust and press to seal. Turn and decoratively crimp or flute the edges.

5   Place the pie on a rimmed baking sheet. Brush the lattice top with egg wash and sprinkle with sanding sugar or granulated sugar.

6   Bake until the filling is bubbly and thick, 45 to 50 minutes. Remove the pie from the oven and place it on a cooling rack. Let cool for 2 to 3 hours. The filling will continue to thicken and set as the pie cools.

PEACH CRUMB PIE

This fresh peach pie is topped with a buttery, crunchy brown sugar and oat crumble. Served warm with a scoop of ice cream, it is a delicious reward well worth the time spent blanching and peeling the peaches.

MAKES
One 9-inch pie

CRUST
All-Butter Pie Dough, Unbaked Single Crust (page 64)

TOPPING
Brown Sugar and Oat Crumble (page 307)

INGREDIENTS	VOLUME	OUNCES
Peaches	8 to 10	3 lb
Sugar	1 cup	7
Lemon juice	2 tsp	-
Cornstarch	¼ cup	1.2
Ground cinnamon	1 tsp	-
Kosher salt	¼ tsp	-

1 Preheat the oven to 375°F and set the rack in the lowest position.

2 Bring a medium pot of water to a boil. In a medium bowl, prepare an ice bath. Lightly cut an X on top of each peach. Gently lower half of the peaches into the boiling water with a slotted spoon and submerge for 30 to 60 seconds. Remove them with a slotted spoon and immediately submerge in the ice bath. Repeat with the remaining peaches. Transfer the blanched peaches to a cutting board. When they are cool enough to handle, remove the skins with a paring knife or peeler. Pit the peaches and cut them into ⅓-inch slices.

3 In a medium bowl, combine the peaches, sugar, lemon juice, cornstarch, cinnamon, and salt. Toss to combine. Immediately transfer the mixture to the prepared bottom crust. Top with the crumble.

4 Place the pie on a rimmed baking sheet. Bake until the filling is bubbly and thick, 45 to 50 minutes. Remove the pie from the oven and place it on a cooling rack. Let cool for 2 to 3 hours. The filling will continue to thicken and set as the pie cools.

BELLINI PEACH LATTICE PIE

If white peaches are in season, they are perfect in this cocktail-inspired pie, but yellow peaches are just as tasty. White peaches have a higher sugar-to-acid ratio, making them delightfully sweet and soft. In this recipe, they are lightly poached in Prosecco, an Italian sparkling white wine, and covered with a buttery, sugar-topped lattice crust.

MAKES
One 9-inch pie

CRUST
All-Butter Pie Dough, Unbaked Double Crust (page 64)

INGREDIENTS	VOLUME	OUNCES
Peaches	8 to 10	3 lb
Prosecco or other sparkling white wine	1 cup	8
Granulated sugar	½ cup	3.5
Fresh lemon juice	2 tsp	-
Instant tapioca, finely ground in a coffee or spice grinder	¼ cup	1.6
Egg wash (page 308), as needed		
Sanding sugar or granulated sugar, as needed		

1   Preheat the oven to 375°F and set the rack in the lowest position.

2   Bring a medium pot of water to a boil. In a medium bowl, prepare an ice bath. Lightly cut an X on top of each peach. Gently lower half of the peaches into the boiling water with a slotted spoon and submerge for 30 to 60 seconds. Remove them with a slotted spoon and immediately submerge in the ice bath. Repeat with the remaining peaches. Transfer the blanched peaches to a cutting board. When they are cool enough to handle, remove the skins with a paring knife or peeler. Pit the peaches and cut them into ¼-inch slices.

3   In a medium saucepan, heat the sparkling wine to a simmer over high heat. Reduce the heat to medium. Lower the sliced peaches into the wine with a slotted spoon and poach them until slightly soft, 2 to 3 minutes. Remove the pan from the heat, and drain the peaches through a fine-mesh, heat-resistant strainer suspended over a bowl. Reserve the poaching liquid.

4 In a medium bowl, combine the poached peaches, ¾ cup of the reserved poaching juice, and the granulated sugar, lemon juice, and tapioca. Toss to combine and set aside for about 30 minutes, or until the tapioca is soft. Stir the filling and pour it into the prepared bottom crust.

5 Roll out the top crust to ⅛ inch thick. Using a fluted pastry wheel, cut twelve 1-inch-wide dough strips. Brush the edge of the bottom crust with water and gently weave and arrange the dough strips on top of the filling to create a lattice top (see page 50). Trim the edges flush with the edge of the bottom crust and press to seal. Turn and decoratively crimp the edges. Brush the lattice top with egg wash and sprinkle liberally with sanding sugar or granulated sugar.

6 Place the pie on a rimmed baking sheet. Bake until the filling is bubbly and thick, 45 to 50 minutes. Remove the pie from the oven and place it on a cooling rack. Let cool for 2 to 3 hours. The filling will continue to thicken and set as the pie cools.

FRESH BLUEBERRY PIE

If you have never had a fresh blueberry pie, this is the classic recipe to try. The top crust is formed with overlapping star cutouts, making it perfect for the Fourth of July—high season for fresh blueberries!

MAKES
One 9-inch pie

CRUST
All-Butter Pie Dough, Unbaked Double Crust (page 64)

INGREDIENTS	VOLUME	OUNCES
Blueberries, rinsed and picked over for stems	6 cups (about 2 pints)	24
Granulated sugar	1¼ cups	8.75
Instant tapioca, finely ground in an electric grinder	3 tbsp	1
Fresh lemon juice	2 tsp	-
Lemon zest	½ tsp	-
Kosher salt	¼ tsp	-
Egg wash (page 308), as needed		
Sanding sugar or granulated sugar, as needed		

1 Preheat the oven to 375°F and set the rack in the lowest position.

2 In a medium bowl, combine the blueberries, granulated sugar, tapioca, lemon juice, lemon zest, and salt. Toss to combine. Set aside for about 30 minutes, or until the tapioca softens. Stir the filling and pour it into the prepared bottom crust.

NOTE *Frozen berries can be substituted for fresh berries. If using, be sure to allow them to partially defrost before combining them with the other filling ingredients.*

3 Roll out the top crust to ⅛ inch thick. Using a 2-inch star cookie cutter, cut out 20 stars. Brush the top edge of the bottom crust with water and arrange the stars around the pie, lightly brushing each star on the pie with water before overlapping it with another star and gently pressing them to attach. Continue in a random pattern, or, if preferred, in concentric circles. Brush the star top with egg wash and sprinkle with sanding sugar or granulated sugar.

4 Place the pie on a rimmed baking sheet. Bake until the filling is bubbly and thick, 45 to 50 minutes. Remove the pie from the oven and place it on a cooling rack. Let cool for 2 to 3 hours. The filling will continue to thicken and set as the pie cools.

LEMON-GLAZED BLUEBERRY HAND PIES

The combination of blueberries wrapped in a flaky, buttery crust and glazed with a lemon icing is delightfully delicious. These little hand pies are a wonderful addition to a picnic or lunch box. They can be made with fresh or frozen blueberries (see Note, page 102).

MAKES

Eight 4½-inch round hand pies or sixteen 4½-inch half-round hand pies

CRUST

Two recipes Cream Cheese Dough (page 76), chilled

TOPPING

Lemon Icing Glaze (page 312; optional)

INGREDIENTS	VOLUME	OUNCES
Blueberries, rinsed and picked over for stems	3 cups (1 pint)	12
Granulated sugar	⅓ cup	2.4
Cornstarch	2 tbsp	-
Fresh lemon juice	1 tsp	-
Lemon zest	½ tsp	-
Kosher salt	¼ tsp	-
Egg wash (page 308), as needed		
Sanding sugar or granulated sugar, as needed (optional)		

1 Preheat the oven to 375°F and set the rack in the lowest position. Line two baking sheets with parchment paper.

2 In a medium saucepan, combine the blueberries, granulated sugar, cornstarch, lemon juice, lemon zest, and salt and stir to combine. Bring to a gentle simmer over medium heat, and cook, stirring, until the juices are thickened and clear, 2 to 3 minutes. Remove the pan from the heat and allow to cool to room temperature, about 30 minutes.

3 Roll out half of the chilled dough to ⅛ inch thick. Using a round 4½-inch cutter, cut 8 discs from the dough, re-rolling scraps as necessary. Transfer the discs to a prepared baking sheet and refrigerate until firm, about 30 minutes. Repeat the rolling, cutting, and chilling process with the remaining half of the dough.

4 Remove the chilled dough discs from the refrigerator. For round hand pies, spoon 1 to 2 tablespoons of the filling into the center of a dough disc. Lightly brush the edges of the disc with water and place a second disc on top. Gently press the edges to seal.

Add a decorative border by pressing the edges of the dough together with the tines of a fork. For half-round pies, using your hands, gently warm the chilled dough discs until pliable. Place 1 tablespoon of the filling in the center of a disc. Lightly brush water around the edge of half of the disc, and then fold the other half over the filling to create a half-circle. Seal and decorate the edges as indicated above. Repeat with the remaining dough discs and filling.

5 Place the hand pies on a prepared baking sheet and brush them with egg wash. Using a paring knife, cut decorative steam vents into the top of each pie. If desired, sprinkle sanding or granulated sugar liberally over the hand pies.

6 Bake until the filling is bubbly and thick and the crust is golden brown, 20 to 25 minutes. Remove the hand pies from the oven and place them on a cooling rack. Let cool for 1 hour. The filling will continue to thicken and set as the pies cool.

7 If desired, use a fork to drizzle the glaze over the top of each hand pie. Allow to set for at least 1 to 2 hours before serving.

CHERRY CHEESECAKE HAND PIES

The slightly tangy cream cheese filling complements the acidity of the fruit in this hand pie. The cream cheese crust is tender yet durable, making these pies perfectly portable.

MAKES

Eight 4½-inch round hand pies

CRUST

Two recipes Cream Cheese Dough (page 76), chilled

INGREDIENTS	VOLUME	OUNCES
Sour cherries, Morello or Montmorency; pitted if fresh; drained if canned or frozen, ¼ cup of juice reserved	2 cups	12
Water, if using fresh cherries	2 tbsp	-
Cornstarch	3 tbsp	-
Granulated sugar	1¼ cups	8.8
Fresh lemon juice	1 tsp	-
Kosher salt	¼ tsp	-
Cream cheese, softened at room temperature	½ cup	4
Egg yolk	1	-
Egg wash (page 308), as needed		
Sanding sugar or granulated sugar, as needed		

1 Preheat the oven to 375°F and set the rack in the lowest position. Line two baking sheets with parchment paper.

2 Add the cornstarch to the reserved juice, if using canned or frozen cherries, or water if using fresh, and stir to combine. Set aside.

3 In a medium saucepan, combine the cherries, ¾ cup of the granulated sugar, the lemon juice, and salt and stir to combine. Bring to a gentle simmer over medium heat and cook, stirring, for 15 to 20 minutes, until reduced and thickened. Remove the pan from the heat and stir in the cornstarch mixture. Return the pan to the stovetop over medium heat and bring the mixture to a simmer. Cook until clear and thick, 3 to 5 minutes. Remove the pan from the heat and allow to cool to room temperature, 30 to 45 minutes.

4 Roll out half of the chilled dough to ⅛ inch thick. Using a 4½-inch round cutter, cut 8 discs, re-rolling scraps as necessary. Transfer the discs to a prepared baking sheet and refrigerate until firm, about 30 minutes. Repeat the rolling, cutting, and chilling process with the remaining dough. To make decorative cutouts for round hand pies as pictured, use a 1-inch round cutter to cut circles from the centers of half the discs.

5 In a small bowl, stir together the cream cheese and the remaining ½ cup granulated sugar. Add the egg yolk and stir to combine. Set aside.

6 Remove the chilled dough discs from the refrigerator and let stand at room temperature until pliable, 2 to 3 minutes. Spoon 1 tablespoon of the cherry filling and 1 tablespoon of the cream cheese filling into the center of a dough disc. Lightly brush the edges of the disc with water and place a second disc (one with a cutout hole) on top. Gently press the edges to seal. Add a decorative border by pressing the edges of the dough together with the tines of a fork. Repeat with the remaining dough discs and filling.

7 Place the hand pies on a prepared baking sheet and brush them with egg wash. If needed, use a paring knife to cut decorative steam vents into the top of each pie. Sprinkle with sanding sugar or granulated sugar.

8 Bake until the filling is bubbly and thick and the crust is golden brown, 20 to 25 minutes. Remove the hand pies from the oven and place them on a cooling rack. Let cool for 1 hour. The filling will continue to thicken and set as the pies cool.

CONCORD GRAPE PIE

Concord grapes have a fleeting season from late August to mid-October. If you are lucky enough to find these dark purple–blue grapes at a farmer's market, baking this unusual but delicious pie is a must. It is a bit time-consuming to separate the grapes from the skins, but it's well worth the effort for a slice of this tart but sweet dessert.

MAKES
One 9-inch pie

CRUST
All-Butter Pie Dough, Unbaked Double Crust (page 64)

INGREDIENTS	VOLUME	OUNCES
Concord grapes, rinsed and stemmed	8 to 10 cups	2½ lb
Cornstarch	3 tbsp	-
Granulated sugar	1 cup	7
Fresh lemon juice	1 tsp	-
Egg wash (page 308), as needed		
Sanding sugar or granulated sugar, as needed		

1 Preheat the oven to 375°F and set the rack in the lowest position.

2 Extract the pulp from each grape by pressing the end opposite the stem end, reserving the grape skins in a small bowl. Place the pulp in a wire-mesh strainer set over a medium bowl. Allow the pulp to drain for about 30 minutes. Reserve ¼ cup of the liquid and discard the rest.

3 In a medium saucepan, cook the pulp over medium heat, stirring frequently with a whisk, until the seeds start to separate from the pulp, 8 to 10 minutes. Place a wire-mesh strainer over the bowl with the grape skins and strain the cooked pulp into the bowl, pressing on the solids in the strainer with the back of a spatula. Discard the seeds and set aside the grape pulp and skin mixture to cool to room temperature, about 30 minutes.

4 Strain the cooled mixture into a medium bowl. Combine the cornstarch and the reserved liquid. To the cooled pulp mixture, add the cornstarch mixture, sugar, and lemon juice. Pour the mixture into the prepared bottom crust.

5 Roll out the dough for the top crust to ⅛ inch thick. Transfer the top crust to the filled pie, carefully setting it over the filling. Trim the edges of the top crust flush with the edge of the bottom crust and press to seal. Turn and decoratively crimp the edges. Using a paring knife, cut vents into the top crust. Brush the top crust with egg wash and sprinkle liberally with sanding sugar or granulated sugar.

6 Place the pie on a rimmed baking sheet. Bake until the filling is bubbly and thick, 45 to 50 minutes. Remove the pie from the oven and place it on a cooling rack. Let cool for 2 to 3 hours. The filling will continue to thicken and set as the pie cools.

NOTE *A grape motif cut into the top crust beautifully highlights the flavor inside. Dust a sheet of parchment paper with flour. On the paper, roll out the dough for the top crust to ⅛ inch thick. Using ¾-inch and 1-inch round cutters, cut out a grape-cluster pattern in the center of the crust. Using a paring knife, cut out a stem-shaped piece from the scraps of dough. Slide the parchment paper with the dough onto a baking sheet and freeze for 15 to 20 minutes, or until firm. Brush the edge of the bottom crust with water and gently slide the top crust over the filling, positioning the grape cluster in the center. Brush the underside of the stem cutout with water and affix it to the top crust near the grape cluster.*

Apricot Galette

MARKET FRUIT GALETTE

A simple free-form pie that highlights the seasonal fruit encased in the flaky, buttery pastry. The technique is easy and quick—fresh fruit is slightly sweetened and then placed in the center of a rolled-out round of pastry dough to create a rustic yet beautiful dessert.

MAKES
One 10-inch galette

CRUST
All-Butter Pie Dough for single crust (page 64) or Cream Cheese Dough (page 76), chilled

INGREDIENTS	VOLUME	OUNCES
STONE FRUIT VARIATION		
Apricots, nectarines, peaches, or plums, pitted and sliced as desired	7 to 8	1 lb
Granulated sugar, plus more as needed	½ cup	3.5
Cornstarch	3 tbsp	-
Unsalted butter	2 tbsp	-
APPLE OR PEAR VARIATION		
Apples or pears, peeled, cored, and diced	3 to 4	2 lb
Granulated sugar	⅓ cup	2.4
Cornstarch	3 tbsp	-
Ground cinnamon	½ tsp	-
Unsalted butter	2 tbsp	-
BERRY VARIATION		
Mixed berries (blueberries, raspberries, blackberries, or strawberries)	About 4 cups	2 lb
Granulated sugar, plus more as needed	⅓ cup	2.4
Cornstarch	3 tbsp	-
Unsalted butter	2 tbsp	-

continued

Sour Cherry Variation

Sour cherries, Morello or Montmorency; pitted if fresh; drained if canned or frozen	3 cups	1¼ lb
Granulated sugar	1¼ cups	8.75
Cornstarch	¼ cup	1.2
Fresh lemon juice	1 tsp	-
Unsalted butter	2 tbsp	-
Egg wash (page 308), as needed		
Sanding sugar or granulated sugar, as needed		

1 Preheat the oven to 375°F and set the rack in the lowest position.

2 On a lightly floured piece of parchment paper, roll out the chilled dough to a ⅛-inch-thick, 13-inch-diameter disc. Transfer the dough on the parchment to a baking sheet and refrigerate until firm, about 30 minutes.

3 Remove the chilled dough from the refrigerator and let stand at room temperature until pliable.

4 Combine the prepared fruit of your choice, the sugar, and cornstarch, as well as the spice or lemon juice, if called for. Toss to combine and immediately pile the filling evenly onto the center of the dough disc, leaving a 2- to 3-inch border. Cut the butter into small pieces and dot them over the top of the filling. Fold the dough border up and over the filling, pleating it every 2 inches and leaving the center area uncovered. Carefully lift each pleat and brush water under each fold to seal. Gently press the dough against the fruit. Brush the outside top crust with egg wash and sprinkle with sanding or granulated sugar.

5 Bake until the filling is bubbly and thick and the edges of the crust are golden brown, 30 to 40 minutes. Remove the galette from the oven and place it on a cooling rack. Let cool for 1 hour. The filling will continue to thicken and set as the galette cools.

INDIVIDUAL FRUIT GALETTES *Follow the recipe for the Market Fruit Galette, but divide the chilled dough into 6 equal pieces and roll each piece into a disc 6 to 7 inches in diameter and ⅛ inch thick. Transfer the dough discs to a rimmed baking sheet lined with parchment paper. Refrigerate until firm, about 30 minutes. Proceed with steps 3 and 4, placing approximately ⅓ cup of fruit in the center of each disc. Continue with step 5, baking for 20 to 30 minutes.*

Individual Apple Galettes

FRESH BERRY TARTLETS

These tartlets are filled with vanilla cream and topped with fresh fruit—a tasty and elegant presentation. You can replace the berries with other fresh fruits, depending on the season.

MAKES
Twelve 3-inch tarts or one 9-inch tart

CRUST
Vanilla Tart Dough (page 70), fitted into twelve 3-inch tartlet pans or one 9-inch tart pan, blind baked, and cooled

INGREDIENTS	VOLUME	OUNCES
Granulated sugar	½ cup	3.5
Cornstarch	3 tbsp	-
Milk	¾ cup	6.5
Egg yolks	4	-
Heavy cream	¾ cup	6.3
Vanilla bean, split lengthwise, seeds scraped	1	-
Seasonal berries	6 cups	-

1 In a medium bowl, combine ¼ cup of the granulated sugar with the cornstarch and whisk together until smooth and free of lumps. Add ½ cup of the milk and the egg yolks to the cornstarch mixture and stir to combine. Set aside.

2 In a small saucepan, combine the remaining ¼ cup milk and the heavy cream with the remaining ¼ cup sugar. Add the vanilla bean seeds and pod. Bring the mixture to a boil over medium heat, stirring with a whisk to dissolve the sugar. Remove the pan from the heat. Set aside and let steep for 10 to 15 minutes. Remove and discard the vanilla bean pod.

3 Gradually add one-third of the hot milk mixture to the egg mixture, while whisking constantly, to temper the eggs. Return the tempered egg mixture to the remaining milk mixture in the saucepan and cook, stirring constantly, over medium heat, just until the mixture reaches a boil. Cook, stirring continuously, for 2 minutes more, or until thick.

4 Pour the filling into a heatproof bowl and press a piece of plastic wrap directly on the surface to prevent a skin from forming. Place the bowl in an ice bath to cool.

5 Fill each tart shell three-quarters full with pastry cream, smoothing the filling with an offset spatula. Arrange the beries on top of each tart. Serve immediately.

STRAWBERRY CRÈME FRAÎCHE TART

A tart piled high with ripe berries on a bed of tangy crème fraîche, complemented with orange zest. The perfect springtime icebox tart.

MAKES
One 9-inch tart

CRUST
Vanilla Tart Dough (page 70), fitted into a 9-inch tart pan, blind baked, and cooled

INGREDIENTS	VOLUME	OUNCES
Strawberries, hulled and halved	2 pints	32
Sugar	½ cup	3.5
Cream cheese, softened at room temperature	½ cup	4
Crème fraîche	¾ cup	6.75
Vanilla extract	1½ tsp	-
Orange zest	½ tsp	-
Heavy cream, whipped to soft peaks	¾ cup	6.3

1 In a medium bowl, combine the strawberries with ¼ cup of the sugar and toss to combine. Let stand, tossing occasionally, until the berries are shiny and softened. Set aside.

2 In the bowl of a stand mixer fitted with the paddle attachment, combine the cream cheese, crème fraîche, remaining ¼ cup sugar, the vanilla, and orange zest and beat on low speed until smooth, 4 to 5 minutes.

3 Whisk one-third of the whipped cream into the cream cheese mixture by hand until combined. Gently fold in the remaining whipped cream using a rubber spatula.

4 Spoon the filling into the tart shell. Smooth and level the filling using an offset spatula. Refrigerate for approximately 1 hour, or until set.

5 Strain the strawberries through a sieve, reserving the berries and discarding the juice. Top the cream cheese mixture with the reserved berries. Serve immediately.

RASPBERRY MASCARPONE TART

A simple but stunning tart that features ripe raspberries on a layer of lemon and honey-sweetened mascarpone. Try substituting other berries depending on what is available at your local farm stand. Strawberries are a typical early summer choice, but as the berry season comes into full swing, a mixture of different types—blackberries, blueberries, and golden and red raspberries—would be phenomenal.

MAKES
One 9-inch tart

CRUST
Vanilla Tart Dough (page 70), fitted into a 9-inch tart pan, blind baked, and cooled

INGREDIENTS	VOLUME	OUNCES
Honey	½ cup	5.9
Vanilla extract	1 tsp	-
Lemon zest	½ tsp	-
Fresh lemon juice	¼ cup	2
Water, cool	1 tbsp	-
Gelatin, powdered	1 tsp	-
Mascarpone, softened at room temperature	¾ cup	6.5
Heavy cream, whipped to soft peaks	⅓ cup	2.8
Raspberries	1½ cups (1 pint)	16
Confectioners' sugar, as needed		

1 In a medium bowl, combine the honey, vanilla, lemon zest, and lemon juice. Whisk to combine and set aside.

2 Place the water in a small saucepan and sprinkle the powdered gelatin on top. Set aside and allow the gelatin to bloom (see page 58), about 10 minutes, or until all of the water has been absorbed by the gelatin.

3 In the bowl of a stand mixer fitted with the paddle attachment, beat the mascarpone on low speed until smooth, 2 to 3 minutes. Add the honey mixture slowly and beat on low speed, scraping down the sides of the bowl as necessary, until smooth, 2 to 3 minutes more.

4 Place the saucepan with the bloomed gelatin over low heat and heat until the gelatin has completely melted.

5 Whisk one-third of the whipped cream into the mascarpone mixture. Add the warm gelatin in a slow but steady stream, whisking to combine. Using a rubber spatula, gently fold in the remaining whipped cream.

6 Immediately pour the filling into the prepared tart shell. Smooth and level the filling using an offset spatula. Arrange the raspberries in concentric circles on top of the filling. Refrigerate for 1 hour, or until set.

7 Dust with confectioners' sugar just before serving.

STRAWBERRY-RHUBARB TART

Strawberries and rhubarb are a natural springtime pairing. In this tart, a lattice top adds a touch of refinement.

MAKES
One 9-inch tart

CRUST
All-Butter Pie Dough, Unbaked Double Crust (page 64), bottom crust fitted into a 9-inch tart pan and chilled

INGREDIENTS	VOLUME	OUNCES
Rhubarb, cut into ½-inch pieces	1⅔ cups	8
Strawberries, hulled and halved	1⅓ cups	11
Cornstarch	¼ cup	1.2
Granulated sugar	1 cup	7
Fresh lemon juice	2 tbsp	-
Egg wash (page 308), as needed		
Sanding sugar or granulated sugar, as needed		

1 Preheat the oven to 375°F and set the rack in the lowest position.

2 In a medium bowl, combine the rhubarb, strawberries, cornstarch, granulated sugar, and lemon juice. Toss to combine and pour the filling into the prepared bottom crust. Set aside.

3 Roll out the dough for the top crust to ⅛ inch thick. Using a fluted pastry wheel, cut ten 1-inch-wide strips of dough. Brush the edge of the bottom crust with water and gently weave and arrange the dough strips on top of the filling to create a lattice top (see page 50). Trim the edges flush with the edge of the bottom crust by gently rolling the pin over the top of the tart, pressing to seal. Brush the lattice top with egg wash and sprinkle with sanding sugar or granulated sugar.

4 Place the tart on a rimmed baking sheet. Bake until the filling is thick and bubbly, 30 to 40 minutes. Remove the tart from the oven and place it on a cooling rack. Let cool for 2 to 3 hours. The filling will continue to thicken and set as the tart cools.

APPLE STREUSEL TART

In this tart, the flavor of apples is enhanced by a simple butter-browning technique called *beurre noisette*, a French term that translates to "hazelnut butter." Golden Delicious apples are a good choice here because they are mild and naturally sweet and require only a little granulated sugar to sweeten the filling. Be sure to use a vanilla bean, as the bits of bean and brown butter will create a filling beautifully "flecked" with flavor.

MAKES
One 9-inch tart

CRUST
Vanilla Tart Dough
(page 70), fitted into
a 9-inch tart pan and
chilled

TOPPING
Streusel (page 304)

INGREDIENTS	VOLUME	OUNCES
Unsalted butter, cubed	4 tbsp (½ stick)	2
Vanilla bean, split lengthwise, seeds scraped	½	-
Apples, peeled and cut into ¼-inch slices	3 to 4	2 lb
Granulated sugar	3 tbsp	-
Apple cider	¼ cup	2.25
Confectioners' sugar, as needed		

1 Preheat the oven to 375°F and set the rack in the lowest position.

2 In a medium sauté pan with a light bottom, melt the butter over medium heat. Add the split vanilla bean and seeds. Swirl the pan occasionally to be certain that the butter is cooking evenly. As the butter melts, it will begin to foam and the color will progress from lemony yellow to golden tan and finally to a toasty brown.

3 When the butter is toasty brown, add the apples and toss to coat. Allow the apples to release their juices and cook until "dry," 5 to 10 minutes, or until the liquid has fully evaporated. Using a heat-resistant spatula, stir in the sugar and cook for 2 to 3 minutes, or until the sugar dissolves. Add the apple cider to deglaze the pan, stirring to loosen any browned apples from the bottom of the pan. Remove the filling from the heat and let cool completely, 1 to 2 hours. Remove and discard the vanilla bean pod.

4 Place the prepared and chilled tart shell on a rimmed baking sheet and pour in the cooled filling. Top with the streusel.

5 Bake until the filling is bubbly and thick, 30 to 40 minutes. Remove the tart from the oven and place it on a cooling rack. Let cool for 2 to 3 hours. The filling will continue to thicken and set as the tart cools. Dust with confectioners' sugar before serving.

LINZER TORTE

The Linzer torte has a three-hundred-year history and is named after the Austrian city of Linz. This raspberry jam tart is baked in a flaky pastry enriched with almonds and flavored with cinnamon and cloves.

MAKES
One 9-inch tart

CRUST
Linzer Torte Dough (page 75), bottom crust fitted into a 9-inch tart pan and chilled

INGREDIENTS	VOLUME	OUNCES
Raspberry preserves	1¾ cups	18.5
Lemon zest	½ tsp	-
Fresh lemon juice	2 tsp	-
Egg wash (page 308), as needed		

1 Preheat the oven to 375°F and set the rack in the lowest position.

2 In a medium bowl, combine the raspberry preserves, lemon zest, and lemon juice and stir to combine. Pour the filling into the prepared tart shell. Smooth and level the filling with an offset spatula. Chill in the freezer while rolling and cutting out the lattice top.

3 Dust a sheet of parchment paper with flour. On the parchment paper, roll out the top crust to ⅛ inch thick. Using a pastry wheel, cut fourteen 1-inch-wide strips of dough. If the strips become too soft, slide the parchment paper onto a flat baking sheet and freeze for 15 to 20 minutes. Once the strips are firm, remove them from the freezer and gently arrange the dough strips on top of the filling to form an unwoven lattice top. Do not try and weave these strips; the dough is delicate and will tear. However, if the dough rips, carefully press it back together. Trim the edges flush with the edge of the pan and press to seal. Place in the freezer until the dough is firm, 20 to 30 minutes.

4 Place the Linzer torte on a rimmed baking sheet and brush the top with egg wash. Bake for 40 to 45 minutes, or until bubbly. Remove the torte from the oven and place it on a cooling rack. Let cool for 1 to 2 hours. The filling will continue to thicken and set as the torte cools.

ROASTED GINGER PLUM TART

Plums are perfect for tart making. There are over three hundred varieties of plums available, plus a long season of availability. The plums that are best for baking will be blue to purple in skin color, sweet in flavor, and with a springy texture. In this tart, the plums are first roasted to release some of their moisture and prevent the tart from becoming soggy.

MAKES
One 9-inch tart

CRUST
Vanilla Tart Dough (page 70), fitted into a 9-inch tart pan and chilled

TOPPING
Nut Streusel (page 306)

INGREDIENTS	VOLUME	OUNCES
Plums, medium, rinsed, halved, and pitted	7 to 8	1½ lb
Light brown sugar, packed	½ cup	4
Finely chopped candied ginger	1 tbsp	-
Cornstarch	3 tbsp	-
Ground cinnamon	½ tsp	-
Ground ginger	½ tsp	-
Fresh lemon juice	1 tsp	-

1 Preheat the oven to 375°F and set the rack in the lowest position.

2 Place the plums on a rimmed baking sheet and roast them until soft, 20 to 30 minutes. Transfer the baking sheet to a cooling rack. Let cool for about 20 minutes, or until the plums can be handled. If necessary, slice or chop the plums into smaller pieces.

3 In a medium bowl, combine the roasted plums, brown sugar, candied ginger, cornstarch, cinnamon, gound ginger, and lemon juice. Toss to combine and then immediately pour the filling into the prepared crust.

4 Top with the streusel.

5 Place the tart on a rimmed baking sheet. Bake until the filling is bubbly and thick, 20 to 30 minutes. Remove the tart from the oven and place it on a cooling rack. Let cool for 1 to 2 hours. The filling will continue to thicken and set as the tart cools.

CREAM

VANILLA CREAM PIE

Every baker's repertoire must have a classic vanilla cream pie. The effect pictured here was created by piping the whipped cream with a ribbon tip.

MAKES
One 9-inch pie

CRUST
All-Butter Pie
Dough, Blind-Baked
Single Crust
(page 64)

TOPPING
Sweetened Whipped
Cream (page 313)

INGREDIENTS	VOLUME	OUNCES
Sugar	¾ cup	5.3
Cornstarch	¼ cup	1.2
Milk	3 cups	26
Large eggs	2	-
Egg yolks	4	-
Kosher salt	¼ tsp	-
Vanilla bean, split lengthwise, seeds scraped	1	-
Unsalted butter	2 tbsp	-

1 In a bowl, combine ¼ cup of the sugar with the cornstarch and whisk until free of lumps. Add ¾ cup of the milk, the eggs, egg yolks, and salt and whisk to combine.

2 In a medium saucepan, combine the remaining 2¼ cups milk with the remaining ½ cup sugar. Add the vanilla bean seeds and pod. Bring the mixture to a boil over medium heat, stirring continuously to dissolve the sugar.

3 Gradually add one-third of the hot milk mixture to the egg mixture, whisking continuously, to temper the eggs. Return the tempered egg mixture to the remaining milk mixture in the saucepan and cook, stirring continuously, until it reaches a boil. Continue to cook the filling, stirring continuously, for 2 minutes more. Remove the pan from the heat and stir in the butter until melted.

4 Transfer the filling to the prepared crust. Smooth and level the filling with an offset spatula. Press a piece of plastic wrap directly on the surface of the filling to prevent a skin from forming. Let the filling cool, then refrigerate the pie for 1 to 2 hours, or until set.

5 Pipe (see page 297) or spoon the whipped cream on top of the filling. Refrigerate the pie for at least 1 hour, but no longer than 2 hours, before serving.

CHOCOLATE MALT PIE

The dense, rich, bittersweet chocolate filling in this cream pie is topped with chocolate whipped cream. It can be garnished with malt balls or a light dusting of cocoa powder.

MAKES
One 9-inch pie

CRUST
Cookie Crumb Crust, made with chocolate wafers (page 69), baked and cooled

TOPPING
Chocolate Whipped Cream (page 314)

INGREDIENTS	VOLUME	OUNCES
Sugar	¾ cup	5.3
Cornstarch	¼ cup	1.2
Milk	3 cups	26
Large eggs	2	-
Egg yolks	4	-
Kosher salt	¼ tsp	-
Malted milk powder	1 cup	5
Unsalted butter	2 tbsp	-
Vanilla extract	1 tsp	-
Chopped bittersweet chocolate (not more than 65%)	-	10
Chocolate malt balls, roughly chopped, as needed		

CHOCOLATE CREAM PIE

Follow the recipe for Malt Pie, omitting the malted milk powder in step 2. Top the pie with Sweetened Whipped Cream (page 313) and garnish with grated bittersweet chocolate.

1 In a medium bowl, combine ¼ cup of the sugar with the cornstarch and whisk until smooth and free of lumps. Add ¾ cup of the milk, the eggs, egg yolks, and salt and whisk to combine. Set aside.

2 In a medium saucepan, combine the remaining 2¼ cups milk, the remaining ½ cup sugar, and the malted milk powder. Bring the mixture to a boil over medium heat, stirring continuously to dissolve the sugar.

3 Gradually add one-third of the hot milk mixture to the egg mixture to temper the eggs, whisking continuously. Return the tempered egg mixture to the remaining milk mixture in the saucepan and cook, stirring continuously, until it reaches a boil. Continue to cook the filling, stirring continuously, for 2 minutes more. Remove the pan from the heat and stir in the butter, vanilla, and chopped chocolate, stirring until smooth and creamy.

4 Transfer the filling to the prepared crust. Smooth and level the filling with an offset spatula. Press a piece of plastic wrap directly on the surface of the filling to prevent a skin from forming. Let the filling cool, then refrigerate the pie until set, 1 to 2 hours.

5 Pipe (see page 297) or spoon the whipped cream on top of the filling and garnish with the chopped malt balls. Refrigerate for at least 1 hour, but no longer than 2 hours, before serving.

CHOCOLATE-NUTELLA CREAM PIE

An addition of Nutella—the ever-popular toasted hazelnut and cocoa spread—perfectly complements this bittersweet-chocolate cream pie.

MAKES
One 9-inch pie

CRUST
Cookie Crumb Crust, made with chocolate wafers (page 69), baked and cooled

TOPPING
Sweetened Whipped Cream (page 313)

INGREDIENTS	VOLUME	OUNCES
Nutella	1 cup	7.2
Sugar	¾ cup	5.3
Cornstarch	¼ cup	1.2
Milk	3 cups	26
Large eggs	2	-
Egg yolks	4	-
Kosher salt	¼ tsp	-
Unsalted butter	2 tbsp	-
Vanilla extract	1 tsp	-
Chopped bittersweet chocolate (not more than 65% cacao), plus grated bittersweet chocolate as needed (optional)	-	10
Chopped toasted hazelnuts, as needed (optional)		

1 Spread ½ cup of the Nutella over the bottom of the prepared crumb crust. Set aside.

2 In a medium bowl, combine ¼ cup of the sugar with the cornstarch, whisking until free of lumps. Add ¾ cup of the milk, the eggs, egg yolks, and salt, whisking to combine. Set aside.

3 In a medium saucepan, combine the remaining 2¼ cups milk with the remaining ½ cup sugar. Bring the mixture to a boil over medium heat, stirring continuously to dissolve the sugar.

4 Gradually add one-third of the hot milk mixture to the egg mixture to temper the eggs, whisking continuously. Return the tempered egg mixture to the remaining milk mixture in the saucepan and cook, stirring continuously, until it reaches a boil.

Continue to cook the filling, stirring continuously, for 2 minutes more. Remove the pan from the heat and stir in the butter, vanilla, chopped chocolate, and remaining ½ cup Nutella, stirring until smooth and creamy.

5 Allow the filling to cool for 10 to 15 minutes, then pour the filling into the prepared crust over the layer of Nutella. Smooth and level the filling with an offset spatula. Press a piece of plastic wrap directly on the surface of the filling to prevent a skin from forming. Let cool, then refrigerate the pie until set, 1 to 2 hours.

6 Top with the whipped cream and, if desired, garnish with grated chocolate or a sprinkling of toasted hazelnuts. Refrigerate for at least 1 hour, but no longer than 2 hours, before serving.

CHOCOLATE–PEANUT BUTTER PIE *Follow the recipe for Chocolate-Nutella Cream Pie, replacing the Nutella with an equal quantity of peanut butter in steps 1 and 5.*

GERMAN CHOCOLATE PIE

German chocolate cake is a favorite, so why not turn it into a pie? A crisp, chocolaty crust is filled with chocolate custard and topped with gooey caramel, coconut flakes, and pecans.

MAKES
One 9-inch pie

CRUST
Cookie Crumb Crust, made with chocolate wafers (page 69), baked and cooled

INGREDIENTS	VOLUME	OUNCES
Sugar	⅓ cup	2.4
Cornstarch	2 tbsp	-
Milk	1½ cups	13
Large eggs	2	-
Egg yolks	2	-
Kosher salt	¼ tsp	-
Vanilla extract	1 tsp	-
Unsalted butter	5 tbsp	2.5
Chopped bittersweet chocolate (not more than 65% cacao)	-	4
Evaporated milk	⅔ cup	5.8
Lightly toasted and chopped pecans (see page 30)	½ cup	2
Flaked or desiccated coconut, lightly toasted (see Note)	⅓ cup	1

1 In a medium bowl, combine 2 tablespoons of the sugar with the cornstarch and whisk until free of lumps. Add ¼ cup of the milk, 1 egg, the egg yolks, and the salt and whisk to combine. Set aside.

2 In a medium saucepan, combine the remaining 1¼ cups milk with the remaining sugar. Bring the mixture to a boil over medium heat, stirring continuously to dissolve the sugar.

3 Gradually add one-third of the hot milk mixture to the egg mixture, whisking continuously, to temper the eggs. Return the tempered egg mixture to the remaining milk mixture in the saucepan and cook, stirring continuously, until it reaches a boil. Continue to cook the filling, stirring continuously, for 2 minutes more. Remove the

pan from the heat and stir in 1 tablespoon of the butter, the vanilla, and the chopped chocolate, stirring until smooth and creamy.

4 Transfer the filling to the prepared crust. Smooth and level the filling with an offset spatula. Press a piece of plastic wrap directly on the surface of the filling to prevent a skin from forming. Let the filling cool, then refrigerate the pie until set, 1 to 2 hours.

5 In a small bowl, beat the remaining egg with a whisk. Set aside.

6 In a medium saucepan, combine the evaporated milk with the remaining 4 tablespoons of butter and cook over medium heat until the mixture is hot and the butter has melted. Remove the pan from the heat.

7 Gradually add one-third of the hot milk mixture to the beaten egg, whisking continuously, to temper it. Return the tempered egg mixture to the remaining milk mixture in the saucepan and cook, stirring continuously, for 1 minute, or until the mixture just thickens. Remove the pan from the heat and stir in the pecans and coconut. Let cool for 10 to 15 minutes, then spread the pecan mixture over the chilled chocolate filling in the prepared crust.

8 Let the topping cool, then refrigerate the pie until set, 1 to 2 hours.

NOTE *To toast the coconut, spread it in an even layer on a baking sheet and toast in a 375°F oven until lightly browned, 8 to 10 minutes.*

BUTTERSCOTCH CREAM PIE

The rich caramel flavor in this pie is achieved by heating the dark brown sugar and butter until it caramelizes and develops a full, buttery flavor. Finished with swirls of whipped cream, this pie is a perennial favorite.

MAKES
One 9-inch pie

CRUST
All-Butter Pie
Dough, Blind-Baked
Single Crust
(page 64)

TOPPING
Sweetened Whipped
Cream (page 313)

INGREDIENTS	VOLUME	OUNCES
Cornstarch	¼ cup	1.2
Milk	3 cups	26
Large eggs	2	-
Egg yolks	4	-
Kosher salt	¼ tsp	-
Unsalted butter	½ cup (1 stick)	4
Dark brown sugar, packed	1 cup	7.8
Light corn syrup	1 tbsp	-
Water	¼ cup	-
Vanilla extract	1 tsp	-

1 In a medium bowl, combine the cornstarch with ½ cup of the milk, the eggs, egg yolks, and salt and whisk until free of lumps. Set aside.

2 In a small saucepan, heat the remaining 2½ cups milk until warm. Remove the pan from the heat. Set aside.

3 In a medium heavy-bottomed saucepan, melt the butter, brown sugar, corn syrup, and water over medium heat, stirring to combine and dissolve the sugar. Bring to a boil; do not stir the mixture. Cook until the mixture registers 250°F on a candy thermometer. Remove the pan from the heat.

4 Stream the warm milk slowly into the hot sugar mixture, whisking continuously to dissolve the sugar and combine the milk. If the sugar is allowed to solidify, the mixture will separate.

5 Gradually add one-third of the hot milk mixture to the egg mixture, whisking continuously, to temper the eggs. Return the tempered egg mixture to the remaining milk mixture in the saucepan and cook, stirring continuously, until it reaches a boil. Continue to cook the filling, stirring continuously, for 2 minutes more. Remove the pan from the heat and stir in the vanilla.

6 Transfer the filling to the prepared crust. Smooth and level the filling with an offset spatula. Press a piece of plastic wrap directly on the surface of the filling to prevent a skin from forming. Let the filling cool, then refrigerate the pie until set, 1 to 2 hours.

7 Pipe (see page 297) or spoon the whipped cream on top of the filling. Refrigerate for at least 1 hour, but no longer than 2 hours, before serving.

COCONUT CREAM PIE

A cool and creamy coconut cream pie, topped with lightly sweetened whipped cream and finished with plenty of toasted coconut!

MAKES
One 9-inch pie

CRUST
All-Butter Pie
Dough, Blind-Baked
Single Crust
(page 64)

TOPPING
Sweetened Whipped
Cream (page 313)

INGREDIENTS	VOLUME	OUNCES
Sugar	¾ cup	5.3
Cornstarch	¼ cup	1.2
Coconut milk, unsweetened	-	one (14-ounce) can
Large eggs	2	-
Egg yolks	4	-
Kosher salt	¼ tsp	-
Milk	1¼ cups	11
Coconut, unsweetened, flaked	½ cup	1.5
Unsalted butter	2 tbsp	-
Vanilla extract	1 tsp	-
Coconut, unsweetened, lightly flaked or shredded, toasted (see Note, page 139), for garnish	½ cup	1.5

1 In a medium bowl, combine ¼ cup of the sugar with the cornstarch and whisk until free of lumps. Add three-quarters of the coconut milk, the eggs, egg yolks, and salt and whisk to combine. Set aside.

2 In a medium saucepan, combine the milk, the remaining coconut milk, the remaining ½ cup sugar, and the flaked coconut. Bring the mixture to a boil over medium heat, stirring to dissolve the sugar.

3 Gradually add one-third of the hot milk mixture to the egg mixture, whisking continuously, to temper the eggs. Return the tempered egg mixture to the remaining milk mixture in the saucepan and cook, stirring continuously, until it reaches a boil. Continue to cook the filling, stirring continuously, for 2 minutes more. Remove the pan from the heat and stir in the butter and vanilla, stirring until smooth and creamy.

4 Transfer the filling to the prepared crust. Smooth and level the filling with an offset spatula. Press a piece of plastic wrap directly on the surface of the filling to prevent a skin from forming. Let the filling cool, then refrigerate the pie until set, 1 to 2 hours.

5 Pipe (see page 297) or spoon the whipped cream on top of the filling and garnish with the toasted coconut. Refrigerate for at least 1 hour, but no longer than 2 hours, before serving.

LEMON MERINGUE PIE

In my family, lemon meringue pie was always front and center at family gatherings and signified a special occasion. My father was especially fond of these pies, and my mother always made one for his birthday. The sharp lemon flavor is especially delicious offset by the crunchy sweetness of the meringue.

MAKES
One 9-inch pie

CRUST
All-Butter Pie
Dough, Blind-Baked
Single Crust
(page 64)

TOPPING
Two recipes Swiss
Meringue (page 309)

INGREDIENTS	VOLUME	OUNCES
Sugar	1¼ cups	8.75
Cornstarch	⅓ cup	2
Water	1¾ cups	14
Egg yolks	4	-
Fresh lemon zest	From 1 lemon	-
Freshly squeezed lemon juice	¾ cup	5.7
Unsalted butter	2 tbsp	-
Kosher salt	¼ tsp	-

1 In a medium bowl, combine ¾ cup of the sugar, the cornstarch, ¼ cup water, and the egg yolks and whisk until free of lumps. Set aside.

2 In a heavy-bottomed saucepan, combine the remaining ½ cup sugar, the remaining 1½ cups water, the lemon zest, and lemon juice. Bring the mixture to a boil over medium heat, stirring to dissolve the sugar.

3 Gradually add one-third of the hot lemon juice mixture to the egg yolk mixture, whisking continuously, to temper the eggs. Return the tempered egg mixture to the remaining juice mixture in the saucepan and cook, stirring continuously, until thick and smooth, 2 to 3 minutes. Remove the pan from the heat and stir in the butter and salt, stirring until smooth.

4 Transfer the filling to the prepared crust. Smooth and level the filling with an offset spatula. Press a piece of plastic wrap directly on the surface of the filling to prevent a skin from forming. Let the filling cool, then refrigerate the pie until set, 1 to 2 hours.

5 Preheat the broiler on low. Pipe (see page 297) or spread the meringue over the filling, making sure to completely cover the filling and anchor the meringue to the edge of the crust to keep it from shrinking, and place it under the broiler until the meringue is lightly browned, 4 to 5 minutes. Alternatively, use a kitchen torch to brown the exterior of the meringue (see page 297).

ORANGE-VANILLA CREAM PIE

This pie is reminiscent of a Creamsicle, a childhood favorite, with a layer of tart and sweet orange filling topped with vanilla cream.

MAKES
One 9-inch pie

CRUST
All-Butter Pie
Dough, Blind-Baked
Single Crust
(page 64)

TOPPING
Sweetened Whipped
Cream (page 313)

INGREDIENTS	VOLUME	OUNCES
For the Orange Filling:		
Sugar	⅔ cup	4.7
Cornstarch	2 tbsp	-
Orange juice	¾ cup	7
Egg yolks	4	-
Unsalted butter	½ cup (1 stick)	4
Orange zest	From 1 orange	-
For the Vanilla Filling:		
Sugar	¼ cup plus 2 tbsp	2.6
Cornstarch	2 tbsp	-
Milk	1½ cups	13
Large egg	1	-
Egg yolks	2	-
Unsalted butter	1 tbsp	-
Vanilla bean, split lengthwise, seeds scraped	½	-
For the Topping:		
Orange zest	1 tsp	-

1 Make the orange filling: In a medium bowl, combine ⅓ cup of the sugar, the cornstarch, ¼ cup of the orange juice, and the egg yolks and whisk until free of lumps. Set aside.

2　In a heavy-bottomed saucepan, combine the butter with the remaining ⅓ cup sugar, the orange zest, and the remaining ½ cup orange juice. Bring the mixture to a boil over medium heat, stirring continuously to dissolve the sugar.

3　Gradually add one-third of the hot orange juice mixture to the egg yolk mixture, whisking continuously, to temper the eggs. Return the tempered egg mixture to the remaining juice mixture in the saucepan and cook, stirring continuously, until it reaches a boil. Continue to cook the filling, stirring continuously, for 2 minutes more.

4　Transfer the filling to the prepared crust. Smooth and level the filling with an offset spatula. Press a piece of plastic wrap directly on the surface of the filling to prevent a skin from forming. Let the filling cool, then refrigerate the pie until set, about 1 hour.

5　Make the vanilla filling: In a medium bowl, combine 2 tablespoons of the sugar with the cornstarch, ¼ cup milk, the egg, and egg yolks and stir with a whisk until smooth and free of lumps. Set aside.

6　In a heavy-bottomed saucepan, combine the remaining sugar, vanilla bean seeds and pod, and the remaining 1¼ cups milk. Bring the mixture to a boil over medium heat, stirring continuously to dissolve the sugar.

7　Gradually add one-third of the hot milk mixture to the egg yolk mixture, whisking continuously, to temper the eggs. Return the tempered egg mixture to the remaining milk mixture in the saucepan and cook, stirring continuously, just until it reaches a boil. Continue to cook the filling, stirring continuously, for 2 minutes more. Remove the pan from the heat and stir in the butter. Let cool 20 to 30 minutes.

8　Pour the vanilla filling over the chilled orange filling in the prepared crust. Smooth and level the vanilla filling with an offset spatula. Press a piece of plastic wrap directly on the surface of the filling to prevent a skin from forming. Let the filling cool, then refrigerate the pie until set, 1 to 2 hours.

9　Pipe (see page 297) or spoon the whipped cream over the filling. Refrigerate for at least 1 hour, but no longer than 2 hours. Sprinkle with the orange zest before serving.

MAPLE CREAM PIE

A pie with a creamy, robust maple filling. In order to get the fullest maple flavor, it is important to use Grade B syrup, as it is the darkest in color and will impart the most intensity.

MAKES
One 9-inch pie

CRUST
All-Butter Pie
Dough, Blind-Baked
Single Crust
(page 64)

TOPPING
Maple Whipped
Cream (page 316)

INGREDIENTS	VOLUME	OUNCES
Sugar	¼ cup	1.75
Cornstarch	¼ cup	1.2
Heavy cream	1½ cups	13
Egg yolks	4	-
Kosher salt	¼ tsp	-
Unsalted butter	2 tbsp	-
Maple syrup. Grade B	¾ cup	9

1 In a medium bowl, combine 2 tablespoons of the sugar with the cornstarch and whisk until free of lumps. Add ¼ cup of the heavy cream, the egg yolks, and salt and whisk to combine. Set aside.

2 In a heavy-bottomed saucepan, combine the remaining 1¼ cups heavy cream with the remaining 2 tablespoons sugar. Bring the mixture to a boil over medium heat, stirring continuously to dissolve the sugar.

3 Gradually add one-third of the hot cream mixture to the egg mixture, whisking continuously, to temper the eggs. Return the tempered egg mixture to the remaining cream mixture in the saucepan and cook, stirring continuously, until it reaches a boil. Continue to cook the filling, stirring continuously, for 2 minutes more. Remove the pan from the heat and stir in the butter and maple syrup, stirring until smooth and creamy.

4 Transfer the filling to the crust and smooth with an offset spatula. Press a piece of plastic wrap directly on the surface of the filling to prevent a skin from forming. Let cool, then refrigerate until set, 1 to 2 hours.

5 Top with the whipped cream. Refrigerate for at least 1 hour, but no longer than 2 hours, before serving.

PEANUT BUTTER–BANANA CREAM PIE

Bananas between layers of vanilla and peanut butter creams, finished with sweetened whipped cream, and garnished with sweet and salty candied peanuts make this pie fit for the King. Elvis! Elvis!

MAKES
One 9-inch pie

CRUST
One Graham Cracker–Crumb Crust (page 67), baked and cooled

TOPPING
Sweetened Whipped Cream (page 313) and Candied Salty Peanuts (page 319)

INGREDIENTS	VOLUME	OUNCES
For the Vanilla Filling:		
Sugar	¼ cup plus 2 tbsp	2.2
Cornstarch	2 tbsp	-
Milk	1½ cups	13
Large egg	1	-
Egg yolks	2	-
Unsalted butter	1 tbsp	-
Vanilla extract	½ tsp	-
Banana, ripe, peeled, cut in half lengthwise and then crosswise into fourths	1	-
For the Peanut Butter Filling:		
Cream cheese, softened at room temperature	⅓ cup	3
Peanut butter (not old-fashioned or freshly ground)	½ cup	6
Sweetened condensed milk	⅓ cup	4.25
Vanilla extract	1 tsp	-
Heavy cream	⅔ cup	5.6

1 Make the vanilla filling: In a medium bowl, combine 2 tablespoons of the sugar with the cornstarch and whisk until free of lumps. Add ¼ cup of the milk, the egg, and egg yolks, and whisk to combine. Set aside.

2 In a heavy-bottomed saucepan, combine the remaining 1¼ cups milk with the remaining ¼ cup sugar. Bring the mixture to a boil over medium heat, stirring continuously to dissolve the sugar.

3 Gradually add one-third of the hot milk mixture to the egg mixture, whisking continuously, to temper the eggs. Return the tempered egg mixture to the remaining milk mixture in the saucepan and cook, stirring continuously, until it reaches a boil. Continue to cook the filling, stirring continuously, for 2 minutes more. Remove the pan from the heat and stir in the butter and vanilla, stirring until smooth.

4 Fold the banana pieces into the vanilla filling and pour into the prepared crust. Take care to press the bananas below the surface of the filling to prevent browning. Smooth and level the filling with an offset spatula. Press a piece of plastic wrap directly on the surface of the filling to prevent a skin from forming. Let the filling cool, then refrigerate the pie until set, 1 to 2 hours.

5 Make the peanut butter filling: In the bowl of a stand mixer fitted with the paddle attachment, combine the cream cheese and peanut butter. Beat on medium speed until well combined and smooth. Gradually beat in the condensed milk and vanilla.

6 In a medium bowl, whip the cream until it forms medium peaks. Gently fold about ¼ cup of the whipped cream into the cream cheese mixture. Fold in the remaining whipped cream in two batches.

7 Spread the peanut butter filling over the chilled vanilla filling in an even layer. Smooth and level the peanut butter filling with an offset spatula.

8 Pipe (see page 297) or spoon the whipped cream onto the peanut butter filling and garnish with the candied peanuts. Refrigerate for at least 1 hour, but no longer than 2 hours, before serving.

SOUR CREAM–AND-RAISIN CREAM PIE

An unusual combination: plump raisins folded into a sweet custard with the tang of sour cream, in a crisp and crunchy oatmeal crust. Capped with whipped cream and dusted with cinnamon—perfect with a glass of milk!

MAKES
One 9-inch pie

CRUST
One Cookie-Crumb Crust, made with crisp oatmeal cookies (page 69), baked and cooled

TOPPING
Sweetened Whipped Cream (page 313)

INGREDIENTS	VOLUME	OUNCES
Sugar	¾ cup	5.3
Cornstarch	¼ cup	1.2
Ground cinnamon, plus more as needed	2 tsp	-
Kosher salt	¼ tsp	-
Milk	½ cup	4.3
Large eggs	2	-
Sour cream	1½ cups	12.4
Raisins, plumped (see Note)	1 cup	4.75
Vanilla extract	½ tsp	-

1 In a medium bowl, combine ¼ cup of the sugar with the cornstarch, cinnamon, and salt and whisk until free of lumps. Add the milk and eggs and whisk to combine. Set aside.

2 In a medium saucepan, combine the remaining ½ cup sugar with the sour cream, stirring continuously over medium heat until the sugar is dissolved and the mixture is hot.

3 Gradually add one-third of the hot sour cream mixture to the egg mixture, whisking continuously, to temper the eggs. Return the tempered egg mixture to the remaining sour cream mixture in the saucepan and cook, stirring continuously, until it reaches a boil. Continue to cook the filling, stirring continuously, for 2 minutes more. Remove the pan from the heat and stir in the raisins and vanilla, stirring until smooth and creamy.

4 Pour the filling into the prepared crust. Smooth and level the filling with an offset spatula. Press a piece of plastic wrap directly on the surface of the filling to prevent a skin from forming. Let the filling cool, then refrigerate the pie until set, 1 to 2 hours.

5 Pipe (see page 297) or spread the whipped cream over the filling and garnish with a light dusting of cinnamon. Refrigerate for at least 1 hour, but no longer than 2 hours, before serving.

NOTE *If the raisins are dry or hard, place them in a small container, cover them with warm water (80°F), and then immediately drain off the water. Cover the container and allow the raisins to rehydrate for 4 hours, or until they are plump and soft. This method of plumping dried fruit prevents the raisins from losing their flavor in a liquid, or from weeping into the filling.*

PANNA COTTA PIE

When it is too hot to turn on the oven, this cool and creamy vanilla cream pie is perfect. For just a bit of kick, pair it with fresh strawberries or raspberries seasoned with a splash of aged balsamic vinegar.

MAKES
One 9-inch pie

CRUST
Graham Cracker–Crumb Crust (page 67), baked and cooled

INGREDIENTS	VOLUME	OUNCES
Water, cool	2 tbsp	-
Gelatin, powdered	2 tsp	-
Heavy cream	3 cups	26
Sugar	¾ cup	5.3
Strawberries, rinsed, hulled, and halved or quartered; or raspberries, rinsed	1 pt	16
Balsamic vinegar	2 tsp	-
Freshly ground black pepper, as needed (optional)		

1 Place the water in a small bowl and sprinkle the powdered gelatin on top. Whisk to combine. Set aside to bloom the gelatin (see page 58), about 10 minutes, or until the gelatin has absorbed all of the water.

2 In a small saucepan, combine 1½ cups of the heavy cream with ½ cup of sugar, stirring continuously over medium heat until the sugar is dissolved and the mixture is hot. Set aside.

3 Place the remaining 1½ cups cream in a medium stainless-steel bowl. Add the gelatin to the cream and gently whisk until the gelatin has dissolved. Add the reserved hot cream and stir to combine. Allow the mixture to cool until it registers 85° to 90°F on a candy thermometer and appears slightly lumpy.

4 Pour the filling into the prepared crust. Smooth and level the filling with an offset spatula. Immediately refrigerate the pie, chilling it for at least 4 hours until set.

5 Meanwhile, in a large bowl, combine the berries, the remaining ¼ cup sugar, and the vinegar. Season with pepper, if desired, and toss to combine.

6 Top the pie with the berries and serve.

MEXICAN CHOCOLATE TART

Traditionally, Mexican chocolate is flavored with cinnamon, almonds, and vanilla. This tart's filling is made with almond milk and milk chocolate, with a hint cinnamon and vanilla.

MAKES
One 9-inch tart

CRUST
Vanilla Tart Dough (page 70), fitted into a 9-inch tart pan, blind baked, and cooled

TOPPING
Sweetened Whipped Cream (page 313)

INGREDIENTS	VOLUME	OUNCES
Sugar	⅓ cup	2.4
Cornstarch	2 tbsp	-
Ground cinnamon, plus more as needed	2 tsp	-
Almond milk, unsweetened	1½ cups	13
Large egg	1	-
Egg yolks	2	-
Unsalted butter	1 tbsp	-
Roughly chopped milk chocolate	-	4
Vanilla extract	1 tsp	-

1. In a medium bowl, combine ¼ cup of the sugar with the cornstarch and cinnamon and whisk until free of lumps. Add ¼ cup of the almond milk, the egg, and the egg yolks and whisk to combine. Set aside.

2. In a medium saucepan, combine the remaining 1¼ cups almond milk with the remaining sugar. Bring the mixture to a boil over medium heat, stirring to dissolve the sugar.

3. Gradually add one-third of the hot almond milk mixture to the egg mixture, whisking continuously, to temper the eggs. Return the tempered egg mixture to the remaining almond milk mixture in the saucepan and cook, stirring continuously, until it reaches a boil. Continue to cook the filling, stirring continuously, for 2 minutes more. Remove the pan from the heat and stir in the butter, chocolate, and vanilla, stirring until smooth and creamy.

4. Transfer the filling to the crust and smooth with an offset spatula. Press a piece of plastic wrap directly on the surface to prevent a skin from forming. Let cool, then refrigerate until set, 1 to 2 hours.

5. Top with the whipped cream and garnish with a light dusting of cinnamon. Refrigerate for at least 1 hour, but no longer than 2 hours, before serving.

SWEET CITRUS RISOTTO TART

This recipe is adapted from a recipe given to me by a student at The Culinary Institute of America, Raewyn Horton, who was given it by her grandmother. It's a vanilla rice pudding, scented with citrus from both a lemon and an orange, in a crispy almond tart shell. It's perfect in the winter when citrus is at its prime.

MAKES

One 9-inch round or square tart

CRUST

Nut Tart Dough, made with almonds (page 74), fitted into a 9-inch round or square tart pan, blind baked, and cooled

INGREDIENTS	VOLUME	OUNCES
Water	1 cup	8.5
Arborio rice	½ cup	4
Kosher salt, plus more as needed	¼ tsp	-
Large egg	1	-
Heavy cream	½ cup	4.2
Milk	1 cup	8.6
Granulated sugar	½ cup	3.5
Lemon zest, plus more as needed	From 1 lemon	-
Orange zest, plus more as needed	From 1 orange	-
Unsalted butter	2 tbsp	-
Vanilla extract	1 tsp	-
Confectioners' sugar, as needed		

1 In a heavy-bottomed saucepan, combine the water, rice, and a pinch of salt. Bring the mixture to a boil over medium heat, stirring continuously. Cover the pot, reduce the heat to low, and cook until the rice is almost tender, 15 to 18 minutes. Uncover, stir, and remove from the heat. Set aside.

2 In a medium bowl, combine the egg, heavy cream, and the ¼ teaspoon of salt and whisk until well combined. Set aside.

3 In a heavy-bottomed saucepan, combine the milk, sugar, lemon zest, and orange zest. Bring the mixture to a boil over medium heat, stirring continuously to dissolve the sugar. Remove the pan from the heat. Set aside.

4 Gradually add one-third of the hot milk mixture to the egg mixture, whisking continuously, to temper the egg. Return the tempered egg mixture to the remaining milk mixture in the saucepan, add the reserved rice, and cook, stirring continuously, until the mixture is creamy and thick, 10 to 15 minutes. Remove the pan from the heat and stir in the butter and vanilla until smooth.

5 Pour the filling into the prepared crust. Smooth and level the filling with an offset spatula. Press a piece of plastic wrap directly on the surface to prevent a skin from forming. Let the filling cool, then refrigerate the tart until set, 1 to 2 hours.

6 Garnish with a dusting of confectioners' sugar and additional lemon and orange zests (sprinkle the zests over the whole tart, or in a pattern as pictured).

SWEET VANILLA-RICE TART IN A SPICED TART CRUST *Blind bake and cool one Spice Tart Crust (page 71). Follow the recipe for Sweet Citrus Risotto Tart, adding a scraped vanilla bean pod and seeds in place of the lemon and orange zests in step 3 and removing the pod before adding the egg mixture in step 4, and garnish with a dusting of cinnamon.*

CHAI VANILLA TART

This is an unusual yet delicious tart. The custard is flavored with chai, a spiced black tea that traditionally includes cardamom, cinnamon, cloves, ginger, and black pepper. Purchase a high-quality chai tea, such as Harney and Sons or Tazo, for the best flavor.

MAKES

One 9-inch round or 4½ by 14-inch rectangular tart

CRUST

Vanilla Tart Dough (page 70), fitted into a 9-inch round or 4½ by 14-inch rectangular tart pan, blind baked, and cooled

TOPPING

Sweetened Whipped Cream (page 313)

INGREDIENTS	VOLUME	OUNCES
Sugar	⅓ cup	2.4
Cornstarch	2 tbsp	-
Milk	1¾ cups	15.2
Large egg	1	-
Egg yolks	2	-
Chai tea bags	2	-
Unsalted butter	1 tbsp	-
Vanilla extract	½ tsp	-
Ground cinnamon, as needed		

1 In a medium bowl, combine ¼ cup of the sugar with the cornstarch and whisk until free of lumps. Add ¼ cup of the milk, the egg, and the egg yolks and whisk to combine. Set aside.

2 In a medium saucepan, combine the remaining 1½ cups milk with the remaining sugar. Bring the mixture to a boil over medium heat, stirring to dissolve the sugar. Remove the pan from the heat, add the tea bags, and let steep for 5 minutes. Remove and discard the tea bags.

3 Gradually add one-third of the hot milk mixture to the egg mixture, whisking continuously, to temper the eggs. Return the tempered egg mixture to the remaining milk mixture in the saucepan and cook, stirring continuously, until it reaches a boil. Continue to cook the filling, stirring continuously, for 2 minutes more. Remove the pan from the heat and stir in the butter and vanilla until smooth and creamy.

4 Transfer the filling to the prepared crust. Smooth and level the filling with an offset spatula. Press a piece of plastic wrap directly on the surface of the filling to prevent a skin from forming. Let the filling cool, then refrigerate the tart until set, 1 to 2 hours.

5 Pipe (see page 297) or spread the whipped cream over the filling and garnish with a light dusting of cinnamon. Refrigerate for at least 1 hour, but no longer than 2 hours, before serving.

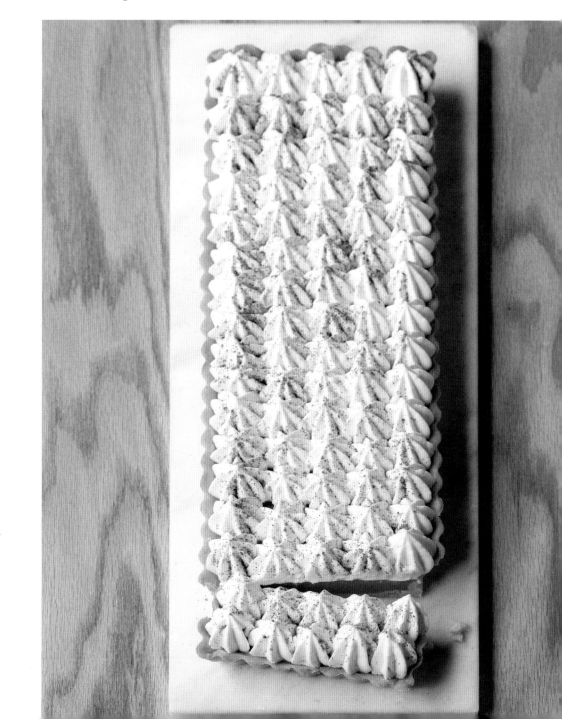

COCOA AND MARSHMALLOW TART

The inspiration for this tart came on a cold and snowy winter day filled with sledding—the perfect time for hot cocoa topped with marshmallows! The filling is rich, dense, and simple to prepare. Piled high with sweet toasted marshmallows—who could resist?

MAKES
One 9-inch tart

CRUST
Graham Cracker–Crumb Crust (page 67), baked and cooled

INGREDIENTS	VOLUME	OUNCES
All-purpose flour	3 tbsp	-
Cocoa powder	⅓ cup	1.2
Sugar	¾ cup	5.3
Heavy cream	1 cup	8.4
Milk	1¾ cups	15.2
Egg yolks	3	-
Vanilla extract	½ tsp	-
Mini marshmallows	2 cups	3.5

1 In a medium heavy-bottomed saucepan, combine the flour, cocoa powder, and sugar and whisk until free of lumps. Set aside.

2 In a medium bowl, whisk together the heavy cream, milk, and egg yolks.

3 Stream the heavy cream mixture into the dry ingredients in the saucepan, whisking until smooth and creamy.

4 Bring the mixture to a boil over medium-high heat, whisking continuously. Continue to cook the filling, stirring continuously, for 2 minutes more. Remove the pan from the heat and stir in the vanilla.

5 Transfer the filling to the crust and smooth with an offset spatula. Press a piece of plastic wrap directly on the surface of the filling to prevent a skin from forming. Let cool, then refrigerate until set, 1 to 2 hours.

6 Preheat the broiler to low. Top the chilled tart with marshmallows and broil until the marshmallows are lightly browned, 4 to 5 minutes. Let stand at room temperature until the marshmallows are cool before serving.

CARAMEL AND BANANA TART

This dessert is bananas Foster in tart form: bananas layered between a creamy rum-and-cinnamon filling and topped with caramel. How could it get any better than that?

MAKES
One 9-inch tart

CRUST
Vanilla Tart Dough (page 70), fitted into a 9-inch tart pan, blind baked, and cooled

INGREDIENTS	VOLUME	OUNCES
FOR THE FILLING:		
Sugar	⅓ cup	2.4
Cornstarch	2 tbsp	-
Ground cinnamon	1 tsp	-
Milk	1½ cups	13
Large egg	1	-
Egg yolks	2	-
Dark rum	1 tbsp	-
Unsalted butter	1 tbsp	-
Banana, ripe, peeled and cut into ¼-inch-thick rounds	1	-
FOR THE TOPPING:		
Heavy cream	⅓ cup	2.8
Light corn syrup	1 tsp	-
Sugar	½ cup	3.5
Unsalted butter	2 tbsp	-

1 Make the filling: In a medium bowl, combine ¼ cup of the sugar, the cornstarch, and the cinnamon and whisk until free of lumps. Add ¼ cup of the milk, the egg, and the egg yolks and whisk to combine. Set aside.

2 In a medium saucepan, combine the remaining 1¼ cups milk with the remaining sugar. Bring the mixture to a boil over medium heat, stirring to dissolve the sugar.

3 Gradually add one-third of the hot milk mixture to the egg mixture, whisking continuously, to temper the eggs. Return the tempered egg mixture to the remaining milk mixture in the saucepan and cook, stirring continuously, until it reaches a boil. Continue to cook the filling, stirring continuously, for 2 minutes more. Remove the pan from the heat and stir in the rum and butter until smooth and creamy.

4 Pour half of the warm filling into the prepared crust. Smooth and level the filling with an offset spatula. Arrange the sliced banana over the filling and top with the remaining filling. Press a piece of plastic wrap directly on the surface of the filling to prevent a skin from forming. Let the filling cool, and then refrigerate the tart until set, 1 to 2 hours.

5 Make the topping: In a small saucepan, bring the cream to a boil over medium heat. Remove the pan from the heat.

6 Place the corn syrup in a small heavy-bottomed saucepan over medium-high heat. Add the sugar in 1- to 2-tablespoon increments, tilting and swirling the pan after each addition until the sugar is melted and is a rich golden brown color.

7 Remove the pan from the heat and slowly stir in the hot cream. The hot mixture will bubble up, so use caution. Stir in the butter until incorporated.

8 Immediately pour the warm caramel over the chilled tart filling. Tilt and rotate the tart so the caramel coats the top evenly. Let cool, then refrigerate the tart for at least 1 hour, until the caramel is firm.

CUSTARD

CUSTARD PIE

Custard pie is simultaneously delicate and light yet very rich. The key to a crisp bottom crust and a smooth custard filling is partially baking the crust at high heat and then reducing the oven temperature partway through the cooking time.

MAKES
One 9-inch pie

CRUST
All-Butter Pie
Dough, Unbaked
Single Crust
(page 64)

TOPPING
Sweetened Whipped
Cream (page 313)

INGREDIENTS	VOLUME	OUNCES
Sugar	¾ cup	5.3
Water	¼ cup	2
Milk	2¼ cups	19.5
Large eggs	3	-
Kosher salt	¼ tsp	-
Vanilla extract	1 tsp	-
Freshly grated nutmeg	¼ tsp	-

1 Preheat the oven to 400°F and set the rack in the lowest position.

2 Place the chilled pie crust on a baking sheet, line the crust with lightly oiled or sprayed parchment, and fill with weights. Partially blind bake the crust until it is a matte, pale golden color, 15 to 20 minutes. Remove the weights and parchment and bake until lightly browned, about 10 minutes more.

EGGNOG CUSTARD PIE

Follow the recipe for Custard Pie, increasing the nutmeg to ½ teaspoon and adding 3 tablespoons rum and ¼ teaspoon ground cinnamon in step 4.

3 Meanwhile, in a small heavy-bottomed saucepan, combine the sugar and water. Bring to a boil over medium heat, stirring, then let the mixture boil without stirring until the sugar has dissolved, 3 to 5 minutes. Remove the pan from the heat.

4 Meanwhile, in a medium bowl, combine the milk, eggs, salt, vanilla, and nutmeg and whisk until smooth. Pour the sugar mixture into the milk mixture in a steady stream, whisking continuously to combine.

5 Reduce the oven temperature to 325°F. Open the oven, pull out the rack slightly, and pour the filling into the pie crust. Bake until the filling has set 3 inches from the edge but the center is still slightly wobbly, 40 to 45 minutes. Remove the pie from the oven and place it on a cooling rack. The center of the filling will continue to solidify as the pie cools.

6 Refrigerate the cooled pie for at least 4 hours before serving with the whipped cream.

PUMPKIN PIE

The perfect pumpkin pie is rich yet slightly spicy, with a smooth texture that yields a nice clean slice. Be sure to remove the pie from the oven while the center is just slightly wobbly or the pie will overbake and the center will crack.

MAKES
One 9-inch pie

CRUST
All-Butter Pie Dough, Unbaked Single Crust (page 64)

TOPPING
Sweetened Whipped Cream (page 313)

INGREDIENTS	VOLUME	OUNCES
Sugar	1 cup	7
Ground cinnamon	1½ tsp	-
Ground ginger	1 tsp	-
Ground cloves	¼ tsp	-
Kosher salt	½ tsp	-
Pumpkin purée	1¾ cups	One (15-oz) can
Large eggs	3	-
Vanilla extract	1 tsp	-
Heavy cream	½ cup	4.25

BROWN SUGAR PUMPKIN PIE

Follow the recipe for Pumpkin Pie, replacing the granulated sugar with packed light brown or dark brown sugar.

1 Preheat the oven to 400°F and set the rack in the lowest position.

2 Place the pie crust on a baking sheet, line with lightly oiled or sprayed parchment, and fill with weights. Partially blind bake the crust until it is a matte, pale golden color, 15 to 20 minutes. Remove the weights and parchment and bake until lightly browned, about 10 minutes more.

3 Meanwhile, in a medium bowl, whisk together the sugar, spices, and salt.

4 In a separate medium bowl, beat together the pumpkin, eggs, vanilla, and heavy cream with a whisk. Whisk the dry ingredients into the pumpkin mixture until well combined.

5 Reduce the oven temperature to 350°F. Pour the filling into the warm pie crust. Bake until the filling has set 3 inches from the edge but the center is just slightly wobbly, 45 to 50 minutes. Remove the pie from the oven and place it on a cooling rack. Let cool for about 2 hours. The center of the filling will continue to solidify as the pie cools.

6 Chill the cooled pie in the refrigerator for at least 4 hours before serving topped with the whipped cream.

PUMPKIN CHEESECAKE PIE

The marbled effect of the deep orange of the pumpkin and the white of the cream cheese makes this a beautiful, unique, and—most importantly—delicious dessert to present to your guests.

MAKES
One 9-inch pie

CRUST
Cookie-Crumb Crust, made with gingersnaps (page 69), baked and still warm

INGREDIENTS	VOLUME	OUNCES
Large eggs	2	-
Heavy cream	½ cup	4.25
Vanilla extract	1 tsp	-
Cream cheese, softened at room temperature	1 cup	8
Sugar	1 cup	7
Pumpkin purée	1¾ cups	One (15-oz) can
Ground cinnamon	1 tsp	-
Ground ginger	½ tsp	-
Freshly grated nutmeg	¼ tsp	-
Kosher salt	¼ tsp	-

1 Preheat the oven to 350°F and set the rack in the lowest position.

2 In a medium bowl, whisk together the eggs, heavy cream, and vanilla until smooth and creamy.

3 In the bowl of a stand mixer fitted with the paddle attachment, combine the cream cheese and sugar and beat on low speed until smooth. Add the egg mixture in two stages, mixing on low speed for 2 to 3 minutes, or until smooth, and scraping the bowl after each addition.

4 Transfer ½ cup of the cream cheese mixture to a pastry bag (or a zip-top plastic bag; snip off one corner before using), and set aside.

5 Combine the remaining cream cheese mixture with the pumpkin, cinnamon, ginger, nutmeg, and salt. Pour the pumpkin filling into the still warm crust.

6 Place the tip of the pastry bag holding the reserved cream cheese mixture just at the surface of the pumpkin filling. Pipe circles of cream cheese mixture, leaving equal spaces between the shapes. Then lightly drag a paring knife or a toothpick in a circular pattern from the center of the filling to the edge of the crust to create a swirled, marbled effect.

7 Bake until the filling has set 3 inches from the edge but the center is just slightly wobbly, 45 to 50 minutes. Remove the pie from the oven and place it on a cooling rack. The center of the filling will continue to solidify as the pie cools.

8 Chill the pie in the refrigerator for at least 4 hours before serving.

MAPLE PUMPKIN PIE

The rich, earthy flavors of pumpkin and maple syrup complement each other well. Be sure to use Grade B maple syrup as it will lend a more pronounced maple flavor to the pie.

MAKES
One 9-inch pie

CRUST
All-Butter Pie Dough, Unbaked Single Crust (page 64), edges crimped or decorated with cutout shapes (see page 52)

TOPPING
Maple Whipped Cream (page 316)

INGREDIENTS	VOLUME	OUNCES
Maple syrup, Grade B	¾ cup	9
Large eggs	3	-
Pumpkin purée	1¾ cups	One (15-oz) can
Heavy cream	½ cup	4.2
Vanilla extract	1 tsp	-
Ground cinnamon	1½ tsp	-
Ground ginger	1 tsp	-
Ground cloves	¼ tsp	-
Kosher salt	½ tsp	

1 Preheat the oven to 400°F and set the rack in the lowest position.

2 In a small heavy-bottomed saucepan, bring the maple syrup to a boil over medium-high heat. Cook the syrup until it registers between 230° and 235°F on a candy thermometer. Remove the pan from the heat and let the syrup cool for 10 minutes.

3 Place the chilled pie crust on a baking sheet, line the crust with lightly oiled or sprayed parchment, and fill with weights. Partially blind bake the crust until it is a matte, pale golden color, 15 to 20 minutes. Remove the crust from the oven, remove the weights and parchment, and bake until lightly browned, about 10 minutes more.

4 While the crust is partially baking, in a medium bowl, whisk together the eggs, pumpkin, heavy cream, vanilla, cinnamon, ginger, cloves, and salt. Pour the warm maple syrup into the pumpkin mixture in a steady stream, whisking continuously to combine.

5 Reduce the oven temperature to 350°F. Pour the filling into the warm pie crust. Bake until the filling has set 3 inches from the edge but the center is still slightly wobbly,

45 to 50 minutes. Remove the pie from the oven and place it on a cooling rack. The center of the filling will continue to solidify as the pie cools.

6 Chill the pie in the refrigerator for at least 4 hours before serving topped with the whipped cream.

SWEET POTATO PIE

This traditional Southern pie features a smooth, orange-colored custard and a hint of mild cinnamon spice, in a slightly spicy gingersnap crumb crust.

MAKES
One 9-inch pie

CRUST
Cookie Crumb Crust, made with gingersnaps (page 69), baked and still warm

TOPPING
Sweetened Whipped Cream (page 313; optional)

INGREDIENTS	VOLUME	OUNCES
Sweet potatoes, preferably Jewel or Beauregard	2 to 3 large	13 to 16
Unsalted butter, melted	4 tbsp (½ stick)	2
Granulated sugar	¼ cup	1.75
Light brown sugar, packed	¼ cup	2
Large eggs	2	-
Egg yolk	1	-
Milk	¾ cup	6.5
Vanilla extract	1 tsp	-
Ground cinnamon	½ tsp	-
Freshly grated nutmeg	¼ tsp	-
Kosher salt	½ tsp	-

1 Preheat the oven to 400°F and set the rack in the lowest position.

2 Cut off the ends of the sweet potatoes and place them on a baking sheet or in a roasting pan. Bake for about 1 hour, or until the potatoes are tender. Remove from the oven and let cool. Peel the potatoes and place the flesh in the bowl of a food processor fitted with the steel blade. Process until smooth. (Alternatively, purée the potatoes with an immersion blender.)

3 Add the melted butter, both sugars, the eggs, egg yolk, milk, vanilla, cinnamon, nutmeg, and salt to the food processor and process until smooth.

4 Pour the filling into the warm crust. Bake until the filling has set 3 inches from the edge but the center is just slightly wobbly, 45 to 50 minutes. Transfer the pie to a cooling rack. The center of the filling will continue to solidify as the pie cools.

5 Refrigerate the pie for at least 4 hours before serving with whipped cream, if desired.

TRIPLE CITRUS PIE

The tart and creamy citrus filling of this play on the classic Key lime pie is offset by the buttery crispness of the graham cracker–crumb crust. If Key limes are not in season or cannot be sourced, use bottled Key lime juice. Nellie and Joe's Famous Lime Juice or Manhattan Key Lime Juice are excellent choices.

MAKES
One 9-inch pie

CRUST
Graham Cracker–Crumb Crust (page 67), baked and cooled

TOPPING
Sweetened Whipped Cream (page 313)

INGREDIENTS	VOLUME	OUNCES
Sweetened condensed milk	1¼ cups	One (14-oz) can
Egg yolks	4	-
Large egg	1	-
Key lime juice	¼ cup	2
Orange juice	½ cup	4
Lemon juice	¼ cup	2
Key lime zest	From 1 lime	-
Orange zest	From 1 orange	-
Lemon zest	From 1 lemon	-

1 Preheat the oven to 350°F and set the rack in the lowest position.

2 In a medium bowl, combine the condensed milk, egg yolks, and egg and whisk until smooth. Add the lime, lemon, and orange juices and whisk until well combined. The mixture will thicken slightly.

3 Pour the filling into the prepared crust.

4 Bake until the filling has set 3 inches from the edge but the center is just slightly wobbly, 10 to 15 minutes. Remove the pie from the oven and place it on a cooling rack. Let the pie cool for about 2 hours. The center of the filling will continue to solidify as the pie cools.

5 Chill the pie in the refrigerator for at least 4 hours before serving topped with the whipped cream and garnished with the lime, orange, and lemon zests.

CHEESECAKE PIE

A classic cheesecake—dense, rich, and creamy—in a pie crust. Add a small amount of melted bittersweet chocolate to a portion of the batter and swirl it in as described in the variation to create a lovely and dramatic marbled effect.

MAKES
One 9-inch pie

CRUST
Graham Cracker–Crumb Crust (page 67), baked and cooled

INGREDIENTS	VOLUME	OUNCES
Large eggs	3	-
Cream cheese, softened at room temperature	1 cup	8
Sugar	⅓ cup	2.5
Heavy cream	1 cup	8.4
Lemon or orange zest	2 tsp	-
Kosher salt	¼ tsp	-

1 Preheat the oven to 350°F and set the rack in the lowest position.

2 In a medium bowl, lightly whisk the eggs until smooth.

3 In the bowl of a stand mixer fitted with the paddle attachment, combine the cream cheese and sugar and beat on low speed until smooth. Add the eggs in two stages, scraping the bowl after each addition. Mix until well combined. Slowly add the heavy cream, zest, and salt and mix until combined.

4 Pour the filling into the prepared crust. Bake until the center of the pie is just slightly wobbly, 40 to 45 minutes. Remove the pie from the oven and place it on a cooling rack. The center of the filling will continue to solidify as the pie cools.

5 Chill the pie in the refrigerator for at least 4 hours before serving.

CHOCOLATE SWIRL CHEESECAKE PIE *Follow the recipe for Cheesecake Pie, omitting the zest in step 3. Reserve one-half of the cream cheese mixture from step 3. Gently melt 2 ounces of bittersweet chocolate. While whisking, stream the warm chocolate into the remaining cream cheese mixture. Transfer the mixture to a pastry bag (or a zip-top plastic bag; cut off one corner before using). Fill the crust with the plain cream cheese mixture, then pipe circles with the chocolate–cream cheese mixture onto the plain cheesecake. Lightly drag a paring knife or a toothpick in a circular pattern from the center of the filling to the edge of the crust, creating a swirled effect. Bake as directed.*

CHESS PIE

This pie is an intensely sweet and rich Southern specialty made of sugar, butter, and eggs. The origins of chess pie are somewhat muddled, and theories abound as to how this pie obtained its name. One charming explanation is that when the baker was asked what kind of pie it was, the response was, "Oh, it's jes' pie."

MAKES
One 9-inch pie

CRUST
All-Butter Pie Dough, Unbaked Single Crust (page 64)

INGREDIENTS	VOLUME	OUNCES
Sugar	1¼ cups	8.75
All-purpose flour	2 tbsp	-
Kosher salt	¼ tsp	-
Unsalted butter, softened at room temperature	½ cup (1 stick)	4
Large eggs	4	-
Vanilla extract	1 tsp	-

LEMON CHESS PIE

Follow the recipe for Chess Pie, replacing the vanilla with the zest of 1 lemon and 2 tablespoons lemon juice, adding them after the addition of the eggs in step 4.

1 Preheat the oven to 400°F and set the rack in the lowest position.

2 Place the chilled pie crust on a baking sheet, line the crust with lightly oiled or sprayed parchment, and fill with weights. Partially blind bake the crust until it is a matte, pale golden color, 15 to 20 minutes. Remove the crust from the oven, remove the weights and parchment, and bake until lightly browned, about 10 minutes more.

3 Meanwhile, in a small bowl, stir together the sugar, flour, and salt.

4 In the bowl of a stand mixer fitted with the paddle attachment, combine the sugar mixture and the butter. Beat on low speed until smooth, 2 to 3 minutes. Add the eggs and vanilla to the mixture in two stages, scraping the bowl after each addition, and mix until combined and smooth.

5 Reduce the oven temperature to 350°F. Pour the filling into the warm crust. Bake until the edges of the filling slightly puff up and become slightly cracked and the center is just set, 45 to 50 minutes. Remove the pie from the oven and place it on a cooling rack.

6 Serve slightly warm or at room temperature.

CHOCOLATE CHESS PIE

Chocolate is not an ingredient normally used in chess pies, but in this version the bittersweet chocolate adds a dense, smooth, and rich complement to the traditional ingredients of butter, sugar, and eggs.

MAKES

One 9-inch pie

CRUST

All-Butter Pie Dough, Unbaked Single Crust (page 64)

INGREDIENTS	VOLUME	OUNCES
Unsalted butter	¾ cup (1½ sticks)	6
Chopped bittersweet chocolate (not more than 65% cacao)	-	4
Sugar	1 cup	7
Large eggs	3	-
Vanilla extract	1 tsp	-
Kosher salt	¼ tsp	-

1 Preheat the oven to 400°F and set the rack in the lowest position.

2 Place the chilled pie crust on a baking sheet, line the crust with lightly oiled or sprayed parchment, and fill with weights. Partially blind bake the crust until it is a matte, pale golden color, 15 to 20 minutes. Remove the weights and parchment and bake until lightly browned, about 10 minutes more.

3 While the crust is partially baking, in a small heavy-bottomed saucepan, melt the butter and chocolate over low heat, stirring to combine. Remove the saucepan from the heat and let cool for 10 minutes.

4 In a medium bowl, combine the sugar, eggs, vanilla, and salt, whisking continuously until thick and smooth. Pour the chocolate mixture into the egg mixture in a steady stream, whisking continuously to combine.

5 Pour the filling into the warm pie crust. Bake until the edges of the filling slightly puff up and become slightly cracked, and the center is just set, 30 to 40 minutes. Remove the pie from the oven and place it on a cooling rack.

6 Serve slightly warm or at room temperature.

SHOO-FLY PIE

This pie is made with alternating layers of streusel-like crumbs and molasses filling, resulting in a cakelike texture with a base of gooey and flavorful molasses. It is a type of traditional Amish pie that is called "wet bottom," for the layer of molasses that settles at the bottom of the pie. For a "dry bottom," stir the crumb mixture into the filling instead of layering it. Both versions are perfect served slightly warm with a hot cup of coffee.

MAKES

One 9-inch pie

CRUST

All-Butter Pie Dough, Unbaked Single Crust (page 64)

INGREDIENTS	VOLUME	OUNCES
All-purpose flour	¾ cup	3.5
Light brown sugar, packed	½ cup	4
Unsalted butter	2 tbsp	-
Kosher salt	¼ tsp	-
Water, boiling	¾ cup	6.25
Baking soda	1 tsp	-
Molasses	½ cup	6
Light corn syrup	½ cup	5.7
Large egg	1	-

1 Preheat the oven to 400°F and set the rack in the lowest position.

2 Place the chilled pie crust on a baking sheet, line the crust with lightly oiled or sprayed parchment, and fill with weights. Partially blind bake the crust until it is a matte, pale golden color, 15 to 20 minutes. Remove the weights and parchment and bake until lightly browned, about 10 minutes more.

3 While the crust is partially baking, in a medium bowl, combine the flour, brown sugar, butter, and salt, using a pastry cutter or rubbing with your fingers, until the butter is broken into pea-size pieces.

4 In a separate medium bowl, combine the boiling water, baking soda, molasses, and corn syrup and stir until the molasses and corn syrup have dissolved. Add the egg and stir to combine.

5 Reduce the oven temperature to 375°F. Sprinkle half of the flour mixture over the bottom of the warm crust. Pour half of the molasses filling into the pie crust over the flour mixture. Add the remaining flour mixture and then the remaining filling. Bake until the edges of the filling slightly puff up and become slightly cracked, and the center is just set, 45 to 50 minutes. Remove the pie from the oven and place it on a cooling rack. Allow the pie to cool for at least 1 hour. Serve warm or at room temperature.

BOILED APPLE CIDER CUSTARD TART

A classic New England specialty typically made in pie form, but upgraded here to an elegant tart. Serve each slice with vanilla ice cream to offset the brightness of the apples. Pears can be easily substituted for the apple.

MAKES

One 11-inch tart

CRUST

Vanilla Tart Dough (page 70), fitted into an 11-inch tart pan and chilled

INGREDIENTS	VOLUME	OUNCES
Apple cider	2½ cups	22.5
Unsalted butter	2 tbsp	-
Light brown sugar, packed	3 tbsp	-
Large eggs	2	-
Vanilla extract	1 tsp	-
Kosher salt	¼ tsp	-
Granny Smith apple, peeled and grated	1	-

1 Preheat the oven to 350°F and set the rack in the lowest position.

2 In a medium heavy-bottomed saucepan, bring the cider to a rapid boil over medium heat. Continue boiling until the cider has reduced to 1 cup, 40 to 45 minutes. Use a heatproof glass volume measuring cup to check the progress of the cider, as needed.

3 Remove the saucepan from the heat and pour the cider through a fine-mesh strainer into a medium stainless-steel bowl. Add the butter and 1 tablespoon of the brown sugar, stirring until the butter has melted and the sugar has dissolved. Let the cider mixture cool for 15 to 20 minutes.

4 Place the chilled crust on a baking sheet, line the crust with lightly oiled or sprayed parchment, and fill with weights. Partially blind bake the crust until it is a matte, pale golden color, 15 to 20 minutes. Remove the weights and parchment.

5 While the crust is partially baking, in a medium bowl, combine the eggs, vanilla, and salt and stir with a whisk. Pour the warm cider mixture into the egg mixture in a steady stream, whisking continuously to combine.

6 Pour the filling into the warm tart crust. Sprinkle the grated apple evenly over the filling. Bake until just set, 10 to 15 minutes.

7 Open the oven, pull out the rack, and sprinkle the remaining 2 tablespoons brown sugar over the apple. Continue baking until the filling is slightly set and the center is just slightly wobbly and lightly browned, 10 to 15 minutes more. Remove the tart from the oven and place it on a cooling rack. Let the tart cool for 1 hour.

8 Serve slightly warm or at room temperature.

LEMON CLOUD TART

The lemon filling in this tart naturally separates into two distinct layers when baked—a fluffy top layer lightened by the whipped cream, and a bottom layer of creamy lemon curd.

MAKES

One 9-inch tart

CRUST

Vanilla Tart Dough (page 70), fitted into a 9-inch tart pan and chilled

TOPPING

Sweetened Whipped Cream (page 313)

INGREDIENTS	VOLUME	OUNCES
Heavy cream	½ cup	4.2
Large eggs	4	-
Sugar	1 cup	7
Fresh lemon zest	From 1 lemon	-
Lemon juice	½ cup (from 4 to 5 lemons)	4.5

1 Preheat the oven to 350°F and set the rack in the lowest position.

2 Place the chilled crust on a baking sheet, line the crust with lightly oiled or sprayed parchment, and fill with weights. Partially blind bake the crust until it is a matte, pale golden color, 15 to 20 minutes. Remove the weights and parchment.

3 While the crust is partially baking, in a medium bowl, whip the cream using a whisk until soft peaks form.

4 In a separate medium bowl, combine the eggs and sugar and whisk until thick and smooth. Add half of the lemon zest and the lemon juice and stir to combine.

5 In three batches, gently fold the whipped cream into the egg mixture.

6 Pour the filling into the warm crust. Bake until the edges of the filling slightly puff up and the center is just slightly wobbly, 30 to 40 minutes. Remove the tart from the oven and place it on a cooling rack. Refrigerate the tart for 2 hours, or until firm enough to slice.

7 Serve topped with the whipped cream and garnished with the remaining lemon zest.

RICOTTA TART

Creamy, rich vanilla custard with the characteristic graininess of ricotta is presented in a pistachio tart crust and topped with bittersweet chocolate shavings. It's like a cannoli in tart form!

MAKES
One 9-inch tart

CRUST
Nut Tart Dough, made with pistachios (page 74), fitted into a 9-inch tart pan and chilled

INGREDIENTS	VOLUME	OUNCES
Large eggs	2	-
Vanilla extract	1 tsp	-
Cream cheese, softened at room temperature	½ cup	4
Sugar	⅓ cup	2.3
Ricotta	2 cups	15
Kosher salt	½ tsp	-
Bittersweet chocolate curls (see page 300), as needed		

1 Preheat the oven to 350°F and set the rack in the lowest position.

2 Place the chilled crust on a baking sheet, line the crust with lightly oiled or sprayed parchment, and fill with weights. Partially blind bake the crust until it is a matte, pale golden color, 15 to 20 minutes. Remove the weights and parchment and bake until lightly browned, about 10 minutes more.

3 While the crust is baking, in a medium bowl, combine the eggs and vanilla and whisk until thick and smooth.

4 In the bowl of a stand mixer fitted with the paddle attachment, combine the cream cheese, sugar, ricotta, and salt and beat on medium speed until smooth. Reduce the mixer speed to low and add the egg mixture in two stages, scraping the bowl and mixing until smooth after each addition.

5 Pour the filling into the warm tart crust. Smooth and level the filling with an offset spatula. Bake until the center of the tart is just slightly wobbly, 15 to 20 minutes. Remove the tart from the oven and place it on a cooling rack. Let the tart cool for about 2 hours.

6 Chill the tart in the refrigerator for at least 4 hours, or until firm, before topping with the chocolate curls and serving.

CREAMY MAPLE TART

If the rich flavor and sweet earthiness of maple syrup appeal to you, you'll love this creamy baked-custard tart. It's served with maple whipped cream for a double dose of maple flavor.

MAKES
One 9-inch tart

CRUST
Vanilla Tart Dough (page 70), fitted into a 9-inch tart pan and chilled

TOPPING
Maple Whipped Cream (page 316)

INGREDIENTS	VOLUME	OUNCES
Maple syrup, Grade B	¾ cup	8.75
Heavy cream	2 cups	16.8
Egg yolks	4	-
Large egg	1	-
Vanilla extract	1 tsp	-
Kosher salt	¼ tsp	-

1 Preheat the oven to 350°F and set the rack in the lowest position.

2 Place the chilled crust on a baking sheet, line the crust with lightly oiled or sprayed parchment, and fill with weights. Partially blind bake the crust until it is a matte, pale golden color, 15 to 20 minutes. Remove the weights and parchment and bake until lightly browned, about 10 minutes more.

3 While the crust is baking, in a medium bowl, combine the maple syrup, heavy cream, egg yolks, egg, vanilla, and salt and whisk until creamy and smooth. Pour the maple filling through a fine-mesh strainer into a bowl.

4 Open the oven, pull out the rack slightly, and pour the filling into the tart crust. Bake until the filling is just slightly wobbly at the center, 25 to 30 minutes.

5 Remove the tart from the oven and place it on a cooling rack. Let the tart cool for about 1 hour.

6 Refrigerate the tart for at least 2 hours. Pipe (see page 297) or spread the whipped cream over the filling and serve.

BITTERSWEET CHOCOLATE MOCHA TART

The combination of dense bittersweet chocolate, a kick of espresso, and sweet toasty meringue makes this tart irresistible, and one you will not easily forget!

MAKES
One 9-inch tart

CRUST
Chocolate Tart Dough (page 72), fitted into a 9-inch tart pan and chilled

TOPPING
Swiss Meringue (page 309)

INGREDIENTS	VOLUME	OUNCES
Heavy cream	1½ cups	13
Sugar	½ cup	3.5
Instant coffee or espresso powder	½ tsp	-
Chopped bittersweet chocolate (not more than 65% cacao)	-	4
Egg yolks	4	-
Kosher salt	¼ tsp	-

1 Preheat the oven to 350°F and set the rack in the lowest position.

2 Place the chilled crust on a baking sheet, line the crust with lightly oiled or sprayed parchment, and fill with weights. Partially blind bake the crust until it has a matte finish and chocolaty aroma, 15 to 20 minutes. Remove the weights and parchment and bake for 10 minutes more.

3 Meanwhile, in a small heavy-bottomed saucepan, combine the heavy cream, sugar, and coffee or espresso powder and stir with a whisk. Bring the mixture to a simmer over medium heat, then remove the pan from the heat. Add the chocolate to the cream mixture and let stand for 5 minutes. Gently stir to combine.

BITTERSWEET CHOCOLATE ORANGE TART

Follow the recipe for Bittersweet Chocolate Mocha Tart, replacing the coffee or espresso powder with the zest of 1 orange in step 3.

4 In a medium bowl, combine the egg yolks and salt and whisk until thick and smooth.

5 Pour the chocolate mixture into the egg mixture in a steady stream, stirring continuously to combine.

6 Open the oven, pull out the rack slightly, and pour the filling into the tart crust. Bake until the center is just set, about 15 minutes. Remove the tart from the oven and place it on a cooling rack. Let the tart cool for about 1 hour. Refrigerate the tart for at least 4 hours, or until set.

7 Preheat the broiler on low. Pipe (see page 297) or spread the meringue over the filling, making sure to completely cover the filling and anchor the meringue to the

edge of the crust to keep it from shrinking, and place it under the broiler until the meringue is lightly browned, 4 to 5 minutes. Alternatively, use a kitchen torch to brown the exterior of the meringue (see page 297).

HONEY ORANGE TART

A simple and easy-to-make creamy tart flavored with orange zest and sweetened with honey. Pair this rich tart with fresh strawberries or raspberries.

MAKES
One 9-inch tart

CRUST
Vanilla Tart Dough (page 70), fitted into a 9-inch tart pan and chilled

TOPPING
Sweetened Whipped Cream (page 313)

INGREDIENTS	VOLUME	OUNCES
Heavy cream	2 cups	16.8
Honey	⅓ cup	4
Vanilla bean, split lengthwise, seeds scraped	½	-
Orange zest	2 tsp	-
Egg yolks	5	-

1 Preheat the oven to 350°F and set the rack in the lowest position.

2 Place the chilled crust on a baking sheet, line the crust with lightly oiled or sprayed parchment, and fill with weights. Partially blind bake the crust until it is a matte, pale golden color, 15 to 20 minutes. Remove the weights and parchment and bake until lightly browned, about 10 minutes more.

3 While the crust is baking, in a medium saucepan, combine the heavy cream, honey, the vanilla bean pod and seeds, and 1 teaspoon of the orange zest and whisk to combine. Bring to just under a boil over medium heat, stirring to dissolve the honey. Remove the pan from the heat. Set aside and let steep for 5 minutes. Remove the vanilla bean pod.

4 In a medium bowl, whisk the egg yolks until creamy and smooth.

5 Pour the heavy cream mixture into the egg yolks in a steady stream, whisking continuously to combine.

6 Open the oven, pull out the rack slightly, and pour the filling into the tart crust. Bake until the filling is just slightly wobbly at the center, about 15 minutes. Remove the tart from the oven and place it on a cooling rack. Let the tart cool for 1 hour.

7 Refrigerate the tart for at least 2 hours, or until set, before serving topped with the whipped cream and garnished with the remaining 1 teaspoon orange zest.

CRÈME BRÛLÉE TART

Crème brûlée is traditionally baked and served in ramekins, but here the classic vanilla custard is baked in a tart shell. Just before serving, the tart is sprinkled with sugar, which is heated and caramelized to create a thin, crispy layer over the cool custard.

MAKES
One 9-inch tart

CRUST
Vanilla Tart Dough (page 70), fitted into a 9-inch tart pan and chilled

INGREDIENTS	VOLUME	OUNCES
Heavy cream	1¼ cups	10.5
Milk	⅓ cup	2.8
Vanilla bean, split lengthwise, seeds scraped	1	-
Granulated sugar	⅓ cup plus 1 tbsp	2.4
Kosher salt	¼ tsp	-
Large egg	1	-
Egg yolks	4	-
Light brown sugar, packed	1 tbsp	-

1 Preheat the oven to 350°F and set the rack in the lowest position.

2 Place the chilled crust on a baking sheet, line the crust with lightly oiled or sprayed parchment, and fill with weights. Partially blind bake the crust until it is a matte, pale golden color, 15 to 20 minutes. Remove the weights and parchment and bake until lightly browned, about 10 minutes more.

3 While the crust is baking, in a medium saucepan, combine the heavy cream, milk, and vanilla bean pod and seeds. Bring to just under a boil over medium heat, then remove the pan from the heat. Set aside and let steep for 15 minutes.

4 In a medium bowl, combine ⅓ cup of the sugar, the salt, egg, and egg yolks and whisk until creamy and smooth.

5 Remove the vanilla bean pod from the cream mixture. Pour the cream mixture into the egg mixture in a steady stream, whisking continuously to combine.

6 Open the oven, pull out the rack slightly, and pour the filling into the tart crust. Bake until the filling is just slightly wobbly at the center, 30 to 40 minutes. Remove the tart from the oven and place it on a cooling rack. Let the tart cool for about 1 hour.

7 Refrigerate the tart for at least 2 hours, or until firm.

8 Just before serving, combine the brown sugar and remaining 1 tablespoon sugar, rubbing them together to combine. Sprinkle the sugar mixture over the tart. (To prevent the sugar from dissolving, first blot any liquid from the top of the tart using a paper towel.) Using a culinary torch, heat the sugar, moving the flame over the sugar until it begins to melt, caramelize, and darken. Let cool for 5 to 10 minutes and then serve.

NOTE *Alternatively, a broiler can be used to caramelize the sugar topping: Preheat the broiler. Place the tart under the broiler and broil, rotating the tart for even browning, until the sugar melts and begins to caramelize, about 1 minute. Remove the tart and let it stand until the topping hardens, about 10 minutes. (Note: The tart will become warm using this method, and the edges of the shell may brown and darken unless covered with a pie edge shield or a foil ring.)*

DULCE DE LECHE TART

Dulce de leche is a rich caramel sauce widely used in Latin American countries. Here, the dulce de leche lends a buttery caramel flavor to the filling, and also serves as a soft glaze for the tart. Canned dulce de leche can be purchased at specialty food shops and Latin American markets. The garnish, a sprinkling of flaky sea salt, turns the tart into a salty-sweet treat.

MAKES

One 9-inch tart

CRUST

Vanilla Tart Dough (page 70), fitted into a 9-inch tart pan and chilled

INGREDIENTS	VOLUME	OUNCES
Heavy cream	1¼ cups	10.5
Milk	⅓ cup	2.8
Dulce de leche	1 cup	10
Vanilla bean, split lengthwise, seeds scraped	1	-
Granulated sugar	⅓ cup	2.4
Kosher salt	¼ tsp	-
Large egg	1	-
Egg yolks	4	-
High-quality flaked sea salt, such as Maldon		

1 Preheat the oven to 350°F and set the rack in the lowest position.

2 Place the chilled crust on a baking sheet, line the crust with lightly oiled or sprayed parchment, and fill with weights. Partially blind bake the crust until it is a matte, pale golden color, 15 to 20 minutes. Remove the weights and parchment and bake until lightly browned, about 10 minutes more.

3 While the crust is baking, in a medium saucepan, combine the heavy cream, milk, ¼ cup of the dulce de leche, and the vanilla bean pod and seeds. Bring the mixture to just under a boil over medium heat, then remove from the heat. Set aside and let steep for 15 minutes.

4 In a medium bowl, combine the sugar, salt, egg, and egg yolks and whisk until creamy and smooth.

5 Remove the vanilla bean pod from the cream mixture. Pour the cream mixture into the egg mixture in a steady stream, whisking continuously to combine.

6 Open the oven, pull out the rack slightly, and pour the filling into the tart crust. Bake until the filling is just slightly wobbly at the center, 30 to 40 minutes. Remove the tart from the oven and place it on a cooling rack. Let the tart cool for about 1 hour.

7 In a small saucepan, heat the remaining ¾ cup dulce de leche over medium heat, stirring, until smooth and melted. Immediately pour the melted dulce de leche over the tart. Tilt and rotate the tart so the dulce de leche coats the top evenly.

8 Refrigerate the tart for at least 1 hour, until the dulce de leche is firm. Serve garnished with a light sprinkle of sea salt.

CHEESE TART

This tart is a more elegant version of a cheesecake. It serves as the perfect foil for the first fresh strawberries of the season. Or, if fresh berries are not at their prime, you could also heat high-quality berry preserves or jam and serve it as a sauce on the side.

MAKES
One 9-inch tart

CRUST
Vanilla Tart Dough (page 70), fitted into a 9-inch tart pan and chilled

INGREDIENTS	VOLUME	OUNCES
Large eggs	2	-
Vanilla extract	1 tsp	-
Cream cheese, softened at room temperature	1 cup	8
Sugar	⅓ cup	2.4
Kosher salt	¼ tsp	-
Heavy cream	½ cup	4.2
Lemon zest	From 1 lemon	-

1 Preheat the oven to 350°F and set the rack in the lowest position.

2 Place the chilled crust on a baking sheet, line the crust with lightly oiled or sprayed parchment, and fill with weights. Partially blind bake the crust until it is a matte, pale golden color, 15 to 20 minutes. Remove the weights and parchment and bake until lightly browned, about 10 minutes more.

3 While the crust is baking, in a medium bowl, whisk the eggs until thick and smooth. Whisk in the vanilla.

4 In the bowl of a stand mixer fitted with the paddle attachment, combine the cream cheese, sugar, and salt and beat on low speed until smooth. Add the beaten egg mixture in two stages, scraping the bowl after each addition. Beat in the heavy cream and lemon zest.

5 Pour the filling into the warm crust and bake until the filling is just slightly wobbly at the center, 15 to 20 minutes.

6 Remove the tart from the oven and place it on a cooling rack. Let the tart cool for about 2 hours.

7 Refrigerate the tart for at least 4 hours before serving.

CHOCOLATE AND NUT

PECAN PIE

The hallmarks of this deliciously rich pie are a distinctive layer of sweet custard filling and the crunchy nuts atop it. It's perfect with Bourbon Whipped Cream or a scoop of vanilla ice cream. Two variations are included here as well—with either bittersweet chocolate or cranberries to contrast the buttery richness of the pecans.

MAKES
One 9-inch pie

CRUST
All-Butter Pie Dough, Unbaked Single Crust (page 64)

TOPPING
Bourbon Whipped Cream (page 314; optional)

CHOCOLATE PECAN PIE

Follow the recipe for Pecan Pie, adding 1 cup chocolate chunks with the chopped pecans in step 4.

CRANBERRY PECAN PIE

Follow the recipe for Pecan Pie, adding 1¼ cups roughly chopped fresh or frozen cranberries with the chopped pecans in step 4.

INGREDIENTS	VOLUME	OUNCES
Sugar	2 tbsp	-
All-purpose flour	2 tbsp	-
Dark corn syrup	1½ cups	17.25
Large eggs	3	-
Kosher salt	¼ tsp	-
Vanilla extract	1½ tsp	-
Unsalted butter, melted	3 tbsp	-
Pecans halves, toasted (see page 30)	3 cups	10.5

1 Preheat the oven to 400°F and set the rack in the lowest position.

2 Place the chilled crust on a baking sheet, line the crust with lightly oiled or sprayed parchment, and fill with weights. Partially blind bake the crust until lightly browned, 15 to 20 minutes. Remove the crust from the oven, remove the weights and parchment, and place the crust on a cooling rack. Reduce the oven temperature to 350°F.

3 In a medium bowl, combine the sugar and flour and whisk together. Add the corn syrup and mix thoroughly. Add the eggs, salt, and vanilla, mixing until smooth and well incorporated. Stir in the melted butter.

4 Roughly chop the pecan halves. Spread one-third of the chopped pecans in an even layer on the bottom of the pie crust and pour the filling over them. Sprinkle the remaining pecans evenly over the filling. (Or, if preferred, roughly chop 1 cup of the pecan halves and leave the remaining ones whole; layer the chopped pecans on the bottom of the crust and then arrange the pecan halves over the filling.)

5 Bake until the filling has set 3 inches from the edge or the edges puff slightly and the center of the filling is just slightly wobbly, 45 to 50 minutes. Remove the pie from the oven and place it on a cooling rack.

6 Serve at room temperature with the whipped cream, if desired.

MAPLE PECAN PIE

The complementary flavors of maple and pecan combine in this pie to create an earthy, buttery, robust dessert. Be sure to purchase Grade B maple syrup as the darker amber color and deeper maple flavor are essential to this pie. In the variation that follows, adding bourbon complements the nuttiness of the pecans.

MAKES
One 9-inch pie

CRUST
All-Butter Pie Dough, Unbaked Single Crust (page 64; use the double crust variation if you are cutting out leaves for the border), edges crimped or decorated with cutout leaves (see page 52)

TOPPING
Maple Whipped Cream (page 316; optional)

INGREDIENTS	VOLUME	OUNCES
Sugar	½ cup	3.5
All-purpose flour	2 tbsp	-
Dark corn syrup	¾ cup	8.62
Maple syrup, Grade B	½ cup	6
Large eggs	3	-
Kosher salt	¼ tsp	-
Vanilla extract	1½ tsp	-
Unsalted butter, melted	2 tbsp	-
Pecans halves, toasted (see page 30) and chopped	3 cups	10.5

1 Preheat the oven to 400°F and set the rack in the lowest position.

2 Place the chilled crust on a baking sheet, line the crust with lightly oiled or sprayed parchment, and fill with weights. Partially blind bake the crust until lightly browned, 15 to 20 minutes. Remove the crust from the oven, remove the weights and parchment, and place the crust on a cooling rack. Reduce the oven temperature to 350°F.

3 In a medium bowl, combine the sugar and flour and whisk together. Add the corn syrup and maple syrup and mix thoroughly. Add the eggs, salt, and vanilla and mix until smooth and well incorporated. Stir in the melted butter.

4 Spread one-third of the chopped pecans in an even layer on the bottom of the pie crust and pour the filling over them. Sprinkle the remaining pecans evenly over the filling.

5 Bake until the filling has set 3 inches from the edge or the edges puff slightly and the center of the filling is just slightly wobbly, 45 to 50 minutes. Remove the pie from the oven and place it on a cooling rack.

6 Serve at room temperature with the whipped cream, if desired.

BOURBON PECAN PIE *Follow the recipe for Maple Pecan Pie, omitting the maple syrup in step 3 and increasing the corn syrup to 1¼ cups. Replace the vanilla with 2 tablespoons of a top-shelf bourbon, such as Maker's Mark, in step 3.*

CHOCOLATE ANY (OR NO) NUT PIE

A perfect pie for summertime, with a rich, creamy, no-bake chocolate filling, a smooth chocolate glaze, and your choice of crunchy nuts. Or if you prefer, serve the pie without nuts and garnish instead with shaved chocolate (see page 300).

MAKES
One 9-inch pie

CRUST
No-Bake Chocolate Cookie–Crumb Crust (page 68), chilled

INGREDIENTS	VOLUME	OUNCES
Heavy cream	1 cup	8. 4
Chopped bittersweet chocolate (not more than 65% cacao)	-	10
Cream cheese, softened at room temperature	1 cup	8
Sweetened condensed milk	⅓ cup	3.5
Vanilla extract	1 tsp	-
Kosher salt	½ tsp	-
Chopped nuts, any type, toasted (see page 30)	¾ cup	3

1 In a small saucepan, bring the heavy cream to a boil over medium heat. Remove the pan from the heat.

2 Place the chocolate in a stainless-steel bowl and pour the hot cream over it. Let stand for 5 minutes and then gently stir to incorporate. Reserve ½ cup of the chocolate mixture and set aside.

3 In the bowl of a stand mixer fitted with the paddle attachment, combine the cream cheese, condensed milk, vanilla, and salt and beat on medium speed until smooth. Gradually add the warm chocolate mixture to the cream cheese mixture and mix until creamy and smooth.

4 Pour the filling into the prepared crust. Smooth and level the filling with an offset spatula. Place the pie in the freezer for 15 to 20 minutes to set the filling.

5 Pour the reserved ½ cup of the warm chocolate mixture over the set pie filling. Smooth and level the chocolate with an offset spatula. Immediately top with the chopped nuts.

6 Chill the pie for about 1 hour, or until firm, before serving cold.

HAZELNUT COFFEE PIE

Rich and sweet coffee custard topped with toasted hazelnuts—this pie is similar to a pecan pie, but with the twist of using hazelnuts and flavoring the custard with coffee. When this recipe was developed, it was prepared with Starbucks Via single-serving instant coffee packs, which are easy to use and inexpensive. To crush the hazelnuts after toasting, wrap them in a clean kitchen towel and use a heavy-bottomed saucepan to break the nuts into halves or pieces.

MAKES
One 9-inch pie

CRUST
All-Butter Pie Dough, Unbaked Single Crust (page 64)

TOPPING
Sweetened Whipped Cream (page 313)

INGREDIENTS	VOLUME	OUNCES
Sugar	2 tbsp	-
All-purpose flour	2 tbsp	-
Dark corn syrup	1½ cups	17.25
Instant coffee or espresso powder	1 tsp	-
Large eggs	3	-
Kosher salt	¼ tsp	-
Vanilla extract	1½ tsp	-
Unsalted butter, melted	3 tbsp	-
Chopped toasted hazelnuts (see page 30)	1¾ cups	8.3

1 Preheat the oven to 400°F and set the rack in the lowest position.

2 Place the chilled crust on a baking sheet, line the crust with lightly oiled or sprayed parchment, and fill with weights. Partially blind bake the crust until lightly browned, 15 to 20 minutes. Remove the crust from the oven, remove the weights and parchment, and place the crust on a cooling rack. Reduce oven temperature to 350°F.

3 In a medium bowl, combine the sugar, flour, corn syrup, and coffee or espresso powder and mix thoroughly. Add the eggs, salt, vanilla, and melted butter and mix until smooth and well incorporated. Pour the filling into the pie crust and sprinkle the hazelnuts on top.

4 Bake until the edges puff slightly and the center of the filling is just slightly wobbly, 45 to 50 minutes. Remove the pie from the oven and place it on a cooling rack.

5 Serve at room temperature topped with the whipped cream.

WALNUT PIE

Not as strong-tasting as pecans and with a subtle earthy flavor, walnuts are a good pairing for a custard filling flavored with honey, orange, and vanilla.

MAKES
One 9-inch pie

CRUST
All-Butter Pie
Dough, Unbaked
Single Crust
(page 64)

TOPPING
Sweetened Whipped
Cream (page 313)

INGREDIENTS	VOLUME	OUNCES
Light brown sugar, packed	½ cup	4
All-purpose flour	2 tbsp	-
Light corn syrup	1 cup	11.5
Honey	½ cup	6
Large eggs	3	-
Orange zest	½ tsp	-
Kosher salt	¼ tsp	-
Vanilla extract	1½ tsp	-
Unsalted butter, melted	3 tbsp	-
Chopped toasted walnuts (see page 30)	1½ cups	6

1 Preheat the oven to 400°F and set the rack in the lowest position.

2 Place the crust on a baking sheet, line the crust with lightly oiled or sprayed parchment, and fill with weights. Partially blind bake the crust until lightly browned, 15 to 20 minutes. Remove the crust from the oven, remove the weights and parchment, and place the crust on a cooling rack. Reduce the oven temperature to 350°F.

3 In a medium bowl, combine the sugar and flour and whisk together. Add the corn syrup and honey and mix thoroughly. Add the eggs, orange zest, salt, and vanilla and mix until smooth and well incorporated. Stir in the melted butter.

4 Spread the walnuts in an even layer over the bottom of the pie crust and pour the filling over the nuts.

5 Bake until the filling has set 3 inches from the edge or the edges puff slightly and the center of the filling is just slightly wobbly, about 50 minutes. Remove the pie from the oven and place it on a cooling rack. Serve at room temperature topped with the whipped cream.

GOOBER PIE

In the South, peanuts are often referred to as "goober peas." This pie features peanuts on top of a sweet, gooey custard, and it is delicious with a scoop of vanilla ice cream—crunchy, salty, and sweet.

MAKES
One 9-inch pie

CRUST
All-Butter Pie
Dough, Unbaked
Single Crust
(page 64)

INGREDIENTS	VOLUME	OUNCES
Sugar	½ cup	3.5
All-purpose flour	2 tbsp	-
Dark corn syrup	1½ cups	17.25
Large eggs	3	-
Kosher salt	¼ tsp	-
Vanilla extract	1 tsp	-
Unsalted butter, melted	3 tbsp	-
Chopped salted dry-roasted peanuts	1½ cups	6

1 Preheat the oven to 400°F and set the rack in the lowest position.

2 Place the chilled crust on a baking sheet, line the crust with lightly oiled or sprayed parchment, and fill with weights. Partially blind bake the crust until lightly browned, 15 to 20 minutes. Remove the crust from the oven, remove the weights and parchment, and place the crust on a cooling rack. Reduce the oven temperature to 350°F.

3 In a medium bowl, combine the sugar and flour and whisk together. Add the corn syrup and mix thoroughly. Add the eggs, salt, and vanilla and mix until smooth and well incorporated. Stir in the melted butter.

4 Pour the filling into the pie crust and sprinkle the peanuts over the filling.

5 Bake until the edges puff slightly and the center of the filling is just slightly wobbly, 45 to 50 minutes. Remove the pie from the oven and place it on a cooling rack.

6 Serve at room temperature.

FUDGY WALNUT BROWNIE PIE

The filling for this pie is reminiscent of a fudgy, dense brownie studded with walnuts and bittersweet chocolate chunks. The crispy chocolate crumb crust is an added bonus in both flavor and texture. If you prefer a moister, denser texture to the filling, bake for 35 minutes instead of the recommended 40 minutes. Serve the pie with ice cream for an extra indulgence.

MAKES
One 9-inch pie

CRUST
Cookie-Crumb Crust, made with chocolate wafers (page 69), baked and cooled

INGREDIENTS	VOLUME	OUNCES
Unsalted butter, melted	½ cup (1 stick)	4
Sugar	1 cup	7
Large eggs	2	-
Vanilla extract	1 tsp	-
All-purpose flour	½ cup	2.3
Cocoa powder	⅓ cup	1
Baking powder	¼ tsp	-
Kosher salt	½ tsp	-
Chopped bittersweet chocolate, (not more than 65% cacao)	-	4
Chopped toasted walnuts (see page 30)	¾ cup	3

1 Preheat the oven to 350°F and set the rack in the lowest position.

2 In a medium bowl, combine the melted butter and sugar and whisk together. Whisk the eggs and vanilla in a small bowl. Add the egg mixture to the butter mixture in two stages, mixing until smooth and well incorporated after each addition.

3 In a separate medium bowl, combine the flour, cocoa powder, baking powder, and salt and whisk together. Add the dry ingredients to the egg mixture and stir until well incorporated. Stir in the chocolate and walnuts.

4 Pour the filling into the crumb crust and bake until the center puffs slightly, about 40 minutes. Remove the pie from the oven and place it on a cooling rack.

5 Serve at room temperature.

CANDY BAR PIE

An icebox pie that is perfect for the times when the oven should not be used. A crispy chocolate crumb crust, followed by a layer of peanuts and gooey caramel, topped with a light and creamy nougatlike peanut butter filling make this pie a perfect combination of salty and sweet—just like a candy bar!

MAKES
One 9-inch pie

CRUST
No-Bake Chocolate Cookie–Crumb Crust (page 68), chilled

INGREDIENTS	VOLUME	OUNCES
FOR THE CARAMEL:		
Water	2 tbsp	-
Sugar	½ cup	3.5
Sweetened condensed milk	⅓ cup	3.5
Light corn syrup	¼ cup	3
Unsalted butter	3 tbsp	-
Salted dry-roasted peanuts, chopped, plus more for garnish	¾ cup	2
Vanilla extract	1 tsp	-
FOR THE PEANUT BUTTER FILLING:		
Cream cheese, softened at room temperature	¼ cup	2
Peanut butter (not old-fashioned or freshly ground)	¼ cup	3
Sweetened condensed milk	¼ cup	2.65
Vanilla extract	1 tsp	-
Heavy cream	½ cup	4.2
FOR THE GANACHE:		
Heavy cream	½ cup	4.2
Roughly chopped bittersweet chocolate (not more than 65% cacao)	-	4

1 Make the caramel: In a medium heavy-bottomed saucepan, combine the water, sugar, condensed milk, corn syrup, and butter. Bring the mixture to a boil over medium-high heat, stirring constantly, and cook until a candy thermometer registers 230°F and the mixture is a rich golden caramel. Be careful not to heat the caramel past 230°F or it will become too firm and the pie will be difficult to slice. Fold in the peanuts and vanilla. Set aside to cool for 20 to 30 minutes, or until slightly set but still pourable.

2 Pour the caramel into the prepared crust. Tilt and rotate the crumb crust so the caramel coats the bottom evenly. Refrigerate until set, 20 to 30 minutes.

3 Make the peanut butter filling: In the bowl of a stand mixer fitted with the paddle attachment, combine the cream cheese and peanut butter and beat on medium speed until smooth and well combined. Gradually add the condensed milk and vanilla.

4 In a medium bowl, whip the heavy cream until it reaches medium peak. Gently fold ¼ cup of the whipped cream into the peanut butter mixture until lightened and combined. Gently fold in the remaining whipped cream in two stages. Spread the peanut butter filling over the chilled caramel layer. Smooth and level the peanut butter filling with an offset spatula. Refrigerate until set, 30 to 45 minutes.

5 Make the ganache: In a small saucepan, bring the heavy cream to a boil. Remove from the heat.

6 Place the chocolate in a stainless-steel bowl and pour the hot cream over it. Let stand for 5 minutes and then gently stir to incorporate.

7 Pour the ganache over the chilled peanut butter filling. Smooth and level the ganache with an offset spatula. Sprinkle the additional peanuts over the ganache.

8 Refrigerate until set, about 1 hour. Alternatively, the tart can be frozen for up to 30 minutes to set the filling faster. Serve chilled.

CHOCOLATE CHERRY TART

A crispy chocolate tart crust paired with tart cherry preserves and bittersweet chocolate ganache and finished with a garnish of chocolate shavings shows off a classic flavor combination.

MAKES

One 9-inch tart

CRUST

Chocolate Tart Dough (page 72), fitted into a 9-inch tart pan, blind baked, and cooled

INGREDIENTS	VOLUME	OUNCES
Bittersweet chocolate, melted, as needed for coating tart shell	-	-
Cherry preserves, made with whole tart cherries	1¾ cups	7
Heavy cream	1 cup	8.4
Roughly chopped bittersweet chocolate (not more than 65% cacao)	-	10
Grated bittersweet chocolate	-	1

1. Using a pastry brush, apply a small amount of melted bittersweet chocolate to the bottom and insides of the prepared tart crust, using just enough to coat. Allow the chocolate to set, 10 to 15 minutes. Spread the preserves in an even layer over the bottom of the tart shell. Smooth and level the preserves with an offset spatula.

2. In a small saucepan, bring the heavy cream to a boil over medium heat. Remove the pan from the heat.

3. Place the chopped chocolate in a stainless-steel bowl and pour the hot cream over it. Let stand for 5 minutes and then gently stir to incorporate.

4. Pour the chopped chocolate filling over the preserves in the tart crust. Smooth and level the filling with an offset spatula.

5. Allow the filling to cool for about 20 minutes at room temperature before topping with the grated chocolate to ensure it does not melt. Refrigerate until fully set, 1 to 2 hours.

6. Serve chilled.

ALMOND, COCONUT, AND CHOCOLATE TART

This tart has a dense chocolate custard layer capped with whole toasted almonds and sweet coconut—reminiscent of an Almond Joy candy bar.

MAKES
One 9-inch tart

CRUST
Chocolate Tart Dough (page 72), fitted into a 9-inch tart pan, blind baked, and cooled

INGREDIENTS	VOLUME	OUNCES
Light corn syrup	¾ cup	8.6
Light brown sugar, packed	½ cup	4
Kosher salt	¼ tsp	-
Unsalted butter	3 tbsp	-
Roughly chopped bittersweet chocolate (not more than 65% cacao)	-	4
Large egg	1	-
Vanilla extract	1 tsp	-
Desiccated or flaked sweetened coconut	1 cup	3
Whole almonds, lightly toasted (see page 30)	1½ cups	6.5

1 Preheat the oven to 350°F and set the rack in the lowest position.

2 In a medium saucepan, combine the corn syrup, brown sugar, salt, and butter, and heat over low to medium heat until both the butter and sugar have melted. Stir thoroughly to combine. Remove the pan from the heat and add the chocolate. Let stand for 5 minutes and then gently stir to incorporate, stirring until smooth and creamy.

3 Add the egg and vanilla and mix until smooth and well incorporated.

4 Sprinkle half of the coconut over the bottom of the tart shell. Pour the chocolate mixture over the coconut. Arrange the almonds in an even layer over the chocolate mixture, then sprinkle with the remaining coconut.

5 Bake until the filling is bubbling slightly, but the center of the filling is just slightly wobbly, 15 to 20 minutes. Remove the tart from the oven and place it on a cooling rack.

6 Serve at room temperature.

CHOCOLATE, PEANUT BUTTER, AND PRETZEL TART

A salty pretzel crust makes the perfect vessel for a creamy milk chocolate and peanut butter filling, glazed with chocolate and garnished with more crunchy crushed pretzels.

MAKES
One 9-inch tart

CRUST
Pretzel Tart Dough (page 73), fitted into a 9-inch tart pan, blind baked, and cooled

INGREDIENTS	VOLUME	OUNCES
FOR THE FILLING:		
Heavy cream	1 cup	8.4
Roughly chopped milk chocolate	-	16
Peanut butter	3 tbsp	-
FOR THE GLAZE:		
Heavy cream	2 tbsp	-
Water, warm	1 tbsp	-
Light corn syrup	1 tbsp	-
Roughly chopped milk chocolate	-	2
FOR THE GARNISH:		
Crushed pretzels	½ cup	1

1 Make the filling: In a small saucepan, bring the heavy cream to a boil over medium heat. Remove the pan from the heat.

2 Place the chocolate and peanut butter in a stainless-steel bowl and pour the hot cream over it. Let stand for 5 minutes and then gently stir to incorporate.

3 Pour the chocolate filling into the prepared tart crust. Smooth and level the filling with an offset spatula.

4 Allow the filling to cool for about 20 minutes, or until set and firm. Alternatively, the tart can be frozen for up to 30 minutes to set the filling faster.

5 Make the glaze: In a small saucepan, heat the heavy cream, water, and corn syrup over medium heat. Remove from the heat and stir in the chocolate, stirring until smooth.

6 Pour the glaze over the chilled filling. Tilt and rotate the tart so the glaze coats the top evenly. Sprinkle the crushed pretzels evenly over the glaze. Allow to set at room temperature for about 1 hour.

7 Serve at room temperature.

CRANBERRY, WHITE CHOCOLATE, AND ALMOND TART

The tart acidity of cranberries is offset by the creamy sweetness of white chocolate and caramel. This dessert uses dried cranberries, which are available year-round, making it perfect for those months when fresh fruit is unavailable.

MAKES
One 9-inch tart

CRUST
Vanilla Tart Dough (page 70), fitted into a 9-inch tart pan, blind baked, and cooled

INGREDIENTS	VOLUME	OUNCES
Heavy cream	1 cup	8. 4
Unsalted butter	4 tbsp (½ stick)	2
Sugar	¾ cup	5.3
Light corn syrup	¼ cup	3
Kosher salt	¼ tsp	-
Roughly chopped white chocolate	-	4
Sliced blanched almonds, toasted (see page 30)	1 cup	4
Roughly chopped dried cranberries	1¼ cups	5

1 Preheat the oven to 350°F.

2 In a small saucepan, bring the heavy cream and butter to a boil over medium heat. Remove the pan from the heat. Set aside.

3 To a medium heavy-bottomed saucepan over medium-high heat, add the sugar in 1- to 2-tablespoon increments, tilting and swirling the pan after each addition until the sugar is melted and is a rich golden brown color. If the sugar cooks unevenly, gently tilt or swirl the pan to evenly distribute the sugar. Add the corn syrup and salt and stir to combine.

4 Remove the pan from the heat and slowly stir in the hot cream mixture. The hot mixture will bubble up, so be cautious. If the caramel mixture seizes (begins to re-crystallize and harden), return it to the heat and stir until smooth. Set aside to cool.

5 Pour the caramel into the center of the prepared tart crust. Tilt and rotate the tart so the caramel coats the bottom evenly. Add the white chocolate, nuts, and cranberries in an even layer over the caramel, pressing them down, if necessary, to level.

6 Bake until the filling is bubbling slightly, 15 to 20 minutes. Remove the tart from the oven and place it on a cooling rack.

7 Serve at room temperature.

CARAMEL MIXED NUT TART

This tart contains four types of nuts—pistachios, hazelnuts, cashews, and macadamias—in buttery caramel with a rich and complex flavor. If you prefer another combination of nuts, substitute enough to total approximately one pound.

MAKES
One 9-inch tart

CRUST
Vanilla Tart Dough (page 70), fitted into a 9-inch tart pan, blind baked, and cooled

INGREDIENTS	VOLUME	OUNCES
Heavy cream	1 cup	8.4
Unsalted butter	4 tbsp (½ stick)	2
Sugar	1 cup	7
Light corn syrup	¼ cup	3
Kosher salt	¼ tsp	-
Vanilla extract	1 tsp	-
Whole pistachios, toasted (see page 30)	1 cup	4.25
Whole hazelnuts, toasted (see page 30)	1 cup	3.65
Whole cashews, toasted (see page 30)	1 cup	4.25
Macadamia nuts, toasted (see page 30)	1 cup	3.65

1 Preheat the oven to 350°F.

2 In a small saucepan, bring the heavy cream and butter to just under a boil over medium heat. Remove the pan from the heat. Set aside.

3 To a medium heavy-bottomed saucepan over medium-high heat, add the sugar in 1- to 2-tablespoon increments, tilting and swirling the pan after each addition until the sugar is melted and is a rich golden brown color. If the sugar cooks unevenly, gently tilt or swirl the pan to evenly distribute the sugar. Add the corn syrup and salt and stir to combine.

4 Remove the pan from the heat and slowly stir in the hot cream mixture. The hot mixture will bubble up, so be cautious. If the caramel mixture seizes (begins to re-crystallize and harden), return it to the heat and stir until smooth. Add the vanilla and nuts to the warm caramel mixture and stir to combine.

5 Pour the caramel-nut filling into the prepared tart crust.

6 Bake until the filling is bubbling slightly, 15 to 20 minutes. Remove the tart from the oven and place it on a cooling rack.

7 Serve at room temperature.

ALMOND AND PEAR TART

Frangipane is a classic and delicious pastry filling that contains almond paste, sugar, eggs, butter, and flour. In this tart, the frangipane's sweet almond flavor complements the spicy sweetness of the pears.

MAKES
One 11-inch tart

CRUST
Vanilla Tart Dough (page 70), fitted into an 11-inch tart pan, blind baked, and cooled

INGREDIENTS	VOLUME	OUNCES
Almond paste	-	4
Sugar	½ cup	3.5
Unsalted butter, room temperature	½ cup (1 stick)	4
Large eggs	2	-
Lemon zest	1 tsp	-
All-purpose flour	⅓ cup	1.5
Pears, such as Anjou or Bartlett, ripe, peeled, halved, and cored	3	-
Honey	1 tbsp	-
Sliced blanched almonds, toasted (see page 30)	¼ cup	1

1 Preheat the oven to 350°F.

2 In the bowl of a stand mixer fitted with the paddle attachment, combine the almond paste and sugar and beat on medium speed until combined. Add the butter and mix until light and smooth. Add the eggs and zest in two stages, scraping down the bowl after each addition. Add the flour and mix to combine.

3 Pour the almond filling into the prepared tart crust. Smooth and level the filling with an offset spatula. Arrange the sliced pears over the filling.

4 Bake until the filling is golden brown, 30 to 35 minutes. Remove the tart from the oven and let cool slightly.

5 Drizzle the honey over the top of the tart and sprinkle with the almonds. Serve at room temperature.

MACADAMIA AND WHITE CHOCOLATE TART

This light vanilla custard, chock-full of buttery, rich macadamia nuts, pairs perfectly with white chocolate. As macadamia nuts are fairly large, they should be cut by hand with a knife—or toasted and then crushed into pea-size pieces with the bottom of a heavy skillet.

MAKES

One 9-inch tart

CRUST

Vanilla Tart Dough (page 70), fitted into a 9-inch tart pan, blind baked, and cooled

INGREDIENTS	VOLUME	OUNCES
Unsalted butter, melted	½ cup (1 stick)	4
Sugar	1 cup	7
Kosher salt	¼ tsp	-
Large egg	1	-
Vanilla extract	1 tsp	-
All-purpose flour	⅓ cup	1.5
Chopped white chocolate	-	6
Chopped or crushed macadamia nuts, toasted (see page 30)	1½ cups	6

1 Preheat the oven to 350°F.

2 In a medium bowl, combine the melted butter, sugar, and salt and whisk together. Add the egg and vanilla and mix until smooth. Add the flour and mix until well incorporated.

3 Pour the filling into the prepared tart crust. Sprinkle the chopped white chocolate and nuts over the filling in an even layer, pressing them down, if necessary, to level.

4 Bake until the filling is bubbling slightly, 15 to 20 minutes. Remove the tart from the oven and place it on a cooling rack.

5 Serve at room temperature.

WALNUT CARAMEL TART

Walnuts have a distinctive flavor that complements many ingredients. In this tart, caramel is combined with the walnuts to bring out their unique rich and nutty flavor.

MAKES

One 9-inch round or square tart

CRUST

Vanilla Tart Dough (page 70), fitted into a 9-inch round or square tart pan, blind baked, and cooled

TOPPING

Sweetened Whipped Cream (page 313; optional)

INGREDIENTS	VOLUME	OUNCES
Heavy cream	1 cup	8.4
Sugar	1 cup	7
Kosher salt	¼ tsp	-
Vanilla extract	1 tsp	-
Chopped walnuts, toasted (see page 30)	1½ cups	6
Large egg	1	-

1 Preheat the oven to 350°F.

2 In a small saucepan, bring the heavy cream to a boil over medium heat. Remove the pan from the heat. Set aside to cool slightly.

3 To a medium heavy-bottomed saucepan over medium-high heat, add the sugar in 1- to 2-tablespoon stages, tilting or swirling the pan after each addition until the sugar is melted and is a rich golden brown color. If the sugar cooks unevenly, gently tilt or swirl the pan to evenly distribute the sugar. Add the salt and stir to combine.

4 Remove the pan from the heat and slowly stir in the hot cream. The hot mixture will bubble up, so be cautious. If the caramel mixture seizes (begins to re-crystallize and harden), return it to the heat and stir until smooth. Remove from the heat and stir in the vanilla. Set aside to cool for 30 minutes.

5 Arrange the walnuts in an even layer over the bottom of the prepared tart crust.

6 Add the egg to the caramel filling and blend until smooth and creamy. Immediately pour the caramel filling over the walnuts.

7 Bake until the filling is slightly bubbling, 15 to 20 minutes. Remove the tart from the oven and place it on a cooling rack.

8 Serve at room temperature topped with the whipped cream, if desired.

SALTED CARAMEL CHOCOLATE TART

Salted caramels have long been a treat in Brittany, France, and now enjoy immense popularity stateside as well. In this tart, a sweet caramel is topped with a sprinkling of fleur de sel—a high-quality flaked sea salt—which enhances the dense, rich bittersweet chocolate filling.

MAKES

One 9-inch tart

CRUST

Vanilla Tart Dough (page 70) or Chocolate Tart Dough (page 72), fitted into a 9-inch tart pan, blind baked, and cooled

CHOCOLATE MACADAMIA TART

Follow the recipe for the Salty Caramel Chocolate Tart, sprinkling ½ cup of roughly chopped toasted macadamia nuts into the chocolate in step 2 and proceeding with the recipe as directed. In step 8, finish the top of the tart with ½ cup of roughly chopped toasted macadamia nuts in place of the salt.

INGREDIENTS	VOLUME	OUNCES
For the filling:		
Heavy cream	1¼ cups	10.5
Roughly chopped bittersweet chocolate (not more than 65% cacao)	-	10
For the caramel topping:		
Heavy cream	⅓ cup	2.8
Sugar	½ cup	3.5
Light corn syrup	1 tsp	-
Unsalted butter	2 tbsp	-
Fleur de sel or other high-quality flaked sea salt, as needed		

1 Make the filling: In a small saucepan, bring the heavy cream to a boil over medium heat. Remove the pan from the heat.

2 Place the chocolate in a stainless-steel bowl and pour the hot cream over it. Let stand for 5 minutes and then gently stir to incorporate.

3 Pour the filling into the prepared tart crust and place the tart in the freezer for up to 30 minutes to cool.

4 Make the topping: In a small saucepan, bring the heavy cream to a boil over medium heat. Remove the pan from the heat.

5 To a medium heavy-bottomed saucepan over medium-high heat, add the sugar in 1- to 2-tablespoon stages, tilting and swirling the pan after each addition until the sugar is melted and is a rich golden brown color. If the sugar cooks unevenly, gently tilt or swirl the pan to evenly distribute the sugar. Add the corn syrup and butter and stir to combine.

6 Remove the pan from the heat and slowly stir in the hot cream. The hot mixture will bubble up, so be cautious. If the caramel mixture seizes (begins to re-crystallize and harden), return it to the heat and continue to stir until smooth.

7 Pour the caramel immediately over the chilled tart filling. Tilt and rotate the tart so the caramel coats the top evenly. Refrigerate the tart until the caramel is firm, at least 1 hour.

8 Garnish with a sprinkling of sea salt just prior to serving. Serve chilled.

CHOCOLATE TRUFFLE TART

If you enjoy dark chocolate, this is a tart for you! Be sure to use a chocolate with no more than 65 percent cacao, or it will be too intense. Garnish each dense, rich slice with a dollop of Sweetened Whipped Crème Fraîche to help offset the bittersweet chocolate.

MAKES
One 9-inch tart

CRUST
Chocolate Tart Dough (page 72), fitted into a 9-inch tart pan, blind baked, and cooled

TOPPING
Sweetened Whipped Crème Fraîche (page 317)

INGREDIENTS	VOLUME	OUNCES
FOR THE FILLING:		
Heavy cream	1 cup	8.4
Chopped bittersweet chocolate (not more than 65% cacao)	-	10
FOR THE GLAZE:		
Heavy cream	2 tbsp	-
Chopped bittersweet chocolate (not more than 65% cacao)	-	1.75
Light corn syrup	1 tbsp	-
Warm water	1 tbsp	-

1 Make the filling: In a small saucepan, bring the heavy cream to a boil over medium heat. Remove the pan from the heat.

2 Place the chocolate in a stainless-steel bowl and pour the hot cream over it. Let stand for 5 minutes and then gently stir to incorporate.

3 Pour the filling into the prepared tart crust. Let cool until set, about 1 hour. If necessary, the tart can be frozen for up to 1 hour to set the filling faster.

4 Make the glaze: In a small saucepan, bring the heavy cream to a boil over medium heat. Remove the pan from the heat.

5 Add the chocolate to the warm cream and stir until smooth. Stir in the corn syrup, and then the warm water.

6 Pour the glaze over the chilled chocolate filling. Tilt and rotate the tart so the glaze coats the top evenly. Refrigerate the tart until the glaze is firm, about 1 hour.

7 Serve chilled slices of the tart topped with the whipped crème fraîche.

CHOCOLATE–PEANUT BUTTER TRUFFLE TART *Follow the recipe for the Chocolate Truffle Tart, adding 2 tablespoons creamy peanut butter to the chopped chocolate in step 2. Garnish with Candied Peanuts (page 319).*

MILK CHOCOLATE–HAZELNUT TART

Creamy-smooth milk chocolate in a crispy hazelnut crust, garnished with crunchy toasted hazelnuts. A slice of this tart is perfect paired with a hot cup of coffee or tea.

MAKES

One 9-inch tart

CRUST

Nut Tart Dough, made with hazelnuts (page 74), fitted into a 9-inch tart pan, blind baked, and cooled

INGREDIENTS	VOLUME	OUNCES
Heavy cream	1 cup	8.4
Chopped milk chocolate	-	16
Roughly chopped hazelnuts, toasted and skins removed (see page 30)	1 cup	5

1 In a small saucepan, bring the heavy cream to a boil over medium heat. Remove the pan from the heat.

2 Place the chocolate in a stainless-steel bowl and pour the hot cream over it. Let stand for 5 minutes and then gently stir to incorporate.

3 Pour the filling into the prepared tart crust. Smooth and level the filling with an offset spatula.

4 Allow the filling to cool for 10 to 15 minutes, or until it is set enough to support the hazelnuts. Sprinkle the hazelnuts evenly over the filling, lightly pressing them into the filling, if necessary, to level. Chill the tart until firm, about 1 hour.

5 Serve chilled.

SAVORY

KALE, BACON, AND ONION QUICHE

Kale, a member of the cabbage family, is widely available during the winter and early spring. It has a mild flavor, and its dark, richly colored green leaves add contrast to the salty bacon in this quiche.

MAKES
One 9-inch quiche

CRUST
All-Butter Pie
Dough, Unbaked
Single Crust
(page 64)

INGREDIENTS	VOLUME	OUNCES
Bacon	6 slices	-
Diced onion	1 cup	5
Coarsely chopped stemmed kale	About 5½ cups	3
Freshly ground black pepper	¼ tsp	-
Balsamic vinegar	2 tsp	-
Sour cream	½ cup	4.25
Heavy cream	1¼ cups	10.5
Large eggs	3	-
Grated Parmesan, packed	½ cup	1.5

1 Preheat the oven to 400°F and set the rack in the lowest position.

2 In a medium sauté pan, cook the bacon over medium heat until crisp, 10 to 15 minutes. With a slotted spatula, transfer the bacon to paper towels to drain. Pour off all but about 2 tablespoons of the bacon fat from the pan and set aside the pan. When the bacon has cooled, chop it into ½-inch pieces.

3 Line the chilled crust with lightly oiled or sprayed parchment and fill with weights. Partially blind bake the crust until it is a matte, pale golden color, 15 to 20 minutes. Transfer the crust to a cooling rack and remove the weights and parchment. Reduce the oven temperature to 350°F.

4 Reheat the bacon fat in the sauté pan over medium heat. Add the onion and sauté until translucent and tender, 5 to 10 minutes. Add the kale, season with the pepper, and sauté until the kale is bright green and tender, 10 to 15 minutes more. Add the vinegar and deglaze the pan, scraping up the bacon bits from the bottom of the pan. Add the chopped bacon back to the pan. Remove the pan from the heat.

5 In a medium bowl, combine the sour cream, heavy cream, and eggs and whisk until thick and smooth.

6 Sprinkle half of the cheese over the bottom of the prepared crust and arrange the kale mixture in an even layer over the cheese. Pour the sour cream mixture over the filling and sprinkle evenly with the remaining cheese.

7 Bake until the center of the quiche is just set and the edges are golden brown, 30 to 40 minutes.

8 Remove the quiche from the oven and place it on a cooling rack.

9 Serve warm or at room temperature.

CHORIZO AND POBLANO QUICHE

Poblanos are dark green, almost black chiles. Their flavor ranges from mild to sharp, and when roasted they take on a rich, almost mellow sweet flavor. In this quiche, the poblano is paired with chorizo, a sausage flavored with garlic and chili powder, and a mild Monterey Jack. If you prefer more heat, use a jalapeño cheese.

MAKES
One 9-inch quiche

CRUST
All-Butter Pie Dough, Unbaked Single Crust (page 64)

INGREDIENTS	VOLUME	OUNCES
Poblano chile	1 medium	3 to 4
Canola oil	2 tbsp	-
Diced onion	½ cup	2.35
Chorizo, casings removed, crumbled	¾ cup	4
Sour cream	½ cup	4.25
Heavy cream	1¼ cups	10.5
Large eggs	3	-
Grated Monterey Jack	1 cup	3

1 Preheat the oven to 400°F and set the rack in the lowest position.

2 Roast the chile over the open flame of a gas burner, turning it frequently with tongs until the skin is completely charred and blistered. (You may also roast it under a broiler.) Place it in a bowl and cover with plastic wrap. Let sit for 15 to 20 minutes, allowing the steam to loosen the skin. Using a knife, cut off the top of the chile and slice the chile down the side. Open the chile and spread it flat, skin side up. Remove the outer skin by gently scraping it away with a knife, and then turn the chile over and cut away the inner membrane and seeds. Slice the chile into strips and roughly chop. Set aside.

3 Line the chilled crust with lightly oiled or sprayed parchment and fill with weights. Partially blind bake the crust until it is a matte, pale golden color, 15 to 20 minutes. Transfer the crust to a cooling rack and remove the weights and parchment. Reduce the oven temperature to 350°F.

4 In a medium sauté pan, heat the oil over medium heat. Add the onion and sauté until translucent and tender, 5 to 10 minutes. Add the sausage and cook until lightly browned, 10 to 15 minutes more. With a slotted spatula, transfer the sausage mixture to paper towels to drain and cool.

5 In a medium bowl, combine the sour cream, heavy cream, and eggs and whisk until thick and smooth.

6 Sprinkle half of the cheese over the bottom of the prepared crust and arrange the sausage mixture in an even layer over the cheese. Pour the sour cream mixture over the filling and sprinkle it with the chopped chile and the remaining cheese.

7 Bake until the center of the quiche is just set and the edges are golden brown, 30 to 40 minutes.

8 Remove the quiche from the oven and place it on a cooling rack.

9 Serve warm or at room temperature.

POBLANO, CORN, AND CHEDDAR QUICHE *Follow the recipe for the Chorizo and Poblano Quiche, replacing the sausage with ¾ cup corn kernels (from 3 large ears; or frozen kernels, thawed and drained), and season with ¼ teaspoon salt and ¼ teaspoon chili powder in step 4. Cook the corn until the kernels release all their liquid and it evaporates, 10 to 15 minutes. Proceed with the recipe from step 4 on, replacing the Monterey Jack with cheddar in step 6.*

BROCCOLI AND WHITE CHEDDAR QUICHE

Broccoli and sharp white cheddar combine in this quiche to create a creamy filling studded with emerald green pieces of broccoli.

MAKES

One 9-inch quiche

CRUST

All-Butter Pie Dough, Unbaked Single Crust (page 64), fitted into a 9-inch pie or quiche pan

INGREDIENTS	VOLUME	OUNCES
Broccoli florets, each 1 inch wide, with 1 to 2 inches of stem attached	6 cups	2 lb
Olive oil	2 tbsp	-
Diced onion	½ cup	2.35
Kosher salt	¼ tsp	-
Ground white pepper	¼ tsp	-
Heavy cream	1½ cups	13
Large eggs	3	-
Coarsely grated white cheddar	1 cup	3

1 Preheat the oven to 400°F and set the rack in the lowest position.

2 Line the chilled crust with lightly oiled or sprayed parchment and fill with weights. Partially blind bake the crust until it is a matte, pale golden color, 15 to 20 minutes. Transfer the crust to a cooling rack and remove the weights and parchment. Reduce the oven temperature to 350°F.

3 In a large saucepan, bring about 1 cup of water to a boil over medium heat. Add the broccoli and cover the pan. Steam the broccoli for 2 minutes, until bright green and still slightly crisp. Remove the saucepan from the heat and drain off the water. Set aside.

4 In a medium sauté pan, heat the oil over medium heat. Add the onion and sauté until translucent and tender, 5 to 10 minutes. Remove the pan from the heat. Add the steamed broccoli and season with the salt and pepper. Set aside.

5 In a medium bowl, combine the heavy cream and eggs and whisk until thick and smooth.

6 Sprinkle half of the cheese over the bottom of the prepared crust and arrange the broccoli mixture in an even layer over the cheese. Pour the heavy cream mixture over the filling and sprinkle it with the remaining cheese.

7 Bake until the center of the quiche is just set and the edges are golden brown, 30 to 40 minutes.

8 Remove the quiche from the oven and place it on a cooling rack.

9 Serve warm or at room temperature.

HAM, ASPARAGUS, AND CHEDDAR QUICHE

Ham and asparagus are a traditional combination of ingredients. Choose a high-quality country ham for this quiche. The saltiness of the ham and the sharpness of the cheddar come together nicely when combined with the sweet, tender asparagus.

MAKES
One 9-inch quiche

CRUST
All-Butter Pie Dough, Unbaked Single Crust (page 64), fitted into a 9-inch pie or quiche pan

INGREDIENTS	VOLUME	OUNCES
Asparagus, trimmed to 4-inch pieces	1 bunch	12 to 16
Olive oil	2 tbsp	-
Kosher salt	½ tsp	-
Ground pepper	½ tsp	-
Heavy cream	1½ cups	13
Large eggs	3	-
Coarsely grated sharp cheddar	1 cup	3
Diced ham (from a high-quality country ham)	1 cup	4

1 Preheat the oven to 425°F.

2 In a medium bowl, toss the asparagus with the oil, ¼ teaspoon of the salt, and the pepper. Spread the asparagus in an even layer on a rimmed baking sheet and roast for 8 to 10 minutes, or until tender. Transfer the pan to a cooling rack. Reduce the oven temperature to 400°F and set the rack in the lowest position.

3 Line the chilled crust with lightly oiled or sprayed parchment and fill with weights. Partially blind bake the crust until it is a matte, pale golden color, 15 to 20 minutes. Remove the crust from the oven and place it on a cooling rack. Remove the weights and parchment. Reduce the oven temperature to 350°F.

4 In a medium bowl, combine the heavy cream, eggs, and remaining ¼ teaspoon salt and whisk until thick and smooth.

5 Sprinkle half of the cheese over the bottom of the prepared crust and arrange the roasted asparagus and the ham in an even layer over the cheese. Pour the heavy cream mixture over the asparagus layer and sprinkle it with the remaining cheese.

6 Bake until the center of the quiche is just set and the edges are golden brown, 30 to 40 minutes. Transfer to a cooling rack. Serve warm or at room temperature.

TOMATO, MOZZARELLA, AND BASIL GALETTE

A galette is a free-form, rustic version of a tart with a savory or sweet filling. One of its main advantages is the ease and simplicity of preparation. For a particularly lovely and tasty presentation, select heirloom tomatoes in a variety of colors.

MAKES

One 9-inch galette

CRUST

Cornmeal Pastry Dough (page 78), rolled into a 13-inch disc, fitted into a 9-inch pie pan (edges left untrimmed)

TOMATO AND GOAT CHEESE GALETTE

Follow the recipe for the Tomato, Mozzarella, and Basil Galette, replacing the mozzarella with a 4-ounce log of goat cheese, crumbled, in step 3 and omitting the Parmesan. Omit the basil and instead sprinkle with 1 tablespoon fresh thyme.

INGREDIENTS	VOLUME	OUNCES
Tomatoes, rinsed, cut crosswise into ⅓-inch-thick slices	2 large	About 1 lb
Olive oil	2 tbsp	-
Kosher salt	½ tsp	-
Freshly ground black pepper	¼ tsp	-
Grated mozzarella	⅔ cup	5.7
Grated Parmesan	¼ cup	0.75
Egg wash, as needed (page 308)		
Basil chiffonade	1 tbsp	-

1 Preheat the oven to 400°F.

2 Spread the sliced tomatoes on a baking sheet. Sprinkle with the oil, salt, and pepper. Roast the tomatoes for 20 to 30 minutes, or until soft and slightly shriveled. Remove the pan from the oven and place it on a cooling rack. Let the tomatoes cool for 10 to 15 minutes. Reduce the oven temperature to 350°F.

3 Spread the mozzarella over the dough, leaving a 2- to 3-inch border. Top the mozzarella with the roasted tomatoes and then sprinkle evenly with the Parmesan.

4 Fold the border of dough over the filling to partially cover, pleating the excess slightly to create a uniform appearance. Carefully lift each pleat and brush egg wash under each fold to seal. Brush the top of the border with egg wash.

5 Bake for 20 to 30 minutes, or until the crust is golden brown.

6 Transfer the galette to a cooling rack. Sprinkle with the basil and serve warm.

SPINACH AND FETA QUICHE

This spanakopita-inspired quiche has the traditional flavors of spinach, onion, and feta baked in kataifi, a grated buttery phyllo crust. This product is available in specialty food stores in the frozen food aisle.

MAKES
One 9-inch quiche

CRUST
One Kataifi
(shredded phyllo)
Shell (see recipe)

INGREDIENTS	VOLUME	OUNCES
Kataifi (shredded phyllo), thawed	About 2 cups	4
Unsalted butter, melted	3 tbsp	-
Olive oil	2 tbsp	-
Small-diced onion	¾ cup	3.7
Garlic, minced	1 clove	-
Coarsely chopped stemmed spinach	About 5 cups	7
Kosher salt	¼ tsp	-
Freshly ground black pepper	¼ tsp	-
Heavy cream	¾ cup	6.3
Ricotta	½ cup	4.3
Large eggs	3	-
Crumbled feta	¾ cup	4

1   Preheat the oven to 350°F and set the rack in the lowest position.

2   Set a 9-inch pie pan on a rimmed baking sheet and line the pan with the thawed kataifi in a layer ½ inch thick, allowing it to extend over the edge of the pan by ½ to 1 inch, as it will shrink during baking. Using a pastry brush, brush the sides and top surface of the dough with the melted butter. Bake until light golden brown, 15 to 20 minutes. Remove the phyllo shell from the oven and place it on a cooling rack.

3   In a medium sauté pan, heat the oil over medium heat. Add the onion and sauté until translucent and tender, 5 to 10 minutes. Add the garlic and sauté until fragrant, 2 to 3 minutes. Add the spinach, salt, and pepper and sauté until the spinach has wilted and all of its liquid has evaporated, 5 to 10 minutes more. Remove the pan from the heat. Transfer the spinach mixture to a colander and allow any remaining liquid to drain.

4 In a medium bowl, combine the heavy cream, ricotta, and eggs and whisk until thick and smooth. Stir in the feta and the spinach mixture.

5 Pour the filling into the phyllo shell. Smooth and level the filling with an offset spatula.

6 Bake until the center of the quiche is just set and the edges are golden brown, 30 to 40 minutes.

7 Remove the quiche from the oven and place it on a cooling rack.

8 Serve warm or at room temperature.

CHICKEN POTPIE

A tender and flaky top crust gives way to reveal chunks of moist chicken and vegetables in gravy when cutting into this homey favorite. This potpie must be baked in a deep-dish pie pan as it will overfill a standard pie plate. Preparing this dish with only the top crust eliminates the always-soggy bottom crust.

MAKES

One 9-inch deep-dish potpie

CRUST

All-Butter Pie Dough for single crust (page 64), rolled out, shaped into a single top crust, and frozen (see Forming a Deep-Dish Pie Topper, page 52)

INGREDIENTS	VOLUME	OUNCES
Chicken breasts, boneless and skinless	2	12
Pearl onions, frozen or fresh (if fresh, see recipe for preparation)	¾ cup	4.25
Unsalted butter	1 tbsp	-
Carrots, peeled and cut crosswise into ¼-inch rounds	3	4
Celery, cut crosswise into ¼-inch slices	2 stalks	1.2
All-purpose flour	¼ cup	1.2
Chicken stock	1¾ cups	15.75
Kosher salt	½ tsp	-
Freshly ground black pepper	½ tsp	-
Peas, frozen	¾ cup	3.45
Egg wash (page 308), as needed		

1 Preheat the oven to 425°F and set the rack in the lowest position.

2 Fill a small saucepan halfway with water. Bring the water to a simmer over medium heat. Add the chicken and cook at a low simmer until the thickest section of the breast registers an internal temperature of 165°F on a thermometer, 10 to 15 minutes. Remove the chicken, transfer it to a cutting board, and let cool. Shred the chicken using two forks, pulling the meat apart into small pieces.

3   If using fresh pearl onions, fill a small saucepan halfway with water and bring to a boil. Add the onions and blanch for 2 minutes. Remove the saucepan from the heat, drain off the water, and let the onions cool until they are able to be handled. Cut off each bulb end and squeeze out the onion from the opposite end. Discard the peels.

4   In a medium sauté pan, melt the butter over medium heat. Add the carrots and celery and sauté until tender, 5 to 10 minutes. Add the flour, stirring until incorporated, and cook, stirring constantly, for 2 to 3 minutes. Slowly stir in the chicken stock and allow the mixture to come to a simmer and thicken while continuing to gently stir, about 5 minutes. Remove the pan from the heat and season the mixture with the salt and pepper. Stir in the chicken, pearl onions, and peas.

5   Pour the filling into a deep-dish pie pan set on a baking sheet. Place the frozen, pre-shaped and egg-washed crust on top of the filling, and brush it with a second coat of egg wash. Immediately transfer the pie to the oven and bake until the crust is golden brown and the filling is bubbling, 45 to 50 minutes.

6   Remove the potpie from the oven and place it on a cooling rack.

7   Let the potpie rest for 20 minutes before serving. The filling will continue to thicken as it cools.

BEEF POTPIE

Hearty chunks of beef and vegetables in a rich, savory sauce are covered by a flaky, golden top crust in this potpie variation. Like the Chicken Potpie (page 261), it must be baked in a deep-dish pie pan.

MAKES

One 9-inch deep-dish potpie

CRUST

All-Butter Pie Dough for single crust (page 64), rolled out, shaped into a single top crust, and frozen (see Forming a Deep-Dish Pie Topper, page 52)

INGREDIENTS	VOLUME	OUNCES
Red potatoes, cubed	3	8
Canola oil	3 tbsp	-
Beef, sirloin steak, cubed	-	12 to 16
Garlic, minced	2 cloves	-
Sherry	2 tbsp	-
Beef stock	1¾ cups	15.75
Carrots, peeled and cut crosswise into ¼-inch rounds	3	4
Mushrooms, halved	6 to 8	6
Tomato paste	2 tbsp	1.2
All-purpose flour	¼ cup	1.2
Kosher salt	½ tsp	-
Freshly ground black pepper	½ tsp	-
Pearl onions, frozen or fresh (if fresh, see page 262 for preparation)	¾ cup	4.25
Peas, frozen	¾ cup	3.45
Egg wash (page 308), as needed		

1 Place the potatoes in a small saucepan and add enough water to cover them by 1 inch. Cover the pan and bring the water to a boil. Cook the potatoes until tender, 10 to 15 minutes. Remove the pan from the heat and drain off the water.

2 In a medium sauté pan, heat 2 tablespoons of the oil over medium heat. Add the sirloin and sauté until browned on all sides, about 10 minutes. Add the garlic and sauté,

stirring, until fragrant, about 30 seconds. Add the sherry to deglaze the pan and scrape up the browned bits from the bottom of the pan. Cook until the sherry has evaporated, about 5 minutes. Pour in 1½ cups of the beef stock. Simmer the sirloin over medium heat for 1 to 1½ hours, or until tender.

3 Meanwhile, preheat the over to 425°F.

4 In a separate medium sauté pan, heat the remaining 1 tablespoon oil over medium heat. Add the carrots and cook until tender, about 5 minutes. Add the mushrooms and cook until they have released their liquid and softened, 4 to 5 minutes. Add the tomato paste and flour and stir until incorporated. Cook, stirring constantly, for 2 to 3 minutes. Slowly pour in the remaining ¼ cup beef stock and stir until smooth. Remove the pan from the heat.

5 Add the vegetable mixture to the sirloin. Bring to a simmer over medium-high heat and cook, stirring, until well combined and thickened, about 5 minutes. Remove the pan from the heat and season the mixture with the salt and pepper. Immediately stir in the potatoes, onions, and peas.

6 Pour the filling into a deep-dish pie pan on a baking sheet. Place the frozen, pre-shaped and egg-washed crust on top of the filling, and brush it with a second coat of egg wash. Immediately transfer the pie to the oven and bake until the crust is golden brown and the filling is bubbling, 45 to 50 minutes.

7 Remove the potpie from the oven and place it on a cooling rack.

8 Let the potpie rest for 20 minutes before serving. The filling will continue to thicken as it cools.

VEGETABLE POTPIE

Bright asparagus, mild leeks, earthy mushrooms, and sweet carrots in a rich and creamy vegetable stock make this a memorable spring potpie. As with the other potpies in this book, it must be baked in a deep-dish pie pan.

MAKES

One 9-inch deep-dish potpie

CRUST

All-Butter Pie Dough for single crust (page 64), rolled out, shaped into a single top crust, and frozen (see Forming a Deep-Dish Pie Topper, page 52)

INGREDIENTS	VOLUME	OUNCES
Red potatoes, cubed	3	8
Canola oil	2 tbsp	-
Leeks, white parts only, cleaned and thinly sliced	1 to 2	-
Carrots, peeled and cut crosswise into ¼-inch rounds	3	4
White button mushrooms, halved	6 to 8	6
Garlic, minced	2 cloves	-
Sherry	2 tbsp	-
All-purpose flour	¼ cup	1.2
Vegetable stock	1¾ cups	15.75
Heavy cream	¼ cup	2.1
Kosher salt	½ tsp	-
Freshly ground black pepper	½ tsp	-
Asparagus, cleaned, trimmed to ¼-inch pieces, and blanched	1 bunch	12 to 16
Peas, frozen	¾ cup	3.45
Egg wash (page 308), as needed		

1 Preheat the oven to 425°F.

2 Place the potatoes in a small saucepan and add enough water to cover them by 1 inch. Cover the pan and bring the water to a boil. Cook the potatoes until tender, 10 to 15 minutes. Remove the pan from the heat and drain off the water.

3 In a medium sauté pan, heat the oil over medium heat. Add the leeks and carrots and sauté until tender, about 5 minutes. Add the mushrooms and cook until they have released their liquid and softened, 4 to 5 minutes. Add the garlic and cook, stirring, until fragrant, about 30 seconds. Add the sherry to deglaze the pan and scrape up the browned bits from the bottom of the pan. Cook until the sherry has evaporated, about 5 minutes. Add the flour and stir until incorporated. Cook, stirring constantly, for 2 to 3 minutes. Slowly stir in the vegetable stock and the heavy cream. Bring the mixture to a simmer and cook until thickened, about 5 minutes. Remove the pan from the heat and season the mixture with the salt and pepper. Immediately stir in the potatoes, asparagus, and peas.

4 Pour the filling into a deep-dish pie pan on a baking sheet. Place the frozen, pre-shaped and egg-washed crust on top of the filling, and brush with a second coat of egg wash. Immediately transfer to the oven and bake until the crust is golden brown and the filling is bubbling, 30 to 40 minutes.

5 Remove the potpie from the oven and place it on a cooling rack.

6 Let the potpie rest for 20 minutes before serving. The filling will continue to thicken as it cools.

BLACK BEAN AND CORN EMPANADAS

Empanadas are a traditional portable turnover or hand pie. Their name is derived from the Spanish word *empanar*, which means "to bake in a pastry." Empanada dough is made with masa harina, a type of corn flour. Mexican oregano is a variety of oregano that has a stronger flavor than the more commonly used kind. Both masa harina and Mexican oregano can be found in most supermarkets or in Latin specialty markets. If you prefer more heat, choose a jalapeño cheese and add a pinch of cayenne powder.

MAKES

Twelve to eighteen 4½-inch empanadas

CRUST

Empanada Dough (page 79), chilled

INGREDIENTS	VOLUME	OUNCES
Canola oil	1 tbsp	-
Small-diced onion	½ cup	2.3
Garlic, minced or pressed through a garlic press	1 clove	-
Mexican oregano	1 tsp	-
Ground cumin	½ tsp	-
Corn kernels (from 2 large ears; or frozen kernels, thawed and drained)	¾ cup	3.3
Kosher salt	½ tsp	-
Freshly ground black pepper	½ tsp	-
Rinsed and drained black beans	1¼ cups	8
Grated Monterey Jack	¾ cup	2.2
Oil for frying, as needed		

1 In a medium sauté pan, heat the 1 tablespoon oil over medium heat. Add the onion and sauté until translucent and tender, 5 to 10 minutes. Add the garlic, oregano, and cumin and cook for 30 seconds. Add the corn and sauté just until heated, about 3 minutes. Remove the pan from the heat, season the mixture with the salt and pepper, and stir in the black beans. Transfer to a bowl and let cool for 20 minutes. Add the cheese and stir to combine.

2 Roll out the empanada dough to ⅛ inch thick and cut it into 4½-inch discs with a round cutter, rerolling scraps as necessary. Make at least 1 dozen discs. Place 2 tablespoons of filling in the center of each disc. Brush the edges of each dough disc with water, fold in half, and seal the seams using the tines of a fork. Transfer the empanadas to sheet pans lined with parchment paper, cover, and refrigerate until very firm, at least 1 hour, before frying so that the butter in the dough does not melt when the empanadas are fried. The empanadas can be wrapped tightly in plastic wrap and refrigerated for up to 24 hours, or frozen for up to 3 weeks. Defrost frozen empanadas before frying them.

3 Fill a deep skillet with 2 inches of oil and heat the oil to 350°F. Fry the empanadas in batches, adding them to the hot oil a few at a time, being careful not to overcrowd the pan. Fry until golden brown and crisp, turning as needed to brown both sides, 3 to 4 minutes. Alternatively, the empanadas can be brushed with egg wash and baked fresh or frozen at 400°F for 20 to 25 minutes, or until golden brown.

4 Drain on paper towels and serve immediately.

BEEF AND CHEESE EMPANADAS

This mild beef and cheese filling can be also prepared with hard-boiled eggs, raisins, and olives—traditional in many South American countries including Chile and Argentina—as described in the variation that follows. If you prefer a spicier filling, add cayenne powder to taste.

MAKES

Twelve 4½-inch empanadas

CRUST

Empanada Dough (page 79), chilled

INGREDIENTS	VOLUME	OUNCES
Canola oil	1 tbsp	-
Finely diced onion	½ cup	2.3
Mexican oregano	1 tsp	-
Ground cumin	½ tsp	-
Garlic, minced or pressed through a garlic press	2 cloves	-
Tomato paste	2 tbsp	-
Ground beef, 85% lean	-	8
Beef stock	½ cup	4.5
Kosher salt	½ tsp	-
Freshly ground black pepper	½ tsp	-
Grated Monterey Jack	1 cup	3
Oil for frying, as needed		

1 In a medium sauté pan, heat the 1 tablespoon oil over medium heat. Add the onion and cook until translucent and tender, 5 to 10 minutes. Add the oregano, cumin, and garlic and cook for 30 seconds. Stir in the tomato paste and continue to cook just until heated, 2 to 3 minutes. Add the beef and cook until browned, 5 to 10 minutes. Drain off the fat from the pan. Pour in the beef stock and allow the mixture to come to a simmer. Cook until thickened and some of the liquid has evaporated, 3 to 5 minutes. Remove the pan from the heat and season the mixture with the salt and pepper. Transfer to a bowl and let cool for 20 minutes. Add the cheese and stir to combine.

2 Roll out the empanada dough to ⅛ inch thick and cut it into 4½-inch discs with a round cutter, rerolling scraps as necessary. Make at least 1 dozen discs. Place 2 tablespoons of the filling in the center of each disc. Brush the edges of each dough disc with water, fold in half, and seal the seams using the tines of a fork. Transfer the empanadas to sheet pans lined with parchment paper, cover, and refrigerate until very firm, at least 1 hour, before frying so that the butter in the dough does not melt when the empanadas are fried. The empanadas can be wrapped tightly in plastic wrap and refrigerated for up to 24 hours, or frozen for up to 3 weeks. Defrost frozen empanadas before frying them.

3 Fill a deep skillet with 2 inches of oil and heat the oil to 360°F. Fry the empanadas in batches, adding them to the hot oil a few at a time, being careful not to overcrowd the pan. Fry until golden brown and crisp, turning as needed to brown both sides. Alternatively, the empanadas can be brushed with egg wash and baked fresh or frozen at 400°F for 15 to 20 minutes, or until golden brown.

4 Drain on paper towels and serve immediately.

BEEF, OLIVE, AND HARD-BOILED EGG EMPANADAS *Follow the recipe for Beef and Cheese Empanadas, adding a pinch of cayenne pepper to the seasoning and 1 roughly chopped hard-boiled egg, 2 tablespoons raisins, and ½ cup of green olives, roughly chopped, to the beef mixture after cooking. Omit the Monterey Jack.*

BACON, CRÈME FRAÎCHE, AND SPRING ONION TART

Spring onions are less pungent than mature onions, and can be found in farmer's markets during early spring. The onions are white and green, similar to scallions in appearance but with a more developed bulb. When roasted or sautéed, spring onions become sweet and mild, a perfect pairing with bacon and crème fraîche.

MAKES

One 9-inch or 11-inch tart

CRUST

All-Butter Pie Dough for single crust (page 64), fitted into a 9- or 11-inch tart pan and chilled

INGREDIENTS	VOLUME	OUNCES
Bacon	5 slices	-
Spring onions, cleaned, pale green and white parts only, cut into diagonal slices (reserve ¼ cup of green tops, sliced into ¼-inch pieces)	5 to 6	12 to 16
Olive oil	2 tbsp	-
Kosher salt	¼ tsp	-
Freshly ground black pepper	¼ tsp	-
Crème fraîche	¾ cup	6.5
Heavy cream	½ cup	4.2
Large eggs	2	-
Coarsely grated Gruyère, packed	¾ cup	1.5

1 Preheat the oven to 400°F.

2 In a medium sauté pan, cook the bacon over medium heat until crisp, 10 to 15 minutes. With a slotted spatula, transfer the bacon to paper towels to drain and cool. When cool enough to handle, chop the bacon into ½-inch pieces. Set aside.

3 In a medium bowl, toss the onions with the oil, salt, and pepper. Spread in an even layer on a baking sheet and roast until soft and golden brown with a slight char on the edges, 20 to 30 minutes. Remove the pan from the oven and place it on a cooling rack. Set the oven rack in the lowest position.

4 Line the chilled crust with lightly oiled or sprayed parchment and fill with weights. Partially blind bake the crust until it is a matte, pale golden color, 15 to 20 minutes. Transfer the crust to a cooling rack and remove the weights and parchment. Reduce the oven temperature to 350°F.

5 In a medium bowl, combine the crème fraîche, heavy cream, and eggs and whisk until thick and smooth.

6 Sprinkle half of the cheese over the bottom of the prepared crust and arrange the roasted onions in an even layer over the cheese. Sprinkle with the bacon. Pour the crème fraîche mixture over the bacon and onions and sprinkle with the remaining cheese.

7 Bake until the center of the tart is just set and the edges are golden brown, 20 to 25 minutes. If more top color is preferred, switch the oven to a broil setting and broil for 3 to 4 minutes, or until the cheese begins to brown.

8 Remove the tart from the oven and place it on a cooling rack.

9 Serve warm or at room temperature.

ROASTED CAULIFLOWER, GRUYÈRE, AND PARMESAN TART

When cauliflower is roasted, its flavor is heightened and becomes buttery sweet. Combined here with nutty, earthy Gruyère and Parmesan, this is a tart not to be missed.

MAKES

One 9-inch or 11-inch tart

CRUST

All-Butter Pie Dough for single crust (page 64), fitted into a 9- or 11-inch tart pan and chilled

INGREDIENTS	VOLUME	OUNCES
Cauliflower, cut into bite-size florets	1 small	12 to 16
Olive oil	3 tbsp	-
Kosher salt	¾ tsp	-
Freshly ground black pepper	¼ tsp	-
Sour cream	1 cup	8.5
Heavy cream	¼ cup	2.1
Large eggs	2	-
Mustard powder	½ tsp	-
Coarsely grated Gruyère, packed	¾ cup	1.5
Grated Parmesan, packed	¼ cup	0.8

1 Preheat the oven to 400°F.

2 In a medium bowl, toss the cauliflower with the oil, ¼ teaspoon of the salt, and the pepper. Spread the cauliflower in an even layer on a rimmed baking sheet and roast until soft and golden brown, 20 to 30 minutes. Remove the pan from the oven and place it on a cooling rack.

3 Line the chilled crust with lightly oiled or sprayed parchment and fill with weights. Partially blind bake the crust until it is a matte, pale golden color, 15 to 20 minutes. Transfer the crust to a cooling rack and remove the weights and parchment. Reduce the oven temperature to 350°F.

4 In medium bowl, combine the sour cream, heavy cream, eggs, the remaining ½ teaspoon salt, and the mustard powder and whisk until thick and smooth.

5 Sprinkle half of the Gruyère and Parmesan over the bottom of the prepared crust and arrange the cauliflower in an even layer over the cheeses. Pour the sour cream mixture over the cauliflower and sprinkle with the remaining cheeses.

6 Bake until the center of the tart is just set and the edges are golden brown, 20 to 25 minutes. If more top color is preferred, switch the oven to a broil setting and broil for 3 to 4 minutes, or until the cheeses begin to brown.

7 Remove the tart from the oven and place it on a cooling rack.

8 Serve warm or at room temperature.

ASPARAGUS GRUYÈRE TART

The first asparagus of the season is the most tender. In this tart the asparagus pairs beautifully with a Gruyère and Parmesan custard. When arranged in a circle, the purple tops and green spears create a beautiful tart for a springtime brunch table.

MAKES
One 9-inch or
11-inch tart

CRUST
All-Butter Pie
Dough for single
crust (page 64), fitted
into a 9- or 11-inch
tart pan and chilled

INGREDIENTS	VOLUME	OUNCES
Asparagus, cleaned and trimmed into 1- to 2-inch pieces	1 bunch	12 to 16
Olive oil	2 tbsp	-
Kosher salt	½ tsp	-
Freshly ground black pepper	¼ tsp	-
Heavy cream	1¼ cups	10.5
Large eggs	3	-
Coarsely grated Gruyère, packed	½ cup	1.25
Grated Parmesan, packed	¼ cup	0.8

1 Preheat the oven to 425°F and set the rack in the center position.

2 In a medium bowl, toss the asparagus with the oil, ¼ teaspoon of the salt, and the pepper. Spread the asparagus in an even layer on a rimmed baking sheet and roast until soft and tender, 8 to 10 minutes. Remove the pan from the oven and place it on a cooling rack.

3 Reduce the oven temperature to 400°F and set the rack in the lowest position. Place the chilled crust on a baking sheet, line the crust with lightly oiled or sprayed parchment, and fill with weights. Partially blind bake the crust until it is a matte, pale golden color, 15 to 20 minutes. Transfer the crust to a cooling rack and remove the weights and parchment. Reduce the oven temperature to 350°F.

4 In a medium bowl, combine the heavy cream, eggs, and remaining ¼ teaspoon salt and whisk until thick and smooth.

5 Sprinkle half of the Gruyère and Parmesan cheeses over the bottom of the prepared crust and arrange the asparagus in a circle over the cheese. Pour the heavy cream mixture over the asparagus, and sprinkle with the remaining cheeses.

6 Bake until the center of the tart is just set and the edges are golden brown, 20 to 25 minutes. If more top color is preferred, switch the oven to a broil setting and broil for 3 to 4 minutes, or until the cheeses begin to brown.

7 Remove the tart from the oven and place it on a cooling rack.

8 Serve warm or at room temperature.

CRAB AND CHIVE TART

In many regions of the United States, fresh pasteurized lump crabmeat is readily available April through November, but it also can be purchased flash-frozen or canned. Here the delicate, sweet flavor of the crab is complemented by mild chives, sweet red bell peppers, and Old Bay Seasoning—the traditional flavors of a crab cake in a crispy cornmeal crust.

MAKES
One 9-inch tart

CRUST
Cornmeal Pastry Dough (page 78), fitted into a 9-inch tart or quiche pan and chilled

INGREDIENTS	VOLUME	OUNCES
Unsalted butter	1 tbsp	-
Diced red bell pepper	½ cup	2.5
Heavy cream	1½ cups	13
Large eggs	3	-
Old Bay Seasoning	½ tsp	-
Grated Gruyère	¾ cup	2.25
Lump crabmeat	¾ cup	4
Chopped chives	2 tbsp	-

1 Preheat the oven to 400°F and set the rack in the lowest position.

2 Line the chilled crust with lightly oiled or sprayed parchment and fill with weights. Partially blind bake the crust until it is a matte, pale golden color, 15 to 20 minutes. Transfer the crust to a cooling rack and remove the weights and parchment. Reduce the oven temperature to 350°F.

3 In a medium sauté pan, melt the butter over medium heat. Add the red peppers and sauté for 5 to 10 minutes, or until tender. Set aside.

4 In a medium bowl, combine the heavy cream, eggs, and Old Bay and whisk until thick and smooth.

5 Sprinkle half of the cheese over the bottom of the prepared crust and arrange the sautéed peppers and the crabmeat in an even layer over the cheese. Pour the heavy cream mixture over the peppers and crabmeat layer and sprinkle it with the remaining cheese and the chives.

6 Bake until the center of the tart is just set and the edges are golden brown, 20 to 25 minutes.

7 Remove the tart from the oven and place it on a cooling rack.

8 Serve warm or at room temperature.

CHERRY TOMATO AND RICOTTA TART

In the summertime, cherry tomato plants often produce more tomatoes than can be eaten out of hand. This tart is the perfect solution. Roasting the tomatoes heightens their sweetness, making them a delicious foil for the crisp, buttery cornmeal crust.

MAKES

One 9-inch or 11-inch tart

CRUST

Cornmeal Pastry Dough (page 78), fitted into a 9- or 11-inch tart pan and chilled

INGREDIENTS	VOLUME	OUNCES
Cherry tomatoes, halved	1 pint	12
Olive oil	2 tbsp	-
Kosher salt	½ tsp	-
Freshly ground black pepper	¼ tsp	-
Ricotta	1 cup	8.7
Heavy cream	¼ cup	2.1
Large eggs	2	-
Chopped chives	1 tbsp	-
Grated Parmesan	¾ cup	2.25

1 Preheat the oven to 400°F.

2 In a medium bowl, toss the tomatoes with the oil, ¼ teaspoon of the salt, and the pepper. Spread the tomatoes in an even layer on a rimmed baking sheet and roast for 40 to 50 minutes, or until the tomatoes are soft and slightly shriveled. Remove the pan from the oven and place it on a cooling rack. Set the oven rack in the lowest position.

3 Line the chilled crust with lightly oiled or sprayed parchment and fill with weights. Partially blind bake the crust until it is a matte, pale golden color, 15 to 20 minutes. Transfer the crust to a cooling rack and remove the weights and parchment. Reduce the oven temperature to 350°F.

4 In medium bowl, combine the ricotta, heavy cream, eggs, remaining ¼ teaspoon salt, and the chives and whisk until thick and smooth.

5 Sprinkle half of the Parmesan over the bottom of the prepared tart crust and arrange the tomatoes in an even layer, cut side up, over the cheese. Pour the ricotta mixture over the tomatoes and sprinkle with the remaining Parmesan.

6 Bake until the center of the tart is just set and the edges are golden brown, 20 to 25 minutes. If more top color is preferred, switch the oven to a broil setting and broil for 3 to 4 minutes, or until the cheese begins to brown.

7 Remove the tart from the oven and place it on a cooling rack.

8 Serve warm or at room temperature.

PROSCIUTTO, SPINACH, AND RICOTTA TART *Follow the recipe for the Cherry Tomato and Ricotta Tart, replacing the tomatoes with ½ cup diced onion, 12 ounces stemmed fresh spinach, and ½ cup chopped prosciutto. For step 2, in a medium sauté pan over medium heat, heat 1 tablespoon of the oil. Add the onion and cook until translucent and tender, 5 to 10 minutes. Add the spinach and cook until it has wilted and all of its liquid has evaporated, 5 to 10 minutes more. Remove the spinach from the pan and set aside in a medium bowl. In the same pan, heat the remaining 1 tablespoon oil over medium heat. Add the chopped prosciutto and cook for 4 to 5 minutes. Add the prosciutto to the spinach mixture and stir to combine. Proceed with the recipe from step 3.*

MUSHROOM AND LEEK TART

For this tart, select dark brown cremini mushrooms, which have a slightly more complex and fuller flavor than the common cultivated white mushroom. The cremini mushrooms' earthy flavor balances the tanginess of the crème fraîche and makes for a memorable tart.

MAKES
One 9-inch or
11-inch tart

CRUST
All-Butter Pie
Dough for single
crust (page 64), fitted
into a 9- or 11-inch
tart pan and chilled

INGREDIENTS	VOLUME	OUNCES
Unsalted butter	2 tbsp	-
Leeks, white parts only, cleaned and thinly sliced	3 to 4	-
Chicken stock	¼ cup	2.25
Kosher salt	¼ tsp	-
Freshly ground black pepper	¼ tsp	-
Cremini mushrooms, thinly sliced	10 to 12 medium	6 to 7
Crème fraîche	¾ cup	6.1
Heavy cream	¼ cup	2.1
Large eggs	2	-
Coarsely grated Gruyère, packed	1 cup	3

1 Preheat the oven to 400°F and set the rack in the lowest position.

2 Line the chilled crust with lightly oiled or sprayed parchment and fill with weights. Partially blind bake the crust until it is a matte, pale golden color, 15 to 20 minutes. Transfer the crust to a cooling rack and remove the weights and parchment. Reduce the oven temperature to 350°F.

3 In a medium sauté pan, melt 1 tablespoon of the butter over medium heat. Add the leeks and sauté until translucent and softened, 8 to 10 minutes. Reduce the heat to low and stir in the chicken stock, salt, and pepper. Simmer until almost all of the liquid has evaporated and the leeks are tender, about 15 minutes. Remove from the pan, transfer to a medium bowl, and set aside to cool.

4 In a medium sauté pan, melt the remaining 1 tablespoon butter over medium heat. Add the mushrooms and sauté over medium heat until they have released their liquid and softened, 4 to 5 minutes. Remove the pan from the heat. Set aside.

5 In another medium bowl, combine the crème fraîche, heavy cream, and eggs and whisk until thick and smooth.

6 Sprinkle half of the cheese over the bottom of the prepared crust and arrange the leeks and the mushrooms in an even layer over the cheese. Pour the crème fraîche mixture over the filling and sprinkle with the remaining cheese.

7 Bake until the center of the tart is just set and the edges are golden brown, 20 to 25 minutes. If more top color is preferred, switch the oven to a broil setting and broil until the cheese starts to brown, 3 to 4 minutes.

8 Remove the tart from the oven and place it on a cooling rack. Serve warm or at room temperature.

ARTICHOKE AND PARMESAN TART

Creamy delicate artichoke hearts pair well with the sharp flavor of Parmesan and the richness of eggs. When choosing canned artichokes, select artichokes packed in water instead of oil, and be sure to thoroughly rinse off the brine before using.

MAKES

One 9-inch or 11-inch tart

CRUST

Parmesan Pastry Dough (page 77), fitted into a 9- or 11-inch tart pan and chilled

INGREDIENTS	VOLUME	OUNCES
Unsalted butter	2 tbsp	-
Artichoke hearts, drained, rinsed, outer leaves removed, and sliced in half	-	One (14-oz) can
Ground pepper	¼ tsp	-
Garlic, diced	1 to 2 cloves	-
Sour cream	1 cup	8.5
Heavy cream	¼ cup	2.1
Large eggs	2	-
Grated Parmesan	1 cup	3

1 Preheat the oven to 400°F and set the rack in the lowest position.

2 Line the chilled crust with lightly oiled or sprayed parchment and fill with weights. Partially blind bake the crust until it is a matte, pale golden color, 15 to 20 minutes. Transfer the crust to a cooling rack and remove the weights and parchment. Reduce the oven temperature to 350°F.

3 In a medium sauté pan, melt the butter over medium heat. Add the artichokes, pepper, and garlic and sauté until the artichokes are softened and tender, 8 to 10 minutes. Remove the pan from the heat. Set aside.

4 In a medium bowl, combine the sour cream, heavy cream, and eggs and whisk until thick and smooth.

5 Sprinkle half of the cheese over the bottom of the prepared crust and arrange the artichokes in an even layer over the cheese. Pour the sour cream mixture over the artichokes and sprinkle with the remaining cheese.

6 Bake until the center of the tart is just set and the edges are golden brown, 20 to 25 minutes. If more top color is preferred, switch the oven to broil and broil for 3 to 4 minutes, or until the cheese begins to brown.

7 Remove the tart from the oven and place it on a cooling rack.

8 Serve warm or at room temperature.

CARAMELIZED ONION AND GOAT CHEESE TART

When onions are caramelized, they develop a deep flavor with nutty undertones. For this tart, it is best to choose sweet onions, such as Vidalia or Walla Walla. Their juicy sweetness produces a richness that, when set alongside the subtle yet earthy goat cheese, results in an exceptional flavor combination.

MAKES
One 9-inch or
11-inch tart

CRUST
All-Butter Pie
Dough for single
crust (page 64), fitted
into a 9- or 11-inch
tart pan and chilled

INGREDIENTS	VOLUME	OUNCES
Unsalted butter	1 tbsp	-
Sweet onion, thinly sliced	1 large	10
Kosher salt	¼ tsp	-
Sugar	Pinch	-
Heavy cream	1 cup	8.4
Large eggs	2	-
Fresh goat cheese, cut into ¼-inch rounds	¾ cup	3

1 Preheat the oven to 400°F and set the rack in the lowest position.

2 Line the chilled crust with lightly oiled or sprayed parchment and fill with weights. Partially blind bake the crust until it is a matte, pale golden color, 15 to 20 minutes. Transfer the crust to a cooling rack and remove the weights and parchment. Reduce the oven temperature to 350°F.

3 In a medium sauté pan, melt the butter over medium-high heat. Add the onion, salt, and sugar and sauté, stirring often to prevent the onions from sticking to the pan and burning, until translucent and soft, 15 to 20 minutes. Reduce the heat to medium-low and continue cooking until the onions are a deep golden brown, 15 to 20 minutes more. Remove from the heat and set aside.

4 In a medium bowl, combine the heavy cream and eggs and whisk until smooth.

5 Spread the onions over the bottom of the crust and arrange the cheese in an even layer over the onions. Pour the heavy cream mixture over the cheese.

6 Bake until the center of the tart is just set and the edges are golden brown, 20 to 25 minutes.

7 Remove the tart from the oven and place it on a cooling rack.

8 Serve warm or at room temperature.

SMOKED HAM AND BRIE TART

Brie is a soft ripened cheese. Its flavor can range from mild to nutty to savory and pungent. Here the saltiness of the smoked ham creates a perfect pairing.

MAKES

One 9-inch or 11-inch tart

CRUST

All-Butter Pie Dough for single crust (page 64), fitted into a 9- or 11-inch tart pan and chilled

INGREDIENTS	VOLUME	OUNCES
Unsalted butter	1 tbsp	-
Leek, white and pale green parts only, cleaned and thinly sliced	1 medium	3
Chicken stock	¼ cup	2.25
Freshly ground black pepper	¼ tsp	-
Heavy cream	1 cup	8.4
Mustard powder	½ tsp	-
Large eggs	2	-
Brie, white rind removed, thinly sliced	-	3
Smoked ham, cut into ¼-inch dice	¾ cup	3

1 Preheat the oven to 400°F and set the rack in the lowest position.

2 Line the chilled crust with lightly oiled or sprayed parchment and fill with weights. Partially blind bake the crust until it is a matte, pale golden color, 15 to 20 minutes. Transfer the crust to a cooling rack and remove the weights and parchment. Reduce the oven temperature to 350°F.

3 In a medium sauté pan, melt the butter over medium heat. Add the leeks and sauté until translucent and softened, 8 to 10 minutes. Reduce the heat to low and stir in the chicken stock and pepper. Simmer until almost all of the liquid has evaporated and the leeks are tender, about 15 minutes more. Transfer the leeks to a medium bowl and set aside to cool.

4 In a medium bowl, combine the heavy cream, mustard powder, and eggs and whisk until thick and smooth.

5 Spread the leeks in an even layer over the bottom of the prepared crust and arrange the cheese and ham over the leeks. Pour the heavy cream mixture over the cheese and ham.

6 Bake until the center of the tart is just set and the edges are golden brown, 20 to 25 minutes.

7 Remove the tart from the oven and place it on a cooling rack.

8 Serve warm or at room temperature.

FINISHING TECHNIQUES AND RECIPES

The recipes beginning on page 304 include crumb toppings, meringues, washes and glazes, jellies and preserves, as well as elements for garnish, such as chocolate and nuts. Uncomplicated and easy to prepare, these recipes will lend that special touch to your pie or tart. Crumb toppings, often used with fruit fillings, help retain moisture during and after baking, while adding texture and crispness; while a sprinkling of coarse sugar on top of a double-crust pie contributes a sweet, satisfying crunch. Adding nuts, chocolate, or a dusting of confectioners' sugar can also add flavor as well as eye appeal. Just remember: A garnish should complement and enhance a pie or tart without distracting from its color, texture, or flavor.

BAKED CRUMB TOPPINGS

These sweet, buttery, baked crumb-top crusts lend a crispy and crunchy finish to pies or tarts. Streusel toppings traditionally are a combination of butter, flour, and granulated sugar and are sandier in texture than crumble toppings. Crumb toppings generally include brown sugar and spices and have a crisper and crunchier texture than streusels. Many crumb toppings also include oats or nuts, which provide chewiness and crunchiness to the topping once baked.

CREATING TEXTURE

Regardless of the method you choose for mixing, you can control the finished texture of the topping. For a larger, softer, more cookielike crumb crust, blend the mixture thoroughly. The more you work it between your fingers or in the food processor or mixer, the more it will clump together in larger pieces. When the butter is left in large, irregular, pea-size pieces, the texture of the baked crumb crust becomes sandier or crispier. To create an even crispier texture, melt the required amount of butter, let it cool until it is lukewarm (never use hot butter), and then add it to the other ingredients. Allow the topping to sit for 15 to 20 minutes before placing it on the pie or tart. This resting time allows the fat to be fully absorbed by the dry ingredients and create a better crumb structure on top of the pie or tart.

When placing the streusel or crumb topping on the pie or tart, do not press it into the filling, or the filling will soak into the crumble and cause it to become soggy.

MIXING STREUSEL OR CRUMB TOPPINGS

As when making pie and tart crusts, the textures of these toppings are also affected by the method of rubbing in (cutting in) or handling the butter.

Mixing by Hand

Place the ingredients into a shallow, medium bowl and cut the small-cubed cold butter into the dry ingredients using your fingertips, a pastry blender, or two forks until the mixture looks like coarse irregular crumbs.

Mixing with a Food Processor

Place the dry ingredients in the bowl of a food processor fitted with the steel cutting blade and pulse for 15 to 20 seconds to combine. With the food processor off, add the cold butter and then pulse for 3 to 5 seconds, or 8 to 10 times. The mixture should look like coarse irregular crumbs.

Mixing with a Stand Mixer

Place the dry ingredients in the bowl of a stand mixer fitted with the paddle attachment and mix on low speed to combine. Cut the cold butter into ½-inch pieces. With the mixer off, add the butter to the mixing bowl and mix on medium speed for 1 to 2 minutes, until the butter is well incorporated.

WASHES AND GLAZES

Egg or dairy washes serve various functions in pie and tart making. Finishing washes and glazes act as a protective coat, sealing the pastry shell from moisture or the drying effects of air. They also provide a decorative element, lending shine and gloss to a finished pie or tart. Washes and glazes can also add sweetness and flavor. Lastly, they can serve as "glue" for attaching pieces of unbaked pastry or for holding the finishing touches of sugar, spices, or salt in place during and after baking.

For any wash or glaze, you should apply a fairly thin coating and avoid puddling any excess glaze or wash. A soft, natural-bristle pastry brush works best for this job. If the wash or glaze seems too thick to apply, whisk in a teaspoon or two of water to thin it out.

EGG AND DAIRY WASHES

Various washes can be applied to a crust prior to baking; each has a distinctive effect (see photo, next page). Selecting a wash is a personal choice. In my opinion, the best wash is the traditional whole egg wash, thinned with a little water if necessary, with a pinch of salt (see page 308 for recipe).

INGREDIENT	RESULT
Milk or cream	Even reddish brown color, matte finish
Whole egg	Intense yellow golden color, shiny finish
Egg yolk	Deep brown color, highly glossy finish
Egg white	No color, very shiny, crisp finish

Different washes produce different colors and shine.

Milk

Heavy Cream

Whole Egg

Egg White

Egg Yolk

MERINGUE TOPPINGS

One of the most common decorative techniques for finishing pies and tarts is to top them with a meringue. Many novice and experienced bakers find meringues difficult and frustrating to produce—meringues can bead or break down, tear or puddle underneath, or shrink after baking. Food safety is also a concern because many recipes call for uncooked, or "common," meringue, which contains raw egg whites, to be added before the pastry is baked. I recommend always using a cooked meringue, such as a Swiss or Italian meringue, for topping so that food safety is never an issue.

The recipe should be consulted to determine the desired peak before whipping. For topping or garnishing a pie or tart, a medium or stiff meringue is most often used. Soft meringues are generally incorporated into dough or batter.

Making Meringue Toppings

The key to topping a pie or tart properly is to use an offset spatula or a rubber spatula to spread the meringue. This prevents air pockets from forming in the meringue top, which detract from the beauty of the pie or tart when sliced. Spread the meringue evenly, bringing it against the side of the pie or tart crust so that the meringue will not shrink away from the sides. To create decorative peaks and swirls on the meringue topping, use the back of the offset spatula or a spoon. (Alternatively, you can also pipe meringue into decorative designs; just be sure to pipe all the way to the edge of the crust as above.) Meringue toppings are typically browned in the oven or using a kitchen torch as shown below.

SERVING AND STORAGE

Meringues are best served on the same day as they are made, otherwise they will begin to break down. Any pie or tart filling containing eggs should be stored in the refrigerator, and herein lies a dilemma: If meringues are stored in the refrigerator, they will bead regardless of how long they have been baked in the oven, so again, it's best to serve the pie on the same day! If you want to make a meringue-topped pie or tart in advance, you can prepare the pie or tart ahead of time, but prepare the meringue and finish the dessert on the day you serve it.

PIPING MERINGUE AND OTHER TOPPINGS

To create beautiful piped garnishes with meringues or whipped cream, you will need a pastry bag and pastry tips (see page 13) and a little creativity. Larger tips work best for meringues and whipped cream. It is a good idea to try a few practice designs on a piece of plastic wrap or parchment paper before piping directly onto the pie or tart.

To assemble and fill a pastry bag, first cut the tip off the bag so that the pastry tip will fit snugly inside without popping out. Insert the tip. Twist the tip end of the bag to close it and tuck a bit of the bag inside the tip. Fold over the edge of the bag by about one-third to form a cuff and set the bag inside a container 4 to 5 inches in diameter and about 8 inches tall.

Fill the bag one-third to one-half full with meringue or whipped cream. (Do not overfill.) Turn up the cuff and twist the top of the bag closed. Lift the bag from the container and gently push the filling toward the tip.

To hold the pastry bag, grasp the top of the bag with the thumb and forefinger of one hand and hold the twisted end closed. Use your other hand to gently hold the bag close to the tip and to guide the movement of the bag. Do not squeeze the bag with both hands; instead, apply gentle pressure from the top of the bag as you pipe and use the hand closest to the tip to control the flow of the bag's contents.

Use a culinary torch to evenly brown the exterior of a meringue topping.

TROUBLESHOOTING MERINGUES

Beading	The sugar was not properly dissolved, or the meringue was overbaked.
Breaking down	The meringue was exposed to moisture or humidity.
Burning	The temperature was too high, or the heat was too direct.
Deflating	The meringue was underbeaten or overbeaten.
Puddling	The meringue was underbaked.
Rubbery	The meringue was overbeaten or overbaked.
Shrinking	The meringue was not attached to the edge of the pie crust or tart crust.
Weeping	The meringue was underbeaten.

JELLIES AND PRESERVES

Like using egg washes, using jellies or preserves is another way to seal in freshness and enhance the appearance of pies and tarts. Apricot is the most widely used preserve as it has the most neutral flavor and complements most fillings, but other jams or jellies can be used with equally successful outcomes. When baking juicy fruit pies, the glaze can be brushed into the bottom of an unbaked pastry shell to prevent the bottom crust from absorbing liquid from the fruit. The glaze can also be brushed into the bottom of a prebaked pie or tart shell before it is filled, to retain crispness.

Before being applied, jellies and preserves should be heated until bubbly but not boiling, and then passed through a fine-mesh strainer to remove any solids. If applying the glaze on top of a baked tart, it should be applied shortly after the tart or pie is removed from the oven, creating a glossy finish and sealing in the freshness of the just-baked item. Alternatively, if finishing a tart topped with fresh fruit or berries, apply the glaze just prior to serving, as the fruit can become soggy if glazed and left to sit.

ICINGS

A simple combination of confectioners' sugar, water, and flavoring creates an icing that can easily garnish and finish hand pies and slab pies. Use the tines of a fork to drizzle the frosting over the pastry. If adding toasted nuts or sugar, sprinkle immediately over the icing while it is still wet, so the topping will adhere.

DAIRY GARNISHES

Whipped cream is the first and seemingly the most basic dairy garnish that comes to mind. But there are also several other dairy-based accompaniments, such as crème fraîche or mascarpone. Whipped cream is a very quick and simple garnish to make, and is easy to flavor with fruit purées, liqueurs, or extracts.

TIPS FOR SUCCESSFUL WHIPPED CREAM

- *Sweeten and flavor the cream after it begins to foam. If ingredients are added too early, the cream will take longer to whip.*

- *Whipping cream on lower speeds results in a more stable product.*

- *To make a whipped cream that last longer, stabilize it with a small amount of gelatin (see page 315).*

- *If whipped cream loses its volume after refrigeration, gently whip it to revive it and increase its volume.*

- *Granulated or superfine sugars are the best sweeteners for whipped creams. Avoid using confectioners' sugar; it contains starch, which, when used in too great a quantity, can add a chalky flavor to the whipped cream.*

- *If you are uncertain about how long to whip your cream, it is helpful to finish it by hand with a whisk, which allows for more control.*

The sparkly garnish of coarse or decorative sugars atop a fruit pie not only makes the dessert appealing, but also lends it a satisfying crunch and sweetness. Typically, garnishes not only lend flavor, but also can communicate the flavor profile of the pie or tart, suggesting elements of the filling. Other decorative garnishes include confectioners' sugar, flaky sea salt, toasted or candied nuts, spices, chocolate shavings or curls, and cocoa powder.

Chocolate Shavings and Curls

Begin with a high-quality bar of chocolate and a vegetable peeler. As chocolate is sensitive to heat, including the heat from your hands, it is important not to touch the chocolate directly with your hands. Keep one end of the chocolate bar wrapped, or wrap it in plastic wrap, and only hold the portion that is covered.

To shave or curl the chocolate, simply shave off the desired amount from the bar using a vegetable peeler held as shown at right. Use short strokes to make short shavings. Use longer strokes to produce longer shavings that may curl slightly. If more delicate curls are desired, slowly shave the chocolate from the narrowest edge.

The temperature of the chocolate determines the appearance of the finished shavings or curls. Use cold chocolate if shards are desired; these will create shattered pieces. Use slightly warmer chocolate for bigger, more rounded curls. Be sure to use a metal offset spatula to transfer any chocolate shaving or curls to a plate; using your hands could cause the chocolate to melt. If not using immediately, store chocolate shavings or curls in the refrigerator.

Making chocolate shavings

STORING AND TRANSPORTING PIES AND TARTS

Homemade pies and tarts are best served fresh, the same day they are prepared, but there are certainly times when you will need to make a pie or tart ahead of time. Fruit or nut pies and tarts, left whole and uncut and properly stored, are better than cream pies for serving the next day. Their texture can also be improved by a brief time in the oven prior to serving. In many cases, pies and tarts can also be prepared ahead of time and then frozen whole (see page 303).

SHELF LIFE OF PIES AND TARTS

TYPE OF PIE OR TART	STORAGE	KEEPING
Fruit	Serve same day	2 to 3 days at room temperature; 3 to 4 days refrigerated
Custard or cream	Immediately refrigerate	Refrigerated: 24 hours if topped with dairy topping; up to 3 days if untopped
Nut or chocolate	Serve same day	3 to 4 days refrigerated

REFRESHING PIES AND TARTS

Many pies and tarts (with the exception of refrigerated or cream based) improve when reheated at low to moderate temperatures (300° to 350°F) for 20 to 30 minutes. Reheating time will vary depending on whether a whole pie or tart is being reheated or just a slice. Refreshing a pie or tart in this manner helps to bring the crust back from soft to crispy and warms the filling. Do not use a microwave to rewarm pies or tarts; the crust will become soggy and limp, losing all of its crispness.

TRANSPORTING PIES AND TARTS

Pies and tarts are communal desserts; they taste even better when shared. Several options are available for transporting your pies and tarts to family events, potlucks, or community events or activities. Pie baskets, often handmade, are one traditional and lovely option. Modern plastic pie holders will protect the *pie during transport. Vintage aluminum stackable holders can be purchased at flea markets. These are available in a wide range of styles, from clean and simple to embellished with decals or hand painting. Additionally, fabric pie or tart totes can be sewn. Many free patterns are available on the Internet.*

FREEZING PIES AND TARTS

For time-saving convenience, many pies and tarts can be frozen either after assembly or after baking. When freezing unbaked pies and tarts after assembly, the advantage is a crispy bottom crust at the time of baking, but the compromise is a filling that may not properly set and may become soupy. If the pie or tart is baked and then frozen, the trade-off is that the filling will properly set, but the crust can become soggy and lose its crispness.

TIPS FOR SUCCESS: FREEZING WHOLE PIES AND TARTS

- *Chose a metal or tin baking dish or pan. Ovenproof tempered glass can break if exposed to sudden temperature extremes.*

- *If freezing a pie or tart in an ovenproof glass dish, take care either to defrost the pie in the refrigerator before baking, or place it in a cold oven and then turn the oven on to preheat the glass as the oven preheats, placing a sheet of foil on the rack.*

- *To freeze a whole pie without the dish, line the pan with plastic wrap before forming the bottom crust. Freeze the pie until firm, then pop the pie out of the baking dish, rewrap in plastic wrap, and store until ready to bake.*

- *Choose a fruit pie or tart recipe with tapioca as the thickener. Flour does not hold up well when frozen.*

- *Freeze the unwrapped pie or tart for 1 to 2 hours, until the surface is hard, to protect the crust or surface from being damaged during wrapping; then wrap well with plastic wrap once firm.*

- *If freezing a double-crust pie, egg wash prior to freezing to improve the gloss and shine. Cut vents after brushing on the egg wash (otherwise they will be sealed shut with the wash) and before freezing.*

STREUSEL

In German, the word *streusel* means "sprinkled" or "strewn." A true streusel topping is similar in texture to sand when mixed. When used to top a pie or tart, it provides a sweet and crisp finish.

MAKES
About 1 cup

INGREDIENTS	VOLUME	OUNCES
Sugar	⅓ cup	2.4
All-purpose flour	½ cup	2.3
Ground cinnamon	½ tsp	-
Kosher salt	¼ tsp	-
Unsalted butter, cold, cut into ½-inch cubes	4 tbsp (½ stick)	2

1 In a medium bowl, combine the sugar, flour, cinnamon, and salt.

2 Add the butter to the flour mixture, tossing to coat. Cut the fat into the mixture using your fingertips, a pastry blender, or two forks until the mixture looks like coarse irregular crumbs.

3 Distribute the streusel evenly over the pie or tart and bake as directed. If not using immediately, store the streusel in an airtight container in the refrigerator.

BROWN SUGAR STREUSEL

This streusel is darker in color and has a deeper and more caramelized flavor.

MAKES
About 1½ cups

INGREDIENTS	VOLUME	OUNCES
Dark or light brown sugar, packed	½ cup	4
All-purpose flour	¾ cup	3.5
Ground cinnamon	½ tsp	-
Kosher salt	¼ tsp	-
Unsalted butter, cold, cut into ½-inch cubes	4 tbsp (½ stick)	2

1 In a medium bowl, combine the sugar, flour, cinnamon, and salt.

2 Add the butter to the flour mixture, tossing to coat. Cut the fat into the mixture using your fingertips, a pastry blender, or two forks until the mixture looks like coarse irregular crumbs.

3 Distribute the streusel evenly over the pie or tart and bake as directed. If not using immediately, store the streusel in an airtight container in the refrigerator.

NUT STREUSEL

A sweet, sandy version of streusel topping with the added crunch of nuts! Any nut can be used in this recipe. The key to the crunch and the full nut flavor is to toast the nuts and then cool them to room temperature before adding them to the other ingredients. This recipe makes enough to cover a pie or tart comfortably. If you end up with extra topping, place it in an airtight container and freeze it; it will keep for up to six months.

MAKES
About 2 cups

INGREDIENTS	VOLUME	OUNCES
Sugar	½ cup	3.5
All-purpose flour	½ cup	2.3
Ground cinnamon	1 tsp	-
Kosher salt	¼ tsp	-
Unsalted butter, cold, cut into ½-inch cubes	4 tbsp (½ stick)	2
Almonds or other nuts, toasted (see page 30) and roughly chopped	½ cup	2.5

1 In a medium bowl, combine the sugar, flour, cinnamon, and salt.

2 Add the butter and chopped nuts to the flour mixture, tossing to coat. Cut the fat into the mixture using your fingertips, a pastry blender, or two forks until the mixture looks like coarse irregular crumbs.

3 Distribute the streusel evenly over the pie or tart and bake as directed. If not using immediately, store the streusel in an airtight container in the freezer.

BROWN SUGAR AND OAT CRUMBLE

The oats in this crumble create chewiness and also lend crispness. For this recipe, either old-fashioned or quick-cooking oats can be used. The texture will be more "toothy" with the larger old-fashioned oats, and more uniform with the smaller quick-cooking oats.

MAKES
About 2 cups

INGREDIENTS	VOLUME	OUNCES
All-purpose flour	⅓ cup	1.5
Oats, old-fashioned or quick-cooking	1 cup	3
Light brown sugar, packed	⅓ cup	2.5
Ground cinnamon	½ tsp	-
Kosher salt	¼ tsp	-
Unsalted butter, cold, cut into ½-inch cubes	4 tbsp (½ stick)	2

1 In a medium bowl, combine the flour, oats, sugar, cinnamon, and salt.

2 Add the butter to the flour mixture, tossing to coat. Cut the fat into the mixture using your fingertips, a pastry blender, or two forks until the mixture looks like coarse irregular crumbs.

3 Distribute the crumble evenly over the pie or tart and bake as directed. If not using immediately, store the crumble in an airtight container in the refrigerator.

NOTE *If making the crumble in a food processor, stir in the oats by hand after pulsing in the butter to avoid chopping the oats.*

EGG WASH

An all-purpose egg wash that yields a deep yellow crust with a shiny, glossy finish.

	INGREDIENTS	VOLUME	OUNCES
MAKES About ¼ cup	Large egg	1	-
	Water	1 tsp	-
	Kosher salt	Pinch	-

1 In a small bowl, combine the egg, water, and salt using a wire whisk.

2 Apply the wash to the crust with a pastry brush. Garnish and bake as directed.

SWISS MERINGUE

In this method, warming the egg whites and sugar dissolves the sugar to create a smooth texture, and heats the eggs for a food-safe and stable meringue.

MAKES
About 6 cups

INGREDIENTS	VOLUME	OUNCES
Egg whites	4	4.8
Sugar	1 cup	7

1 Fill a medium saucepan halfway with water and bring to a simmer.

2 In the heatproof bowl of a stand mixer fitted with the whip attachment, whip the egg whites on low speed for 1 to 2 minutes, or until frothy and soft peaks begin to form. With the mixer off, add the sugar, and then whip for 1 minute until the sugar is blended into the whites.

3 Remove the bowl from the stand mixer and place it over the pan of simmering water. Using a whisk, foam the eggs by hand until the mixture registers 140°F on a candy thermometer.

4 Transfer the bowl back to the stand mixer and whisk on high speed until thick and glossy and the desired peak is reached. Use as directed or desired.

ITALIAN MERINGUE

A meringue made with a cooked sugar syrup is called an *Italian meringue*. This extremely stable, food-safe foam works well for topping pies and tarts.

MAKES
About 7 cups

INGREDIENTS	VOLUME	OUNCES
Sugar	¾ cup	5.25
Water	¼ cup	2.4
Egg whites	5	6

1 Spray a heatproof glass measuring cup with nonstick cooking spray and set it aside.

2 In a heavy-bottomed saucepan, combine ½ cup of the sugar with the water. Cook over medium heat without stirring until the mixture registers 230°F on a candy thermometer. Gently stir and continue to cook while you foam the egg whites.

3 Meanwhile, in the bowl of a stand mixer fitted with the whip attachment, whip the egg whites on medium speed until frothy and light. Add the remaining ¼ cup sugar and whip the meringue to medium peaks. Reduce the mixer speed to low.

4 When the sugar syrup reaches 240°F (soft-ball stage), remove the pan from the heat and pour the syrup into the greased measuring cup. Pour the syrup into the meringue in a slow, steady stream.

5 Raise the mixer speed to high and whip until the mixture cools to room temperature. Use as directed or desired.

BASIC JELLY GLAZE

Select a high-quality preserve or jelly. The less expensive products often have a higher percentage of water and will become too thin when heated. If you want to brighten up the flavor of the jelly, add a teaspoon of lemon or orange juice—or add another layer of flavor with a tablespoon of a liqueur, such as Cointreau, Grand Marnier, or cognac.

MAKES
About 1 cup

INGREDIENTS	VOLUME	OUNCES
Preserves or jelly	1 cup	8
Lemon juice (optional)	1 tsp	-
Liqueur (optional)	1 tbsp	-

1　In a small saucepan, melt the preserves over medium heat. Simmer the melted preserves, taking care not to allow them to boil, for 5 to 10 minutes, or until thickened. Remove the pan from the heat. Stir in the lemon juice or liqueur, if using.

2　Pass the melted preserves through a fine-mesh strainer into a small bowl and allow to cool for 5 minutes. If the glaze is refrigerated after this point, or is allowed to cool too long, it will have to be reheated before being applied to a pie or tart. Use a pastry brush to brush the glaze evenly over the pie or tart.

VANILLA ICING GLAZE

An infinite variety of flavors can be created by adding extracts, liqueurs, or fruit juices to this simple and easy-to-make recipe.

MAKES
About 1 cup

INGREDIENTS	VOLUME	OUNCES
Confectioners' sugar	½ cup	2
Vanilla extract	½ tsp	-
Milk, plus more as needed	2 tbsp	-

1 In a small bowl, mix together the confectioners' sugar and vanilla. Add the milk and stir to combine. If necessary, add more milk, 1 tablespoon at a time, until the glaze is smooth and fluid.

2 With a fork, drizzle the glaze over the pie or tart. If garnishing with nuts or decorative sugar, add the topping immediately before the glaze has time to set.

LEMON ICING GLAZE *Follow the recipe for Vanilla Icing Glaze, substituting 2 teaspoons of lemon juice for some of the milk in step 1.*

SWEETENED WHIPPED CREAM

Lightly sweetened, delicate and airy, this is a basic recipe for whipped cream. Omit the sugar for an unsweetened cream.

MAKES
About 2 cups

INGREDIENTS	VOLUME	OUNCES
Heavy cream, cold	1 cup	8.4
Granulated or superfine sugar	1 tsp	-
Vanilla extract	1 tsp	-

1 Chill the bowl and whip attachment of a stand mixer in the freezer for 30 minutes.

2 In the chilled bowl with the chilled whip attachment, beat the heavy cream on low speed until frothy, about 1 minute. Slowly add the sugar and vanilla. Raise the mixer speed to medium and continue beating for about 1 minute. Raise the speed to medium-high and continue beating until the cream is smooth, thick, and doubled in volume. If you are uncertain about how long to whip the cream, finish it by hand with a whisk.

3 Serve immediately, or refrigerate for up to 3 hours before using.

BOURBON WHIPPED CREAM

This is a basic way to add your own signature flavor to whipped cream. Multiple flavor variations can be added to this recipe. Simply substitute any liqueur, fruit juice, or purée for the bourbon.

	INGREDIENTS	VOLUME	OUNCES
MAKES About 2 cups	Heavy cream, cold	1 cup	8.4
	Bourbon	1½ tsp	-
	Granulated sugar	1 tbsp	-

1 Chill the bowl and whip attachment of a stand mixer in the freezer for 30 minutes.

2 In the chilled bowl with the chilled whip attachment, beat the heavy cream on low speed until frothy, about 1 minute. Slowly add the bourbon and sugar. Raise the mixer speed to medium and continue beating for about 1 minute. Raise the speed to medium-high and continue beating until the cream is smooth, thick, and doubled in volume. If you are uncertain about how long to whip your cream, finish it by hand with a whisk.

3 Serve immediately, or refrigerate for up to 3 hours before using.

CHOCOLATE WHIPPED CREAM *Follow the recipe for Bourbon Whipped Cream, omitting the bourbon and adding 2 tablespoons sifted Dutch-process cocoa powder with the sugar in step 2.*

STABILIZED WHIPPED CREAM

When whipped cream is stabilized with gelatin, it will not break down or weep, and it will stay firm much longer than traditional whipped cream.

MAKES
About 2 cups

INGREDIENTS	VOLUME	OUNCES
Water, cold	1 tbsp	-
Powdered gelatin	½ tsp	-
Heavy cream, cold	1¼ cups	10.5
Sugar	1 tbsp	-

1 Chill the bowl and whip attachment of a stand mixer in the freezer for 30 minutes.

2 Place the water in a heatproof glass bowl and then sprinkle the gelatin over the water. Do not stir. Set aside for 10 minutes to let the gelatin bloom (see page 58).

3 Set the bowl over a small saucepan of simmering water. With a spatula, stir the gelatin until it is clear and the gelatin has dissolved. Set aside to cool at room temperature until the mixture is tepid, but still liquid.

4 In the chilled bowl with the chilled whip attachment, beat the heavy cream on low speed until frothy, about 1 minute. Slowly add the sugar and gelatin. Raise the mixer speed to medium and continue beating for about 1 minute, or until the cream forms medium peaks.

5 Spread the whipped cream on top of a cooled filling or serve immediately. If you reserve this cream before using, you will need to rewhip it to lighten it before use.

MAPLE WHIPPED CREAM

With a strong maple flavor, this whipped cream is perfect for nut pies and tarts, as well as for pumpkin pies!

MAKES
About 2 cups

INGREDIENTS	VOLUME	OUNCES
Heavy cream, cold	1 cup	8.4
Maple syrup, Grade B	¼ cup	-
Vanilla extract	1 tsp	-

1 Chill the bowl and whip attachment of a stand mixer in the freezer for 30 minutes.

2 In the chilled bowl with the chilled whip attachment, beat the heavy cream on low speed until frothy, about 1 minute. Slowly add the maple syrup and vanilla. Raise the mixer speed to medium and continue beating for about 1 minute. Raise the speed to medium-high and continue beating until the cream is smooth, thick, and doubled in volume. If you are uncertain about how much to whip the cream, finish it by hand with a whisk.

3 Serve immediately, or refrigerate for up to 3 hours before using.

SWEETENED WHIPPED CRÈME FRAÎCHE

This tangy and nutty-flavored cultured dairy product is an especially pleasant accompaniment to chocolate or fruit pies and tarts. It has a rich velvety texture due to its high fat content. Crème fraîche can be found in the specialty dairy area of most major supermarkets.

MAKES
About 2 cups

INGREDIENTS	VOLUME	OUNCES
Crème fraîche, cold	1 cup	8.4
Heavy cream, cold	1 cup	8.4
Sugar	¼ cup	1.75

1 Chill the bowl and whip attachment of a stand mixer in the freezer for 30 minutes.

2 In the chilled bowl with the chilled whip attachment, combine the crème fraîche and heavy cream and beat on low speed until frothy, about 1 minute. Slowly add the sugar. Raise the mixer speed to medium and continue beating for about 1 minute. Raise the speed to medium-high and continue beating until the cream is smooth, thick, and doubled in volume. If you are uncertain about how much to whip the cream, finish it by hand with a whisk.

3 Serve immediately, or refrigerate for up to 3 hours before using.

WHIPPED MASCARPONE TOPPING

Mascarpone is a mild, soft Italian cheese with a smooth and velvety texture. Here, it is lightened with whipped cream and lightly sweetened, a perfect garnish for chocolate or fruit pies and tarts.

MAKES
About 2 cups

INGREDIENTS	VOLUME	OUNCES
Mascarpone, room temperature	1 cup	8.4
Heavy cream, cold	½ cup	4.2
Sugar	3 tbsp	-
Vanilla extract	1 tsp	-

1 In the bowl of a stand mixer fitted with the whip attachment, combine the mascarpone and cream and beat on low speed until smooth, about 1 minute. Slowly add the sugar and vanilla. Raise the mixer speed to medium and continue beating for about 1 minute. Raise the speed to medium-high and continue beating until the mixture is smooth and thick. If you are uncertain about how far to whip the cream, finish it by hand with a whisk.

2 Serve immediately, or refrigerate for up to 3 hours before using.

WHIPPED ESPRESSO MASCARPONE TOPPING *Follow the recipe for Whipped Mascarpone Topping, adding ½ teaspoon Starbucks Via Ready Brew Italian Roast Coffee Powder to the cream in step 1, stirring to combine.*

CANDIED WHOLE NUTS

Caramelized nuts, when sprinkled on just before serving, create a sweet and crunchy contrast to a cream-filled pie or tart.

MAKES
About 2 cups

INGREDIENTS	VOLUME	OUNCES
Nuts (any type)	½ cup	1.5
Sugar	¼ cup	1.75
Water	¼ cup	2.1
Kosher salt	¼ tsp	-

1 Preheat the oven to 350°F. Line a rimmed baking sheet with parchment paper.

2 In a medium saucepan, combine the nuts, sugar, water, and salt. Bring to a boil over medium heat and cook for 1 minute. Strain through a fine-mesh sieve, discarding the liquid, and spread the nuts in an even layer on the prepared baking sheet.

3 Bake for 15 minutes, or until golden brown. Let cool to room temperature before using.

SALTY CANDIED PEANUTS *Follow the recipe for Candied Whole Nuts, using peanuts and increasing the salt to ½ teaspoon.*

SPICED CANDIED WHOLE NUTS *Follow the recipe for Candied Whole Nuts, substituting brown sugar for granulated sugar and adding a pinch of cayenne pepper and ¼ teaspoon cinnamon in step 2.*

INDEX

Note: Page references in *italics* indicate photographs.